GRAMMATICAL COMPETENCE AND
PARSING PERFORMANCE

BRADLEY L. PRITCHETT

GRAMMATICAL COMPETENCE AND PARSING PERFORMANCE

THE UNIVERSITY OF CHICAGO PRESS

Chicago and London

Bradley L. Pritchett is assistant professor in the Department
of Philosophy at Carnegie Mellon University.

The University of Chicago Press, Chicago 60637
The University of Chicago Press, Ltd., London
© 1992 by The University of Chicago
All rights reserved. Published 1992
Printed in the United States of America

01 00 99 98 97 96 95 94 93 92   5 4 3 2 1

ISBN (cloth): 0-226-68441-5
ISBN (paper): 0-226-68442-3

Library of Congress Cataloging-in-Publication Data

Pritchett, Bradley L.
    Grammatical competence and parsing performance / Bradley L.
Pritchett.
        p.   cm.
    Includes bibliographical references and index.
    1. Grammar, Comparative and general.   2. Competence and
performance (Linguistics)   3. Computational linguistics.
4. Psycholinguistics.   5. Parsing (Computer grammar)   I. Title.
P151.P75   1992
415—dc20   91-43480

To

my parents

Louis and Barbara Pritchett

and

the memory of

Alma H. Burnette

CONTENTS

PREFACE

This work has benefitted immensely from the research of scholars too numerous to mention. Special appreciation, however, is due Susumu Kuno and Amy Weinberg, each of whom has provided a wealth of invaluable comments on earlier versions of this manuscript. I am also grateful to David Swinney and Janet Fodor for providing early encouragement from the psychologists' quarter. Additionally, Susan Mary Power is especially appreciated for her interest in the existence and not the content of this book. Above all, I would like to express my gratitude and respect to John B. Whitman, without whose intellectual influence this work would never have been conceived and without whose eternal friendship it could never have been completed.

This work is intended to be accessible to theoretical and computational linguists and to psycholinguists with interests in natural language processing. Although a basic familiarity with current syntactic theory, and to a lesser extent the Government and Binding framework, is assumed, crucial theory-dependent concepts are defined as introduced. Readers with distinct backgrounds in psycholinguistics may wish to approach chapter 2 in somewhat different fashions. That chapter establishes the primary data through critiques of some well-known model of human natural language processing. Each of its sections is intended to be more or less self-contained and consequently the chapter may be read in its entirety or treated as a reference. However, those who are not familiar with the fundamental phenomena or who assume a largely adequate theory of human natural language processing to exist, are strongly encouraged to read chapter 2 before proceeding to the alternative theory developed in the remainder of this work.

ABBREVIATIONS AND GLOSSES

A	argument or adjective
A′	non-argument or projection of adjective
ACC	accusative
AP	adjective phrase
APPL	applicative
ASP	aspect
ATN	Augmented Transition Network
C	complementizer
CAT	category
CAUSE	causative
CED	Constraint on Extraction Domains
CF	context free
CMGC	Complete Minimal Governing Category
COMP	complementizer
CP	complementizer phrase ($= S'$)
CRT	cathode ray tube
CSS	Canonical Sentoid Strategy
DAT	dative
DEF	definite
Det	determiner
DP	determiner phrase
DS	d-structure; deep structure
DTC	Derivational Theory of Complexity
e	empty category
ECM	Exceptional Case Marking
ECP	Empty Category Principle
GB	Government and Binding
GEN	genitive
GP	garden path
GPSG	Generalized Phrase Structure Grammar
HPSG	Head-driven Phrase Structure Grammar
I	inflection

IND	indicative
INFL	inflection
IP	inflection phrase (= S)
LC	Late Closure
LFG	Lexical Functional Grammar
MA	Minimal Attachment
N	noun
NLP	natural language processing
NOM	nominative
NP	noun phrase
O	operator
OBJ	object
OBJ2	second object
OLLC	On-Line Locality Constraint
P	preposition
PCOMP	prepositional phrase complement
PERF	perfect
PP	prepositional phrase
PPP	Preliminary Phrase Packager
PRED	predicate
PRES	present
PRO	
PS	phrase structure
PST	past
RA	Right Association
REST	Revised Extended Standard Theory
S	Sentence (= IP)
S'	sentence-bar (= CP)
SCH	Semantic Checking Hypothesis
SCOMP	sentential complement
SP	subject agreement prefix
SS	s-structure; surface structure
SSS	Sentence Structure Supervisor
ST	Standard Theory
STM	Short-Term Memory
SUBJ	subject
t	trace
TG	Transformational Grammar
TOP	topic
TRC	theta reanalysis constraint
UG	Universal Grammar
V	verb
VP	Verb Phrase
X'	X-bar
Ø	gap

The garden path leads to the

mirror of the mind

Henry Best
Herbs and the Earth,
1935

CHAPTER ONE

The Garden Path Phenomenon

1.0 The Problem

This work investigates two logically independent but fundamentally related questions central to theories of universal grammar (UG) and human natural language processing (NLP):

    i. How is it that humans are able to (rapidly and automatically) assign grammatically licit structure to incoming strings of words?

and

    ii. What is the relationship between the parser and the grammar which makes this possible?

Throughout the next several chapters, a detailed investigation of human processing breakdown will be found to provide a single answer to both questions:

    iii. The core of syntactic parsing consists of the local application of global grammatical principles.[1]

The remainder of this introduction reviews the fundamental assumptions and problems underlying questions (i) and (ii) and briefly outlines the particular competence-based theory of human natural language processing to be developed throughout the text. Chapter 2 examines a range of influential but problematic performance-based models of human NLP in order to establish the fundamental empirical data as well as reveal the sources of these models' failings and the consequent need for a fundamentally distinct alternative approach. The third chapter develops an initial formalization of (iii), outlining a model of processing transparently derived from aspects of competence grammar which are common to virtually all major grammatical frameworks. Fundamental principles of attachment (theta attachment) and reanalysis (the theta reanalysis constraint) are proposed and subsequently applied to a wide range of performance data. Chapters 4 and 5 reveal that increased linkage between the parsing model and the particular theoretical constructs of the Government and Binding syntactic framework both strengthens its empirical coverage and increases its theoretical simplicity. Chapter 4 further reduces the theta reanalysis constraint to grammar and explores the empirical benefits of this move. The final chapter presents a generalization of theta attachment, re-examining some previously problematic cases and introducing certain additional English and cross-linguistic facts. The ultimate result is both a specific cognitively plausible model of human NLP and a demonstration that approaches to parsing which do not make direct use of principles of competence grammar are both cognitively insufficient and unnecessary.

1.1 Grammar and Parser

If one accepts the hypothesis that the structural descriptions generated by some particular theory of grammar are necessary determinants of both the well-formedness and the interpretation of word strings, a syntactic parser must by definition assign structures equivalent to those of the postulated competence grammar. In some sense then, both parser and grammar have similar tasks—the association of a structural analysis with a string. How active the competence grammar itself is in the parsing process, however, remains an open question. For example, one may easily imagine a completely static grammar consisting of a list of rules which an active parser attempts to match based on its own changing internal state. Given this common conception of parsing, it is not the grammar but how the grammar is traversed which actively determines the course of the parse (for example, Early 1970 among many others). The assumption that the parser and the competence grammar are distinct is almost universally held by those espousing syntactic theories of human natural language processing (cf. Fodor, Bever, and Garrett 1974), and this dichotomy is usually taken to follow naturally from the competence-performance distinction originally drawn by Chomsky (1964). In more modern idiom, the grammar may be said to represent knowledge which the parser puts to use. In keeping with this perspective, researchers in the subfield of (applied) computational linguistics have typically required of a parser only that it yield, in some fashion, structures compatible with the grammar—that is, simply that there be input-output correspondence between the two. While this may be understandable when the primary goal is a practical machine-implementable NLP system, the same is not true where the goal is to model human cognition.

Within the discipline of psycholinguistics where issues of human performance are paramount, the theoretical question of the relationship between grammar and parser has received somewhat more attention. Contra the usual assumptions of parser-grammar independence, models have been occasionally proposed in which the relationship between the grammar and the parser is quite close, with the latter largely dependent upon the former. By far the best known exemplar of such an approach is the processing model associated with the Derivational Theory of Complexity (DTC, cf. Fodor, Bever, and Garrett 1974), a hypothesis which equates a sentence's derivational history with its surface perceptual complexity. The DTC was typically associated with a conceptually independent hypothesis that the parser was the grammar "run backwards" in some sense, an assumption clearly motivated by the superficial similarity between the Standard Theory (ST) model of transformational grammar current at the time and production models which map meaning to sound. Though this interpretation of the grammar-parser relationship proved unworkable given the particular ST model of grammar it assumed (cf. Bresnan 1978), its failure in no way invalidated the more general hypothesis that the grammar and parser are not distinct entities. Unfortunately, the perceived failure of the DTC (actually a failure of the corollary hypotheses concerning the nature of the grammar and of the parser) convinced many psycholinguists that transformational grammar could not be "psychologically real" and as a result most psycholinguistic researchers began to deemphasize the explicit role of the grammar and grammatical theory within models of language use.[2] Among those researchers explicitly concerned with human performance, focus generally shifted toward a search for independent processing principles which putatively reflected general human cognitive functions and were neither derived from a particular model of grammar nor even necessarily specific to language (e.g., Milne 1982). Such approaches typically assume a very static and surface oriented rule-based syntactic formalism (often simple unannotated Context-Free Phrase Structure Rules), but, as models of parsing rather than grammar, often ignore questions concerning the adequacy of this representation (see, for example, §5.1 below). This deemphasis on grammatical theory and the structures it motivates has remained widespread among psycholinguists (cf. Frazier 1978, 1989).

More recently, in an attempt to argue for a closer grammar-parser relationship within the Transformational Grammar tradition, some researchers have suggested that the grammar may be dependent upon the parser rather than vice versa. For example, there have been several attempts to derive specific grammatical constraints such as subjacency or c-command from the architecture of the parser (cf. Marcus 1980; Berwick and Weinberg 1984; Pritchett 1991c). The putative success of the endeavor is construed as evidence of the parser's psychological reality. From this perspective it is the grammar rather than the parser which is held (to varying degrees) to be a derivative construct. In its weak form this constitutes an appealing hypothesis, but it is one which clearly cannot be taken to its logical extreme. The operation of the parser cannot wholly determine the form of the grammar for the simple reason that this would prevent any account of language variation. If there is content to the notion that parsing strategies reflect fundamental and automatic human cognitive processes (whether or not they are specific to language), then they are not expected to vary radically across the species, and consequently, as is virtually uncontroversial, if one's theory of language processing is to have any claims to universality, a separate grammar must be postulated regardless of the design and capabilities of the parser. Quite simply, not all grammatical constraints are parsing constraints.[3] Nevertheless, as the structures the two components assign are necessarily compatible, the grammar and the parser must be related in some fairly direct way, with the precise nature of their relationship remaining to be discovered.

Further complicating this issue are recent developments within grammatical theory itself. All of the major REST-descended theories of grammar (e.g., Government and Binding (GB), Generalized/Head-driven Phrase Structure Grammar (G/HPSG), Lexical Functional Grammar (LFG)) emphasize the importance of conditions on representation over rule systems for deriving those representations, while traditional parsing algorithms, as alluded to above, have typically assumed rather rigidly rule-based grammatical formalisms. Although certain current syntactic theories, such as G/HPSG (Gazdar et al. 1985; Pollard and Sag 1988) and LFG (Kaplan and Bresnan 1982) possess explicit phrase structure rule components, for most linguists the true interest of these theories lies in the conditions they impose on possible representations: for example, the *Head Feature Convention* in GPSG, *coherence* and *completeness* in LFG, or the *Empty Category Principle* in GB. This shift in the conception of Grammar from a system of rules to a system of constraints on representation has been most pervasive within the Government and Binding (a.k.a. Principles and Parameters) framework adopted here, where individual rules have been almost entirely eliminated in favor of parameterized universal principles (cf. Chomsky 1981, 1986b).[4] The relationship between parsers and principle-based grammar(s) is by no means self-evident, but the development of such non-rule-based grammatical models has raised the possibility that a similar refocusing might also be appropriate with respect to natural language processing. A primary goal of this work is to bring data concerning human processing breakdown to bear on this very question and to demonstrate that rather deep and abstract grammatical principles strongly influence surface processing performance, revealing an intimate grammar-parser relationship. Specifically, the core of parsing is in essence simply the local application of global grammatical principles.

1.2 Local and Global Ambiguity

It is well known that certain grammatical sentences prove extremely difficult for humans to process and result in severe processing breakdown. Unlike the vast majority of utterances, which are parsed quickly and automatically with no noticeable effort, a certain range of sentences relinquish their grammatical interpretations only upon conscious reanalysis if they do so at all.[5] The following well-known example, originally provided by Bever (1970), exemplifies this so-called garden path (GP) phenomenon:

(1)   ¿The boat floated down the river sank.[6]
      (The boat which was floated down the river sank.)
      (cf. The boat ridden down the river sank.)

In the literature on syntactic processing in general, the potential difficulty in interpreting such sentences has been hypothesized to result from the existence of some type of ambituity during processing.[7] For example, before the final verb *sink* is encountered in sentence (1), the string *the boat floated down the river* is ambiguous between a main clause

(2) $[_{CP}[_{IP}[_{NP}$ The boat$][_{VP}$ floated $[_{PP}$ down the river$]]]]$

and a reduced relative

(3) $[_{NP}$ The $[_{N'}[_{N'}$ boat$][_{CP}[_{NP}$ $O_i][_{IP}[_{NP}$ $e_i][_{VP}$ floated e_i $[_{PP}$ down the river$]]]]]]$

interpretation.[8] This phenomenon would be largely uninteresting were it restricted to this single structure, but, of course this is not the case, as a structurally distinct example reveals:

(4)   ¿Without her contributions would be impossible.[9]
      (Contributions would be impossible without her.)
      (cf. Without him contributions would be impossible.)

At the point when *contributions* is encountered, it is unclear whether that nominal will ultimately serve as the head of the NP object of the preposition, as in *Without her contributions, it would be impossible,* or as the subject of a forthcoming clause, as in the proper interpretation of the example cited.

However, it is also clear but striking that ambiguity per se cannot be the source of the processing difficulty associated with garden path sentences. Natural language appears both to exhibit and tolerate a large amount of syntactic ambiguity. For example, sentences of English and other languages frequently admit more than one legitimate interpretation. Consider a well-known example:

(5)   a. $[_{IP}[_{NP}$ The sun's rays$]$ $[_{VP}$ meet$]]$ *Time flies*
      b. $[_{IP}[_{NP}$ The sons$]$ $[_{VP}$ raise $[_{NP}$ meat$]]]$

These sentences, while phonologically identical (at least at the segmental level), have distinct lexical, syntactic, and semantic representations. In contrast to the ambiguous and problematic sentences of (1) and (4), examples such as (5) present no difficulty. Such a string is said to be globally ambiguous as there is more than one valid linguistic structure that may be assigned to it as a whole. Other representative examples include:

(6)   Visiting relatives can be a nuisance.
      a.   To visit relatives can be a nuisance.   *JPN X*
      b.   Relatives who are visiting can be a nuisance.
(7)   The boy shot the man with the gun.
      a.   The boy used the gun to shoot the man.
      b.   The boy shot the man who had the gun.   *X*

cf. The boy ate the wokies in the box

(8)   Japanese push bottles up Chinese.
      a.   The Japanese shoved bottles up the Chinese.
      b.   The Japanese advance blocked the Chinese.
(9)   The dark-haired man said that Lobo died yesterday.
      a.   Yesterday the dark-haired man said that Lobo died.
      b.   The dark-haired man said that yesterday Lobo died.
(10) The beagle saw the basset which was attractive.
      a.   The beagle which was attractive saw the basset.
      b.   The beagle saw the attractive basset.

In some cases, such as (8), the global ambiguity is attributable to a combination of lexical and resultant structural ambiguity, while in other cases, such as in (7), it is purely structural. Languages apparently are not designed to avoid such indeterminacy, which cannot in itself be considered problematic. In general, it simply goes unnoticed.

Quite obviously, both garden path and globally ambiguous sentences exhibit ambiguous attachment possibilities during processing (adopting the nearly universally accepted hypothesis that human processing is performed temporally "left-to-right" in something resembling real time). That is, the correct global identity and structural attachment of a constituent is at some point locally indeterminate in both cases. For example, when initially encountered, the adverb in the globally ambiguous example (9) might legitimately be attached directly to either a matrix or embedded constituent. Similarly, as mentioned, when first identified, the nominal *contributions* in the garden path sentence (4) might be attached as the head of the NP object of *without* or as the subject of a forthcoming clause—the ultimately required analysis. There is of course an obvious factor that distinguishes the two cases. By definition, where global ambiguity is involved, multiple local decisions will lead to a grammatical structure, but in the case of a garden path sentence, some locally tenable choice will ultimately lead to global ungrammaticality and resultant processing failure. Ambiguity associated with GPs might therefore more accurately be referred to as *strictly* local, and upon first consideration this fact in itself might appear to provide a reasonable account of the contrast between sentences which are difficult to parse and those which are not.

1.3 Problematic and Unproblematic Ambiguity

Perhaps somewhat surprisingly however, strict locality does not constitute a sufficient characterization of problematic ambiguity. For example, the two sentences in (11) each display such an indeterminacy, but are nevertheless both completely unproblematic:

(11) a.   Ned knew the man hated Rex passionately.
      b.   Ned knew the man extremely well.

At the point when *the man* is encountered, it might be attached as the direct object of the verb, as will prove correct with respect to sentence (b), or as the subject of a forthcoming clause, as will be required in sentence (a). The resolution of the ambiguity in favor of the attachment of *the man* as the object of *know* in (11a) will lead to a globally ungrammatical sentence with *hated Rex* stranded without a subject, while the converse attachment as the subject of a forthcoming S in (11b) will lead to an ungrammatical structure where the complement has a subject but no predicate. Both the NP and S attachment will prove correct in certain instances and untenable in others, but neither sentence presents any conscious processing difficulty whatsoever despite the fact that only a single and distinct choice is grammatical in either case.[10] No single parsing heuristic (for example, always attach as a direct object or always attach as an embedded subject) will prove adequate either in achieving the correct parse or accounting for relative processing difficulty, which cannot evidently be explained simply in terms of the operation of some invariant attachment strategy in a strictly locally ambiguous environment.

With these issues in mind, a garden path sentence must therefore be characterized not simply as a sentence displaying a strictly local ambiguity, but as a grammatical but unprocessable sentence which results from the combination of (a) a local parsing decision which ultimately proves not to be consonant with a global grammatical representation, and (b) the parser's inability to perform the reanalysis necessary to obtain a grammatical representation.[11] GPs thus represent unrecoverable parsing errors which cannot be corrected without the conscious invocation of higher rational and nonautomatic cognitive processes; why those errors occur and why they are unrecoverable is what remains to be discovered. Serving a role similar to that of ungrammatical sentences within linguistic theory, the diverse range of garden path structures provide rich evidence which may be brought to bear on the fundamental issues under consideration: how input strings are assigned structures compatible with the competence grammar and what this reveals about the greater question of the grammar-parser relationship. The ultimate goal of course is not a theory of garden path effects, but a general cognitive model of human language processing.

1.4 Deep and Surface Factors in Processing Breakdown

Consider the contrast between sentences like (11) above or (12) with (13):

(12) a. √I knew the ugly little professor well.
      b. √I knew the ugly little professor disliked me.
(13) a. √I warned the ugly little professor loudly.
      b. ¿I warned the ugly little professor disliked me.
          (I warned that the ugly little professor disliked me.)
          (cf. Rex warned I would regret my actions.)

Were (13b) considered in isolation, it would be quite natural to attribute its garden path status to the fact that it lacks an overt complementizer with the consequent ambiguity of the post-verbal NP between an object and the subject of a potentially forthcoming complement S. Of course, it is vital to note that the *warn* sentences, although unacceptable, are completely grammatical, as structurally parallel but unproblematic examples reveal:

(14)   a.   The president warned (that) he would veto the bill.
       b.   The weatherman warned (that) there would be an earthquake quite soon.
       c.   Frank warned (that) he was getting fed up.

Clearly, the verb *warn* may grammatically co-occur with a single sentential complement, and the complementizer *that* may also optionally be omitted. The sentences in (14) are rendered acceptable as well as grammatical given morphological and syntactic restrictions on the distribution of *he* and *there* or the presence of a complementizer. However, the minimally contrasting set of sentences in (12) quite strikingly demonstrates the impossibility of attributing the garden path effect to these accidental surface factors per se (i.e., the absence of an overt complementizer, of nominative case, or of a pleonastic subject). Each set of sentences displays precisely the same ambiguity however, only when the embedded subject reading is required and then only in (13b) is the sentence costly to process. Since precisely the same coincidence of ambiguities is completely unproblematic in examples such as (12), this contrast reveals that while certain aspects of the garden path phenomenon are clearly arbitrary, the processing difficulty associated with the phenomenon cannot be attributed to these random factors per se (coupled of course with some parsing strategy). In other words, although ambiguity may arise only in the absence of various syntactic and morphological cues, it merely sets the stage for processing breakdown but does not itself explain the phenomenon.

   Similarly, distinct but arbitrary factors also conspire to permit misanalysis in canonical garden path structures:

(15)   ¿The horse raced past the barn fell.
       (The horse which was raced past the barn fell.)
       (cf. The horse ridden past the barn fell.)
(16)   [NP The [N′ [N horse] [CP [NP O_i] [IP [NP e_i] [VP raced e_i [PP past the barn]]]]]]

Two rather random surface facts about English admit the processing difficulty: the homophony of the past tense and passive participle verb form, and the possibility of omitting the relative pronoun and *be* (the *whiz*-deletion of Ross 1967). Were there no homophony, the unproblematic situation exemplified in the gloss of (15) would obtain, where *ridden* and *rode* contrast. Were it not possible to omit the relative pronoun and copula, an acceptable sentence would result, where the *wh*-word effectively prevents *the horse* from being locally interpreted as the main clause subject of *race* in the substring *the horse raced*.

One somewhat deeper fact also appears potentially relevant, the possible transitivity alternation of the verb *race*. When there is no such alternation, unproblematic examples such as (17) result:

(17)   a.   The spaceship destroyed in the battle vanished.
         b.   The teachers instructed by the Berlitz method passed the test.

While the homophony and the deletability of the relative pronoun lead to the ambiguity in a rather straightforward fashion, the contrasting lexical (and hence syntactic) properties of *destroy* and *instruct* versus *race*, however, raise some rather more important questions which will be discussed in §3.3.2.

To summarize, although matrix clause–relative NP ambiguities represent the most widely recognized class of garden path structure in English, examples such as (4) and (13) demonstrate that though the particular ambiguities they display are sufficient, they are not necessary in order to induce severe processing difficulty; there is a much wider variety of garden path structures. Conversely, the contrast between (12) and (13) demonstrates that although some arbitrary ambiguity may be necessary it is not itself sufficient. In fact, as will become clear, the nature of the accidental surface ambiguity itself is of virtually no theoretical interest. Rather, it is purely accidental that in certain constructions a confluence of morphological and syntactic cues which would otherwise prevent the violation of certain grammar-derived processing principles (yet to be characterized) may be missing and may lead to (unrecoverable) processing errors.

Nevertheless, even those researchers who have recognized the arbitrariness of these surface ambiguities have tended to attribute the garden path effect directly to such mere performance factors, independent from issues of linguistic theory. Discussing the well-known *[$_{NP}$ NP tense VP]* filter, Chomsky and Lasnik (1977) remark that it should in no way be construed as ruling out canonical reduced relative garden paths as ungrammatical, precisely because syntactically parallel structures, which are morphologically distinct, must be permitted. In contrast, the filter does prohibit sentences that would always be misanalyzed independent of arbitrary surface ambiguity. For example, in English a sentence initial NP V could always be misinterpreted as the onset of a matrix clause and is hence proscribed as the onset of a sentential subject:

(18)   a.   *The man met you is my friend.
         b.   *He left is obvious.

Unfortunately, it is a short step from the rather uncontroversial conclusion that the grammar licenses structure independent of the shape of the terminal elements, to the notion that an account of processing breakdown falls purely within the realm of a theory of performance. This simply reiterates the long held belief that the parsing and grammatical theory are essentially independent and not related in any particularly interesting fashion.

Unlike most researchers (see chapter 2), Chomsky and Lasnik do attempt some integration between the grammatical filter and the parsing phenomenon. They posit an indirect linkage between the two by informally associating both with what they refer to as a "reasonable perceptual strategy":

(19)   In analyzing a construction C, given a structure that can stand as an independent clause, take it to be a main clause of C. (Chomsky and Lasnik 1977, 436)

Although, if developed, such an analysis could begin to address questions of the grammar-parser relationship, this formulation is unfortunately entirely construction specific and ad hoc. Not only does (19) obviously fail to address numerous questions surrounding ambiguity in English, it also cannot be a universal heuristic even within its own limited domain. Compare an example from Japanese:

(20)   *Japanese*
John wa hon o   yonda to   omotte inai
John TOP book ACC read   COMP thinking is-not
'John doesn't think that (someone) read the book'

The NP NP V sequence, *John wa hon o yonda,* could be interpreted as a matrix clause (*John read the book*), and consequently should be according to the perceptual strategy in (19). Nevertheless, the sentence is both perfectly grammatical and perfectly processable, even though such structures would have to be consistently reinterpreted with *hon o yonda* as embedded. Of course, there are clear syntactic differences between (18) and (20), but both do not exhibit similar processing ambiguities with respect to (19). It therefore seems unlikely that this "reasonable perceptual strategy" reflects any particularly deep constraint on the grammatical limits of ambiguity if human perceptual strategies are held to have any significant degree of universality. Consequently, though the argument that garden path sentences are grammatical is sound, the conclusion that they are directly attributable to trivial surface ambiguity (coupled with some parsing strategy or strategies) independent of deeper grammatical principles has not been demonstrated.

In contrast, what will be argued below is that the connection between grammar and parser is far more general and direct than typically supposed and consequently that independent perceptual strategies such as (19) are not only empirically inadequate but fundamentally unnecessary (for example, see §2.0.1 for a complete discussion of strategy similar to (19)). Specifically, only ambiguity which locally violates certain fundamental grammatical or transparently grammar-derived principles results in processing breakdown.

Other sorts of ambiguities, though they may lead to local misanalyses and the need for restructuring (which may be detected experimentally), will not result in processing failure. Multiply ambiguous sentences demonstrate this point quite strikingly. For instance, examples like (21) are processed without difficulty even though they present repeated structural ambiguities throughout the parse. Each NP is interpretable as a plural NP or a possessive up until the occurrence of the final head noun:

(21)   The woman kicked her sons dogs houses doors . . .

This is unproblematic despite the multiple ambiguities, and what will be discovered is that this may be satisfactorily accounted for only given a direct link between grammatical theory and parsing performance.

To summarize briefly, in contrast with global ambiguities wherein more than one local syntactic analysis will prove well formed, sentences whose ambiguity is strictly local present parsing options which may prove globally untenable. However, as many such sentences may be resolved without difficulty in multiple fashions, the question to ask is what the common feature of garden path sentences is which thwarts the normal processing strategies. By investigating the actual breakdown of the NLP system, much can be revealed about its operation in general. Moreover, these data are robust, widely accepted within the literature, and open to introspection (but only of course with respect to the fact that parsing becomes conscious—not the parser's internal operation) in a fashion similar to judgements of grammaticality.[12] While GPs are commonly adduced as evidence for or against particular processing models, there has been no comprehensive study to date focusing on conscious processing breakdown. Furthermore, processing effects in general, and garden path phenomena in particular, have been studied almost solely with respect to English for reasons that are at least partially linguistic. Clearly, particular sentences that induce processing failure in one language most likely will not do so in another since much is trivially dependent upon the accidental and idiosyncratic aspects of the surface syntax and morphology of the language under consideration. It will be argued in what follows that a model of human natural language processing derived from grammatical theory succeeds in being highly general and predictive not only with respect to English but also cross-linguistically in contrast to the numerous surface-oriented approaches that have been proposed.

1.5 Theta Attachment

A survey of the processing literature yields the following partial taxonomy of garden path phenomena (to be expanded and discussed in detail throughout chapter 2), here classified according to the type of structural ambiguity displayed and the direction of resolution:

(22) *Taxonomy of Garden Path Phenomena*
   a.   Main Clause–Relative NP Ambiguity
        The boat floated down the river.
        ¿The horse raced past the barn fell.
   b.   Complement Clause–Relative Clause Ambiguity
        The tourists persuaded the guide that they were having trouble
           with their feet.
        ¿The doctor told the patient he was having trouble with to leave.
   c.   Object-Subject Ambiguity
        John believed the ugly little man hated him.
        ¿After Susan drank the water evaporated.
   d.   Double Object Ambiguity
        Rex gave her presents to Ron.
        ¿Todd gave the boy the dog bit a bandage.
   e.   Lexical Ambiguity[13]
        ¿The old train the children.
        The church pardons many sinners.

The local ambiguities displayed here represent potential GP contexts, and
the fact that actual garden path effects occur only when ambiguities must be
resolved in favor of certain structures demonstrates the (as yet unexplained)
finding that the garden path effect is directional. For instance, a local object-
subject ambiguity (22c) constitutes a potential GP context, while the fact that
processing difficulty may occur (though, as discussed, it need not) just in
those cases where the ambiguity must be resolved in favor of an attachment of
the NP as subject reflects the directionality of garden path effects.[14]

To foreshadow the analysis which will be developed in chapters 3 through
5, the range of garden path structures as presented in (22) suggests an interesting formulation of the principle of attachment that guides the human language
processor. Without further elaboration for the moment, consider the following
proposed parsing heuristic:[15]

(23) **Theta Attachment:** The theta criterion attempts to be satisfied at
        every point during processing given the maximal theta grid.

For concreteness, assume the formulation of the theta criterion given in
Chomsky (1986b):

(24) **Theta Criterion:** Each argument α appears in a chain containing a
        unique visible theta position P, and each theta position P is visible in
        a chain containing a unique argument α. (Chomsky 1986b, 97)

Informally, each argument must bear exactly one theta role and each theta role
must be assigned to exactly one argument. This may be expressed more formally as

(25)   **Theta Criterion:** Given the structure S, there is a set K of chains, $K = (C_i)$, where $C_i = (\alpha_1^i, \ldots, \alpha_n^i)$, such that:

    i. if α is an argument of S, then there is a $C_i \in K$ such that $\alpha = \alpha_j^i$ and a theta role is assigned to C_i by exactly one position P.

    ii. if P is a position of S marked with the theta role R, then there is a $C_i \in K$ to which P assigns R, and exactly one α_j^i in C_i is an argument. (Chomsky 1981, 335)

but the characterization in (24) is sufficient for current purposes. Theta attachment is intended to insure that the processor recovers a theta assigner's maximal theta grid[16] from the Lexicon and attempts *to match the roles and the data locally in accordance with the theta criterion at every point during processing.* That is, the processor eschews having either undischarged theta roles or non-theta marked targets available locally at any point throughout the parse—precisely as it does in a global representation. Consequently, when a theta role is available, it will be discharged onto any available target, and when a target is available, it will assume any available role. This insures that, where possible, a constituent will be attached into the parse tree in a position in which it may receive a theta role in accord with independent principles of the grammar.[17]

Consider very briefly a simple example. For the time being, certain details are left vague as the analysis postulated here is developed in depth throughout subsequent chapters and grammatical principles beyond the theta criterion also invoked on-line. First consider a non–garden path sentence:

(26)   Without her contributions the orphanage closed.

Initially, *without* is lexically identified as a preposition with an associated theta grid. Although it assigns a single thematic role, there is at this point no target NP available which could potentially serve as an argument and consequently no action can be taken. Next however, the lexical item *her* occurs and is identified as an NP which might locally function either as the preposition's complement or as the determiner of an as-yet-unseen head noun. Hence, there is a local ambiguity. However, since *without* has a theta role available to assign and *her* may function as an argument, by hypothesis the principle of theta attachment forces *her* to be attached in the configurational position in which it may receive the available role, adopting the standard minimal assumption that theta roles are assigned to sisters under government, cf. Chomsky (1986a). The globally possible specifier attachment is not pursued since *her,* as a result, would locally receive no role in the absence of a governing head noun.[18] Next, *contributions* may be identified as an N. The processor again faces a local ambiguity and has two choices: *contributions* might be taken to head a new NP which would lack a theta role, forcing a local violation of the theta criterion, or, alternatively, the larger NP *[NP her contributions]* could be constructed. It is this latter option which is selected in accordance with the principle in (23) as it locally satisfies the theta criterion. The entire NP *her contributions* receives a role from *without*, which is consequently able to discharge its internal role. Additionally, *her* receives a role by virtue of its structural position (possibly under government from the head noun, *contributions,* which itself receives its role as the head of the larger NP). Next, after the identification of the determiner *the,* the NP *the orphanage* is processed, but at this point, no theta role is available since without has already discharged its role, no NP *[$_{NP}$ her contributions the orphanage]* is licensed by the grammar, and no additional theta assigners are available. Subsequently however, when the new theta assigner *closed* does occur, the parse may be completed without difficulty with the unmarked NP *the orphanage* being attached as its subject.

Notice crucially that theta attachment does not predict the temporary stranding of the (potential) argument *the orphanage* to be problematic. Indeed, given the time course of natural language parsing, such situations are unavoidable. Furthermore, inverse but parallel environments arise whenever a theta assigner is encountered in the absence of a target upon which to discharge its role (as with *without* above). Theta attachment is a parsing heuristic which resolves local ambiguity by building a structure which maximally satisfies a particular grammatical constraint (or constraints), but this does not in any way imply that there is inherent cost associated with the temporary inability to satisfy the constraint where not grammatically possible. Were such situations hypothesized to be a significant problem for the processor, parsing difficulty would be vastly overpredicted contra the prima facie empirical evidence. Consequently, temporary unavoidable violations of parsing principles which arise because of the inherently incremental nature of natural language processing cannot be considered significantly costly.[19]

Contrast now a sentence which is problematic for the human natural language processor:

(27)   ¿Without her contributions failed to come in.

As previously suggested, it would be tempting to appeal to the simple notion that any syntactic reanalysis during parsing is costly. Informally, as seen, theta attachment here initially forces *her contributions* to be interpreted as a unitary object NP which may receive a theta role from *without*. As this is globally incorrect, reanalysis will be required in order to obtain *contributions* as a subject for *failed to come in,* and this does seem to correctly predict the processing difficulty. Unfortunately, it was shown in §1.3 that strict locality is not a sufficient condition for processing failure. Consequently, as expected, not all sentences which have global interpretations locally inconsistent with theta attachment yield processing difficulty. For example, in (26) the reinterpretation of *her* as a determiner rather than a head proved costless. More strikingly, the following example involves an initial misattachment of the NP *her contributions* as a complement, parallel to (27):

(28)   We knew her contributions failed to come in.

As in the previous example, reanalysis will be required in order to obtain a subject for *failed to come in,* but in this case there is no processing failure. Complicating matters even further is a minimally contrasting sentence along the lines of (13) above:

(29)   ¿Ned warned Rex hated him.

Here, misattachment of an NP (*Rex*) as a complement does yield difficulty as in (27) in contrast to (28). This is particularly striking as it is the surface syntax of (28) and (29) which is apparently similar. Clearly, with theta attachment as with any invariant parsing strategy, some but not all syntactic local misanalyses will prove costly. Consequently, it would appear that the parser must have a limited ability to correct local attachment errors.

1.6 The Theta Reanalysis Constraint

As a first approximation, consider then the following proposed constraint on syntactic reanalysis:

(30)   **Theta Reanalysis Constraint (TRC):** Syntactic reanalysis which re-interprets a theta-marked constituent as outside of a current theta domain is costly. [*Version 1*][20]

Here "costly" by definition entails that *conscious* processing is required, as discussed previously. Theta domain is defined as follows:

(31)   **Theta Domain:** α is in the γ theta domain of β iff α receives the γ theta role from β or α is dominated by a constituent that receives the γ theta role from β.

The diagram in (32) provides a graphic representation of this simple notion with respect to the predicate *warn.*

(32)

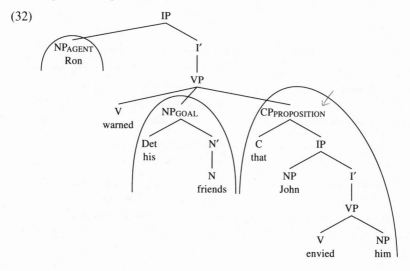

The TRC is directly derived from primitives of grammatical theory—it appeals to a combination of the notions of dominance and thematic role. (The fact that it is not absolutely identical to any existing theoretical construct is an issue which will be investigated in detail in chapter 4.) Hence both the fundamental attachment heuristic (theta attachment) and the constraint on on-line reanalysis (the TRC) are closely linked to grammatical theory. Together they maintain that both the principles of attachment and the constraints on reanalysis during processing are essentially grammatical and not to be explained in terms of general cognitive factors (e.g., short term memory constraints)—a perhaps unexpected situation.

Before exemplifying the effects of the TRC, a few additional notes on theoretical assumptions are necessary. The terms *thematic* or *theta role* have been employed above as apparent synonyms for *semantic role*. However, within the Government and Binding framework, the semantic content of theta roles is generally considered irrelevant to syntax (cf. Chomsky 1986b). For instance, observe the contrast between *know* and *warn*. The verb *know* clearly assigns a role to its subject, call it AGENT, and a role to a single complement, call it THEME, which may be realized either as an NP or an S':

(33)   a.   Ned$_{\text{AGENT}}$ knows Ron$_{\text{THEME}}$.
        b.   Ned$_{\text{AGENT}}$ knows [Ron isn't a fool]$_{\text{THEME}}$.

but not both simultaneously:

(34)   *Ned knows [Ron] [Tom isn't a fool].

Sentence (34) involves a theta criterion violation as the clause, *Tom isn't a fool,* lacks a semantic role. The verb *warn,* on the other hand, assigns an AGENT role to its subject and a role to up to two complements, call them GOAL:

(35)   Ned$_{\text{AGENT}}$ warned Ron$_{\text{GOAL}}$.

and PROPOSITION:

(36)   Ned$_{\text{AGENT}}$ warned [that the criminal was after him]$_{\text{PROPOSITION}}$.
(37)   Ned$_{\text{AGENT}}$ warned Tom$_{\text{GOAL}}$ [that the criminal was after him]$_{\text{PROPOSITION}}$.

The structural difference in the position of the sentential complement has empirical ramifications. For example the sentential complement of *warn* differs from the sentential complement of *know* in its inability to be passivized:

(38)   a.   *That the criminal was after him was warned (Steve) by John.
        b.   That the criminal was after him was known by John.

As will become increasingly clear, with respect to processing as with grammar, it is only the number of roles and the configurational position to which they are assigned which crucially distinguishes verbs and other theta assigners. Actual role content, as opposed to configuration, will prove irrelevant to the analysis developed. However, in order to facilitate discussion for the time being, traditional role labels will be used, such as AGENT, GOAL, THEME, etc. Furthermore, it will also temporarily be assumed that the role PROPOSITION may only be assigned to a sentential element, perhaps triggered by INFL or perhaps for semantic reasons as suggested by Chomsky (1986b). In practice, it will only rarely be necessary to appeal to theta role content, and in chapter 5, all reference to such information will be eliminated, motivating in turn a very desirable and natural extension of the general parsing theory which will be examined in some detail. Consequently, these simplifying assumptions should be viewed only as temporary expository devices.

A full explication of the theta attachment model will be delayed until after chapter 2, which explores certain important issues raised by an examination of alternative processing models. A few brief examples should serve to foreshadow the general approach which will be developed. Recall the following three-way contrast involving object-subject ambiguity:

(39) ¿Without her contributions failed to come in.
(Without her the contributions failed to come in.)
(cf. Without him the contributions failed to come in.)
(40) ¿Susan warned her mother loathed kale.
(Susan warned her that mother loathed kale.)
(cf. Susan warned him mother loathed kale.)
(41) Susan knew her mother loathed kale.

Consider now what the account of a garden path sentence such as (39) will be given the newly proposed TRC. Initially, *without* is identified as a preposition which may assign an internal theta role. When *her* is identified as an NP, theta attachment insures that it is attached as a complement of the preposition rather than as a determiner, as discussed previously. At the next stage, *contributions* is encountered and integrated into a larger NP, *her contributions* via theta attachment even though this requires syntactic restructuring. Although as a result *her* comes to receive a different theta role (POSSESSOR) than was originally assigned, the constituent remains within the theta domain of *without* (being dominated by the NP which receives a role from *without*), and hence the TRC correctly predicts this reanalysis to be unproblematic (cf. example (26)). Subsequently however, when *fail* is processed, an additional theta role becomes available which must be assigned to a subject, forcing another syntactic reanalysis. In contrast to the previous instance, however, this restructuring moves the constituent *contributions* out of its current theta domain in violation of the TRC. As subject of *fail*, the nominal neither directly receives, nor is dominated by a constituent that receives, a role from *without* and the result is processing breakdown.[21]

Compare now the situation with respect to sentence (40). Initially, *Susan* is identified as an NP. Since no theta assigner is initially available in the case of preverbal subjects, there is an unavoidable violation of theta attachment, which as discussed above is not predicted to be considered problematic. Next, *warn* is identified and its theta grid recovered. It may assign maximally one external and two internal roles: AGENT, GOAL, and PROPOSITION.[22] At this point, the AGENT role may be assigned to the subject *Susan* by projecting the appropriate structure: *[$_{IP}$ [$_{NP}$ Susan] [$_{I'}$ [$_{I}$] [$_{VP}$ [$_{V}$ warned]]]]*. Next, *her* is encountered and, in compliance with theta attachment, attached as the GOAL, since PROPOSITION may only be assigned to sentential elements. Immediately thereafter, *mother* is identified, and the larger NP *her mother* constructed as GOAL. Failure to build *[$_{NP}$ her mother]* leaves the NP *mother* without a theta role in local violation of the theta criterion, and as an NP it cannot be construed as the PROPOSITION. As in the previous examples, the reinterpretation of *her* as a specifier does not violate the constraint on reanalysis since *her* remains within the GOAL domain of *warn*, though as a POSSESSOR. The following identification of *loathe*, however, reveals the existence of an external argument role which must be assigned to the subject. This requires syntactic reanalysis wherein *mother* is moved outside the GOAL theta domain of *warn* and attached as the subject of the proposition *mother loathed kale*. This clause is of course not within the GOAL domain as it does not itself receive the GOAL role nor is it dominated by a constituent that receives that role since the PROPOSITION forms a separate internal theta domain. In other words, a constituent which was once the head of the GOAL must be reinterpreted as the subject of the PROPOSITION. As a result, the theta reanalysis constraint is violated and an unacceptable (garden path) sentence is correctly predicted.

Now contrast the situation with respect to the apparently very similar sentence (41). Initially, the processing parallels that of *warn*. When *know* is identified and its theta grid recovered, the AGENT role is assigned to *Susan*, leaving only a single role, THEME. Subsequently, *her* is encountered and assigned the THEME role. Immediately thereafter *mother* is processed and incorporated into the larger THEME NP *her mother* for the now familiar reasons. Crucially, this reanalysis does not violate the TRC. Although *her* ceases to head the THEME, it remains within the THEME NP as its specifier, which is correctly predicted to be unproblematic. Subsequently, the appearance of *loathe* forces syntactic reanalysis as in the previous example. However, in this instance, the theta reanalysis constraint is not violated since the restructuring required does not move either *her* or *mother* outside of their THEME theta domain as the entire clause, *her mother loathed kale*, itself comes to be the THEME. In other words, *her mother*, which was once the THEME, is reinterpreted as the subject of the THEME. Although it is quite true that *her mother* itself comes to receive an AGENT rather than a THEME role, it is crucial to recognize that this is *not* predicted to be problematic. It is not the assignment of a new semantic role per se which is costly, but rather the structural configuration in which such reassignment occurs which is relevant. If the new role is received within the same theta domain, the reanalysis is not costly. The unproblematic reinterpretation of *her* from a head to a specifier in each of the three previous examples is accounted for in precisely the same fashion, even though it receives a new POSSESSOR role in each case. For similar reasons (as will become clearer in chapter 3) it is also unimportant if *know,* like *warn,* actually assigns the semantic content PROPOSITION rather than THEME to a sentential complement since the relevant configurational position of either argument will be identical. Finally, notice that it cannot be the necessity of "splitting" the local constituent $[_{NP}$ *her N']* in (39) and (40) but not in (41) which is the source of the difficulty, for there is a precisely parallel contrast between the following two structures, as further discussed in chapter 3:

(42) ¿I warned Bob wielded an axe.
     (I warned that Bob wielded an axe.)
     (cf. I warned he wielded an axe.)
(43) I know Bob wielded an axe.

Again, the crucial contrast between *know* and *warn* is that the former licenses a single internal thematic role, while the latter licenses two; the labels associated with the roles are irrelevant as far as the TRC is concerned.

Although not all of the details are fully apparent at this point, it is clear that the combination of theta attachment and the theta reanalysis constraint begins to provide an account of one of the most striking facts about natural language processing—that only certain classes of structurally ambiguous sentences cause severe processing difficulty and that these sentences do so consistently within and across individuals (with a few interesting exceptions to be discussed in §4.0.4). The basic facts reported in the literature and amenable to introspective verification can be summarized as follows, somewhat expanded from (22) above:

i. Main Clause–Relative NP Ambiguity is resolved in favor of a main clause analysis (cf. Bever 1970; Chomsky and Lasnik 1977).

   (44) a. √The horse raced past the barn.
        b. ¿The horse raced past the barn fell.

ii. Complement Clause–Relative Clause Ambiguity is resolved in favor of a complement clause analysis (cf. Wanner, Kaplan, and Shiner 1975, Frazier 1978).

   (45) a. √The patient persuaded the doctor that he was having trouble with his feet.
        b. ¿The patient persuaded the doctor that he was having trouble with to leave.

iii. Object–Subject Ambiguity is resolved in favor of an object interpretation (cf. Hakes 1972; Frazier 1978; Frazier and Rayner 1982).

(46) a. √Without her it would be impossible.
      b. ¿Without her contributions would be impossible.
(47) a. √While Ron was sewing the sock it fell on the floor.
      b. ¿While Ron was sewing the sock fell on the floor.
(48) a. √I suspect John.
      b. √I suspect John will come soon.
(49) a. I warned John.
      b. ¿I warned John would come soon.

iv. Double Object Ambiguity appears to be resolved variously.

(50) a. √I gave her gifts.
      b. √I gave her gifts to Ron.
(51) ¿Joe put the candy in the jar into my mouth.
(52) ¿Ned gave the boy the dog bit a bandage.
(53) √¿Katy gave the man who was reading the book.
(54) √¿Katy gave the man who was reading the book the
      magazine.

v. Lexical Ambiguity appears to be resolved variously (cf. Fodor and
   Frazier 1980; Frazier and Rayner 1987).

(55) a. √The warehouse fires destroyed all the buildings.
      b. √The warehouse fires a dozen employees each year.
(56) a. √The old train chugged down the track.
      b. ¿The old train their dogs.

Any parsing model which attempts to mirror human performance, to possess
psychological reality, must capture these facts and predict both the initial direction of the ambiguity resolution as well as the contrasts between those
cases in which initial local misanalyses, arrived at through adherence to the
postulated processing strategies, are ultimately problematic, and those which
are not. In the next chapter, an investigation of prior approaches to such sentences in a variety of frameworks establishes the primary empirical facts and
reveals a wide range of related issues. In chapters 3 through 5, the theta attachment model is developed in detail as numerous empirical and theoretical
questions raised in chapter 2 are considered.

CHAPTER TWO

Performance-Based Models of Human Natural Language Processing

This chapter critically surveys a range of approaches to human language processing, with particular attention paid to the predictions made concerning parsing failure. With the fundamental data and issues thus established, chapters 3 through 5 provide a detailed explication of the theta attachment model. For expository purposes, the various parsing models to be considered will be grouped into four classes. This taxonomy is based largely on the functional motivation of the parsing algorithms and heuristics the models employ: perceptual, computational, lexical, and semantic, though it should be quite clear that the distinctions are not at all rigid. Quite broadly, perceptual accounts postulate processing principles motivated in terms of general cognitive faculties, such as short term (i.e., working) memory. Computational approaches distinguish themselves primarily through attention to the practical and efficient implementability of their models.[23] Lexical models emphasize the role of very specific knowledge of individual words in determining parsing decisions, and semantic models stress the importance of contextual knowledge over independent, parsing-specific strategies. The characterization of these models as performance-based reflects the fact that in each case the proposed fundamental attachment heuristics and reanalysis constraints (or equivalents) are entirely independent of grammatical theory. With the exception of certain radical semantic accounts, all approaches acknowledge that a primary task of the parser is the recovery of the syntactic structure(s) of the input string as licensed by some competence grammar.

2.0 Perceptual Approaches

As stated, perceptual approaches to human natural language processing emphasize attachment strategies for the resolution of local structural ambiguities which are specific to language perception but functionally motivated in terms of more general cognitive faculties, such as short-term memory limitations.[24] Though specific to language processing, the particular strategies are not dependent on or derived from any aspects of grammatical theory. In fact, being oriented toward the recovery of surface phrase structure, perceptual approaches are not generally associated with particular theories of linguistics, though they typically are completely dependent on particular rules of grammar. Given their functional motivation in terms of low-level human cognitive capabilities, the heuristics are themselves generally presumed universal, though this is problematic, as will become apparent.

As earlier demonstrated, for any (serial) parsing model to be adequate, it must incorporate not only an attachment strategy but also some limited form of error recovery since not all local ambiguity is problematic. Many perceptual models have failed to address this issue directly and consequently fail to make clear predictions concerning parsing breakdown. Nevertheless, a somewhat detailed examination of the various approaches is instructive and reveals data and issues which any theory of human language processing must ultimately acknowledge.

2.0.1. The Canonical Sentoid Strategy

In what are some of the first explicit formulations of human parsing strategies, Bever (1968, 1970) and Fodor, Bever, and Garrett (1974) present a very simple heuristic which states that a string having a possible reading as an NP V (NP) sequence necessarily receives a Subject Verb (Object) interpretation over any alternative readings. This so-called Canonical Sentoid Strategy (CSS) clearly foreshadows Chomsky and Lasnik's "reasonable perceptual strategy" presented in (19) above: [25]

(57)   Canonical Sentoid Strategy
       . . . whenever one encounters a surface sequence NP V (NP), assume
       that these items are, respectively, subject, verb, and object of a deep
       sentoid. (Fodor, Bever, and Garrett 1974, 345)

In the discussion which follows, the CSS will be used, perhaps somewhat unjustly, as something of a straw man. In its historical context, the approach was a perfectly reasonable one and had the virtue of being explicit enough to make specific predictions in numerous cases. For precisely this reason, a fairly detailed critical examination of its successes and failures is instructive, if, at times somewhat unfair to an approach that initiated much subsequent research in the psycholinguistics of natural language processing.

Part of the original motivation for the CSS derived from experimental evidence showing that center-embedded sentences such as

(58)   The editor the authors the newspapers hired liked died.

were easier to process than structurally parallel sentences in which the second NP was homophonic to a verb:

(59)   The editor authors the newspapers hired liked died.

This was attributed to the fact that *The editor authors the newspaper* has a legitimate reading as a NP V NP sequence and was thus first interpreted as a sentoid (essentially a clause; cf. Katz and Postal 1964). This same strategy was also capable of accounting for the greater difficulty in processing object relative clauses (60c) over subject relatives (60b). Only in the latter case does the word order in the relative clause itself correspond to the canonical form:

(60) a. I know [Bill hit Mary]. (SVO)
     b. I know the boy [who hit Mary]. (SVO)
     c. I know the boy [who Bill hit]. (OSV)

Further supporting evidence was adduced from the putatively greater difficulty in interpreting certain passive sentences over their active counterparts. This requires an interpretation of the principle in terms of semantic roles rather than simply syntactic structure but might naturally be attributed to the fact that the strategy is intended to recover a "deep" sentoid:

(61) a. John$_{\text{AGENT}}$ hit Bill$_{\text{PATIENT}}$.
     b. Bill$_{\text{PATIENT}}$ was hit by John$_{\text{AGENT}}$.

Thus motivated, this appealingly simple heuristic was found capable of accounting for paradigmatic garden path sentences such as:

(62) ¿The dealer sold forgeries complained.
     (The dealer who was sold forgeries complained.)
     (cf. The dealers given forgeries complained.)

The CSS insures that *The dealer sold forgeries* first receives a subject object verb interpretation which must subsequently be reanalyzed, apparently predicting the difficulty. However, as becomes readily apparent, the strategy provides no account of other garden path sentences to which it might reasonably be applied:

(63) *Relative Clause–Complement Clause Ambiguity*
     ¿The doctor told the patient that he was having trouble with to leave.
     (The doctor told the patient whom he was having trouble with to leave.)
     (cf. The doctor expected the patient that he was having trouble with to leave.)
(64) *Object-Subject Ambiguity*
     ¿Mary warned her professors couldn't be trusted.
     (Mary warned her that professors couldn't be trusted.)
     (cf. Mary warned him professors couldn't be trusted.)
(65) *Lexical N-V Ambiguity*
     ¿The prime number few.
     (There are few prime numbers.)
     (cf. The prime displease mathematicians.)

In (63) the GP effect certainly cannot be attributed to the Canonical Sentoid Strategy since the trouble seems to result from the initial interpretation of *that he was having trouble with* as a complement S' rather than a relative clause. In fact, one can imagine that the CSS should actually force the globally correct relative clause analysis over the complement clause reading since in that instance the analysis of the entire string prior to *to leave* would conform to the canonical NP V NP pattern:

(66)   [$_{NP}$ The doctor] [$_V$ persuaded] [$_{NP}$ the patient that he was having trouble with.]

On the other hand, contrast (63) with (64), where the difficulty seems to result from the incorrect initial interpretation of *her professors* as a single noun phrase. Arguably, this is what the CSS predicts since it forces an NP V NP structure up to the point where the lower auxiliary is encountered. This contrasts with the situation in example (63), where a complement clause rather than a relative NP interpretation is primary, though globally incorrect. The question is why the main clause S is mistakenly closed late in sentence (64) (after *professors* rather than immediately after *her*) while it is incorrectly closed early in sentence (63) (after *the patient* rather than *the patient that he was having trouble with*). In each case, it seems that a consistent reading of the CSS should favor that the maximally large NPs be admitted if any predictions are made at all. Bever stipulates a further principle which might account for the contrast:

(67)   After a Det, which signals the beginning of a Noun Phrase, the end of the NP is indicated by one of the following: (i) a plural morpheme, such as -s, (ii) a morpheme that indicates the beginning of a new phrase, such as *the, that, will, may,* or *should,* (iii) a word that is probably not a noun, for example a verb that is only rarely used as a noun. (Bever 1970)

This can be interpreted to insure maximal NPs only in those cases not involving relative clauses but (67) is quite clearly both extremely ad hoc and hopelessly specific to English.[26] Empirically also, though (67) may arguably account for the misanalysis in (64), it fails even with respect to structurally similar garden paths such as:

(68)   ¿Mary convinced her professors friends would be hard to find.
        (Mary convinced her professors that friends would be hard to find.)
        (cf. Mary convinced her professor friends would be hard to find.)

Though *professors* is interpretable as a plural NP, the plurality is apparently not taken as a signal of the end of the NP constituent, *friends* also being incorrectly included with resulting parsing difficulty. One cannot reasonably attribute the difficulty to the plural-possessive morpheme ambiguity since this is virtually always present.

The CSS also makes clear, but unfortunately incorrect, predictions concerning a class of data which, as foreshadowed in section §1.6, will become increasingly crucial:

(69)   John knew Rex was a fool.
(70)   I doubted her story could be true.

These are completely unproblematic despite the fact that *Rex* in (69) and *her story* in (70) should first be misinterpreted as verbal objects rather than correctly parsed as the subjects of forthcoming clauses. This contrasts strongly with sentences such as (64) and similar examples where early misconstrual of a subject as an object does lead to processing difficulties:

(71)   a.   ¿I warned the ugly man would attack.
              (I warned that the ugly man would attack.)
              (cf. I warned there would be hell to pay.)
        b.   ¿I convinced the students parents were not all bad.
              (I convinced the students that parents were not all bad.)
              (cf. I convinced the student parents were not all bad.)

   Finally, the processing difficulty encountered in the class of garden paths which display a Noun-Verb ambiguity, such as (65) or (72) below results from the failure to interpret an ambiguous string as N V N:

(72)   ¿The old train their cats.
        (Old people train their cats.)
        (cf. The old loathe their cats.)

This error is of course in direct conflict with the predictions of the Canonical Sentoid Strategy, which should predict no GP effects in these instances, since if it is possible for something to be interpreted as a subject verb object sequence, it should be.

   Essentially, the CSS accounts for canonical GP effects but provides no explanation of processing breakdown involving anything other than main clause–relative clause ambiguity. Of course, additional ad hoc and language specific principles, along the lines of (67) might be developed, but this abandons the goal of any general theory of human language processing. Perhaps the most crucial point raised in the previous discussion, however, is one merely implicit in the actual formulation of the Canonical Sentoid Strategy itself. This is the hypothesis that when the actual occurrence of an NP V NP string is inconsistent with the CSS and reanalysis is required, that that reanalysis will be costly. The extent of that cost is far from clear as one certainly does not wish to equate passives and object relatives on the one hand with paradigmatic garden path sentences on the other, though all violate the CSS. The importance of this issue has only begun to be appreciated very slowly within the literature, although a characterization of problematic versus unproblematic ambiguity is crucial, as demonstrated in chapter 1. For this reason, it is useful to continue to review these models chronologically, next turning to the extremely influential model of Kimball (1973).

2.0.2. Kimball's Seven Surface Principles

In a seminal paper, Kimball (1973) posited seven quite general surface structure parsing principles intended to account for a wide range of established, but at that point largely unexplained, perceptual data. The two principles to which Kimball himself explicitly attributes garden path effects are:

(73) *Principle Five (Closure):* A phrase is closed as soon as possible, i.e., unless the next node parsed is an immediate constituent of that phrase. (Kimball 1973, 36)

(74) *Principle Six (Fixed Structure):* When the last immediate constituent of a phrase has been formed, and the phrase E closed, it is costly in terms of perceptual complexity ever to have to go back to reorganize the constituents of that phrase. (Kimball 1973, 37)

These interact with five other general processing heuristics:[27]

(75) *Principle One (Top Down):* Parsing in natural language proceeds according to a top-down algorithm. (Kimball 1973, 20)

(76) *Principle Two (Right Association):* Terminal symbols optimally associate to the lowest nonterminal node. (Kimball 1973, 24)

(77) *Principle Three (New Nodes):* The construction of a new node is signalled by the occurrence of a grammatical function word. (Kimball 1973, 29)

(78) *Principle Four (Two Sentences):* The constituents of no more than two sentences can be parsed at the same time. (Kimball 1973, 33)

(79) *Principle Seven (Processing):* When a phrase is closed it is pushed down into a syntactic (possibly semantic) processing stage and cleared from short term memory. (Kimball 1973, 38)

Principles 1, 2, 3, and 5 constitute the actual attachment heuristics, while 4, 6, and 7 characterize processing cost. It is Kimball's general hypothesis that the number of nodes which must be kept open on-line contributes significantly to processing load and these principles are generally intended to reduce that number or characterize its limits. The first principle, Top Down, is in keeping with the widespread intuition that the parser operates by assuming that it is building a matrix sentence and attempts immediately to attach incoming material to an S node on the basis of that assumption. Given the rules S → NP VP and VP → V NP, a strictly top down parsing algorithm will seek subject-verb-object patterns, yielding effects similar to those of the Canonical Sentoid Strategy and therefore subject to roughly the same criticisms.

Right Association (RA), Kimball's second principle, has remained extremely influential, surviving in some form in virtually all psycholinguistic processing models. RA, as defined above, is intended to account for the contrast in interpretation between the (a) and (b) sentences below as well as the relative unacceptability of the (b) sentences.

(80) a. Joe figured that Susan wanted to take the cat out.
     b. Joe figured that Susan wanted to take the train to NYC out.
(81) a. The girl took the job that was attractive.
     b. The girl went to NY that was attractive.

In Kimball's system, RA is largely redundant with Closure, which he employs explicitly in order to account for GP effects. For this reason, and because RA is so important a component of certain later models, further discussion of its effects will be postponed.[28]

The third principle, New Nodes, is straightforward and is relevant here only insofar as it explicitly recognized that one surface factor leading at least to canonical garden path sentences is the lack of an (largely) unambiguous indicator of a new S' node (e.g., a complementizer or relative pronoun). Kimball hedges on a stronger claim that the existence of functional categories is actually motivated by processing concerns, recognizing that COMP-final languages such as Japanese would appear quite maladaptive from such a perspective. Though "function words" may indeed indicate new nodes, neither their existence nor distribution seem obviously functionally motivated.[29]

Two Sentences, the fourth principle, provides a static complexity metric, irrelevant with respect to processing difficulty which results from local ambiguity. All of the garden path structures to be considered consist of at most two S's. The principle does, however, account for the extreme processing difficulty encountered in multiply center-embedded structures where the difficulty is not obviously due to ambiguity:[30]

(82) The mouse the cat the dog chased bit died.
    (The mouse died which was bitten by the cat which the dog chased.)

Kimball did not actually consider principle 7, Processing, to be a separate principle, but rather a possible explanation of number 6, Fixed Structure (see below). As noted, it had been a tacit assumption that any and all reanalysis is problematic to some degree. Principle 7 represents an attempt to refine that notion through the hypothesis that phrases which have been closed are cleared from memory and hence constitute the domain of problematic reanalysis. (A similar but more developed theory is discussed in §2.3.1.)

It is to the fifth principle, Closure, in combination with the sixth principle, Fixed Structure, motivated in terms of principle 7, Processing, that Kimball attributes the difficulty of both canonical garden paths (83) as well as other sorts of local ambiguity (84):

(83) ¿The girl pushed through the window cried.
    (The girl who was pushed through the window cried.)
    (cf. The girl thrown through the window cried.)

(84)   They knew the girl was in the closet.

Of course, Kimball recognizes that the second example involves absolutely no conscious processing difficulty despite the ambiguity of the postverbal NP between a direct object and an embedded subject. He claims only that it exhibits greater processing time complexity than the corresponding sentence with an overt complementizer (cf. Hakes 1972):

(85)   They knew that the girl was in the closet.

According to Kimball, sentence (84) is closed after *the girl*, while sentence (83) is closed by principle 5 after the PP *through the window*. In contrast, early closure is circumvented in sentence (85) where the occurrence of *that* causes a new S node to be opened in accordance with principle 3, New Nodes.[31] The processing breakdown is explained by principle 6, Fixed Structure which states that once a sentence is closed, reorganization is costly.

As should be clear, there are certain empirical problems with this treatment, primarily due to its general lack of discrimination between problematic and unproblematic reanalysis. On the face of it, Kimball appears to predict that (84) should be just as difficult to process as (83), which is clearly false, as he freely admits. Furthermore, it fails to explain why (86), which is very similar to (84), is, in contrast, a severe GP:

(86)   ¿The girl persuaded her enemies were in the closet.
        (The girl persuaded her that enemies were in the closet.)
        (cf. The girl persuaded him enemies were in the closet.)

"look ahead"!

If closure takes place after *her*, then *enemies were in the closet* should be processed correctly as an S, incorrectly predicting unproblematic processing. On the other hand, if closure occurs after *her enemies*, reorganization must occur, but why its effects are here far more severe than with sentence (84), which also requires similar restructuring, is entirely unclear. An analogous problem is demonstrated by the now familiar contrasting pair in (87) and (88) where only the latter sentence is a garden path:

(87)   Katrina knew the ugly man was dangerous.
(88)   ¿Katrina warned the ugly man was dangerous.
        (Katrina warned that the ugly man was dangerous)
        (cf. Katrina warned he was dangerous.)

As discussed in chapter 1, in both instances an NP which originally may have been attached directly to a VP as a direct object must be reinterpreted as a complement subject. According to these principles, the two sentences should be processed identically, yet only the latter causes difficulty.[32]

Even more simply, sentences such as

(89)   I hate my friends neighbors babies mewling.
(90)   We admire her intelligence agency policies.

are apparently predicted to yield severe garden path effects. Example (89) displays a local genitive-plural, and (90) a compound ambiguity. In each case, closure potentially occurs after each N, yielding the following local analyses:

(91)   i. I hate my [$_{NP}$ friends]
       ii. I hate my [$_{NP}$ friend's neighbors]
       iii. I hate my [$_{NP}$ friend's neighbor's babies]
       iv. I hate my [$_{NP}$ friend's neighbor's babies' mewling]
(92)   i. We admire [$_{NP}$ her]
       ii. We admire [$_{NP}$ her intelligence]
       iii. We admire [$_{NP}$ her intelligence agency]
       iv. We admire [$_{NP}$ her intelligence agency policies]

By principle 5, closure is certainly predicted after each potential NP, but the syntactic reorganization required at each stage is not problematic as predicted by Fixed Structure.

Furthermore, it is difficult to see how to extend Closure and Fixed Structure to account for a range of severe garden path structures which Kimball did not consider:

(93)   ¿The mortician cautioned the relatives that he was taking great pains
       with to arrive at five.
       (The mortician cautioned the relatives whom he was taking great pains
       with to arrive at five.)
       (cf. The mortician expected the relatives that he was taking great pains
       with to arrive at five.)

In fact, Kimball's model actually appears to favor the relative clause interpretation since it is consistent with the early (complete) closure of S after *with* as in a sentence such as:

(94)   ¿The mortician cautioned the bereaved that he was taking great pains
       with.
       (The mortician cautioned the bereaved with whom he was taking great
       pains.)
       (cf. The mortician murdered the bereaved that he was taking great
       pains with.)

The complement clause interpretation, on the other hand, must delay (complete) closure until additional information (an object NP) is encountered—but it appears nevertheless that that is the reading which is anticipated. That (94) is itself a garden path is also completely unexplained by these principles, as is the contrasting absence of GP effects in (95) if these strategies operate by blindly matching PS rules without regard to lexical information, an assumption shared by many current perceptual models (cf. Frazier 1989):

(95)   The mortician forced the relatives that he was taking great pains with
       to arrive at five.

Some further cases which Kimball did not consider and which do not appear to be accounted for include examples such as:

(96)   ¿Without the scorecard that he lost remained unknown.
       (Without the scorecard the fact that he lost remained unknown.)
       (cf. Without Susan that he lost remained unknown.)
(97)   ¿Without her contributions would be impossible.

Early Closure incorrectly predicts primacy of the non–garden path interpretation in these examples. The locally ambiguous fragments, *without her* and *without the map* should be closed as PPs with *contributions* and *that he lost* consequently remaining free to serve as the higher subject. This cannot be the case, however, since both examples yield severe processing difficulty.

With principles 6 and 7, Kimball took initial steps toward defining a domain of problematic reanalysis. All of the various counterexamples to Kimball's principles raise the same question: why do different on-line "re-organizations" result in extreme variations in processing difficulty which may or may not rise to consciousness? A consistent interpretation of Closure does not provide an answer. As was the case with Fodor, Bever, and Garrett's approach, Kimball's strategies handle (certain) canonical garden paths but cannot distinguish them from clearly unproblematic, though locally ambiguous, examples. Nevertheless, Kimball's strategies are of extreme historical importance, by and large initiating the effort to characterize simple, comprehensive, and potentially universal human parsing heuristics. The remaining perceptual models to be discussed continue very much within the spirit established by Kimball, and, like his approach, serve to reveal the crucial necessity for a more refined theory of reanalysis to accompany any theory of attachment.

2.0.3. The Sausage Machine

Frazier and Fodor (1978) propose a two-stage model of human sentence parsing, known as the Sausage Machine, whose primary objective is to remedy the perceived stipulative and ad hoc nature of numerous processing strategies of the sort discussed so far. For the most part, Frazier and Fodor do not challenge the descriptive adequacy of those principles but rather attempt to construct a model which is more theoretically appealing than a mere descriptive list of strategies. Despite a relative lack of explicit concern with processing breakdown, it will nevertheless prove useful, in light of the paper's influence, to consider what might be extrapolated in that regard.

Parsing in the Sausage Machine proceeds in two stages, with the division of labor motivated in large part by the authors' observation that the parser appears to be both very smart and very stupid. While it apparently is untroubled by the necessity of making certain very long-distance associations, as in construing a *wh*-word with a gap (e.g., *Who$_i$ do you believe John suspects the vampire will bite e$_i$*), it nevertheless makes certain very local errors, as in the range of garden path examples discussed. The authors account for this as follows. In the first stage of the model, referred to as the *Preliminary Phrase Packager* (PPP) or the *Sausage Machine* proper, phrasal as well as lexical nodes are assigned to substrings of approximately six words, this limit being loosely associated with the putative size of short-term memory. In the second stage, the *Sentence Structure Supervisor* links these phrasal "packages" together through the construction of higher nodes. So-called "shortsighted" (local) errors are accounted for by the six-word limit on this first stage, while the ability to handle long-distance dependencies of various sorts is to be explained by the global perspective of the second stage. Frazier and Fodor hypothesize that the PPP initially scans the entire sentence with its six-word window,[33] while the SSS sweeps behind it, operating on its output, globally viewing the entire parse tree.

The preferred interpretations of ambiguous sentences are largely determined by the interaction of two parsing heuristics which Frazier and Fodor claim actually result from the structure of the Sausage Machine model itself. The first principle, Right Association (RA), states that, "terminal symbols optimally associate to the lowest nonterminal node," and is obviously derived from Kimball's second principle. However the authors depart from Kimball's approach and maintain that RA need not actually be stipulated but is instead the natural result of the limited size of the window, which simply prevents higher attachment possibilities from being viewed in certain instances. The second parsing principle is the extremely influential Minimal Attachment (MA), which will also be discussed in the next section:

(98)   **Minimal Attachment:** Ambiguous attachment possibilities are to be resolved in favor of attachment to the nodes already present which introduces into the tree the fewest possible number of non-terminal nodes.[34]

For example, consider the sentence

(99)   Malcolm bought the book for Susan.

which has a preferred interpretation of (100a) rather than (100b):

(100)   a.   [$_{IP}$ Malcolm [$_{VP}$ bought [$_{NP}$ the book] [$_{PP}$ for Susan]]]
        b.   [$_{IP}$ Malcolm [$_{VP}$ bought [$_{NP}$ [the book] [$_{PP}$ for Susan]]]]

Since the string is six words long, the entire sentence is visible to the PPP. If the attachment of the prepositional phrase were resolved according to a stipulated principle of Right Association, à la Kimball, the PP *for Susan* would preferentially be associated with the lowest nonterminal node, the NP *the book*, incorrectly predicting interpretation (100b) to be primary. According to Frazier and Fodor however, RA is merely an epiphenomenon determined by what is visible within the six-element window available to the PPP, with the actual ambiguity resolved by Minimal Attachment. As shown, there are two attachment possibilities for the PP—it could be introduced directly into the VP or Chomsky-adjoined to the NP, creating an additional higher NP. MA correctly predicts the former, corresponding to the preferred reading in (100a) which requires only the introduction of a PP node in contrast to (100b) which also requires a higher NP.[35] Minimal attachment appears to overrule Right Association because, as just noted, there is actually no principle of RA, its apparent effects being derivative. When the PP is first visible within the six-word window, the PPP is still able to view the VP node as a possible locus of attachment and the principle of Minimal Attachment applies as stipulated.

Now contrast a situation in which pure Right Association effects are truly predicted:

(101)   Joe bought the book that I had been trying to obtain for Susan.

Here, the primary interpretation is one in which the PP *for Susan* is construed with the lower verb *obtain* rather than the higher verb *buy*. This effect results from the fact that when *for Susan* enters the buffer, the earlier VP is simply no longer visible to the PPP because of the limited size of the scanning window and consequently the only possible point of attachment is within the lower VP.

Thus, modulo the complications introduced by the PPP and the SSS themselves, it would at first glance appear that a desirable simplification of several of Kimball's processing principles is possible, requiring only the single principle of MA. Arguably, MA may partially or fully replace Kimball's principles Top Down, New Nodes, and Closure in addition to the more obvious Right Association.[36] Of course, the size of the window itself and the identity of the elements in which that size is stated are themselves stipulated, though this is not necessarily undesirable if the model as a whole is successful.

The above sketch provides enough information for consideration of Frazier and Fodor's (brief) treatment of processing breakdown and extrapolation to a somewhat broader range of data than they explicitly consider. The authors attribute garden path phenomena to the necessity of syntactic reanalysis given shortsighted errors made by the Preliminary Phrase Packager. (Note that the authors label any local error a garden path and reserve the term severe garden path for sentences which yield conscious difficulty.)

(102)   In general, "garden path" explanations of processing difficulty account for asymmetries between sentences where pure memory load explanations do not. Our own model is of the garden path variety. The parser chooses to do whatever costs it the least effort; if this choice turns out to have been correct, the sentence will be relatively simple to parse, but if it should turn out to have been wrong, the sentence will need to be reparsed to arrive at the correct analy-

> sis. The fact that hearers are not always conscious of having made
> a mistake in the analysis of such sentences (as they are for notori-
> ous garden path sentences like *The horse raced past the barn fell*)
> is not, we submit, a good argument against this kind of perceptual
> complexity. (Frazier and Fodor 1978, 295–96)

Of course, Frazier and Fodor do functionally motivate the Sausage Machine in
terms of the size of working memory. What the authors apparently intend by
the claim that the model does not appeal to memory load is rather than the
parsing complexity of a sentence is not a static function of sentence structure
in terms of its memory requirements (for example, the number of open nodes
which must be stored on-line during the parse).[37] Instead, Frazier and Fodor's
model shares with all of the other models so far discussed the fundamental
assumption that reanalysis per se is costly.

A somewhat disturbing aspect of their approach is reflected in the statement that unawareness of reanalysis does not imply a lack of complexity.
Though this is certainly true, this fact in no way exempts a model from accounting for the difference between conscious and unconscious difficulty. As
discussed in chapter 1, it is a simple and unavoidable empirical fact that some
reanalysis rises to consciousness and that this correlates with particular grammatical structures. One can of course choose to ignore this, but that in no way
renders it unimportant. Conscious reflection may reveal little about the internal operation of the parser, but the *fact* of conscious reflection is extremely
informative. Although Frazier and Fodor do briefly suggest that mispackaging
words that do not belong together is an extremely costly error, worse than late
or premature closure, they provide few details on how this is to be interpreted
and essentially ignore the issue. In contrast, a model found on this distinction
will by its very nature account for unproblematic "minor" garden paths as
well as "severe" GPs as a matter of course, thus constituting a more explanatory model of human NLP.

With these issues in mind, consider how their model handles classical
matrix-relative garden paths of the form: *The horse raced past the barn fell.*
The initial ambiguity resolution in favor of a main clause interpretation is
claimed to result from the application of Minimal Attachment. As the PPP
sweeps through the sentence, its six-word window will initially contain

(103)   ❮[NP the horse] [VP [raced] [PP past the barn]]❯
       1   2   3   4 5 6

after it has recognized the lexical items and grouped them into its phrasal
packages. On its heels, the SSS must group these phrases into a higher constituent. Viewing the global tree geometry, as Frazier and Fodor put it, the
SSS will recognize that attachment as either a relative NP or a matrix S is
possible. Crucially, the latter analysis will be adopted in compliance with the
principle of Minimal Attachment since this will require the introduction of

fewer nonterminal nodes into the tree. As can be seen in (104), it lacks (at least) the extra (complex) NP node which dominates the NP head of the relative and the following relative S'.

(104)   a.   b.

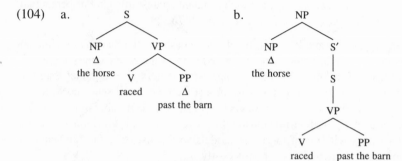

When the Sausage Machine sweeps onward, the presence of *fall* will reveal this analysis to be incorrect and force reprocessing. Furthermore, as Frazier and Fodor note, an appeal to MA also explains the preference for complement clause over relative clause readings. Though the authors do not discuss the processing breakdown associated with this preference:

(105)   ¿The soldier persuaded the radical student that he was fighting in the
             war for to enlist.
             (The soldier persuaded the radical student who he was fighting in the
             war for to enlist.)
             (cf. The soldier expected the radical student that he was fighting in
             the war for to enlist.)

they could account for this effect along the same lines as canonical GP examples. Though precisely how the details would be worked out is not entirely clear, attachment as a complement rather than a relative clause is consistent with the principle of Minimal Attachment since the former does not necessitate an additional NP node. Thus the resulting reanalysis required to obtain the relative clause reading would presumably yield some (unspecified degree of) complexity. Consequently, this is the first model examined which appears to offer a unified account of more than canonical garden path structures.

    Now, however, consider a sentence such as the following:

(106)   ¿The horse raced yesterday fell.

Such examples are simply variations of the paradigmatic garden path pattern, and are clearly grammatical, as a parallel structure reveals:

(107)   The horse ridden yesterday fell.

What is crucial about this example is that the entire sentence will be simultaneously visible to the Preliminary Phrase Packager as it sweeps through the sentence. The GP effect in (103) is accounted for by the invisibility of right-hand information, the verb *fell,* to the PPP, causing it to misanalyze the initial six words via MA. However, in the case of (106), the entire S fits within the window and since the SSS will not make attachments which it knows to be globally ill-formed, no processing difficulty is predicted. Misattachments are the result of local ambiguity, and (106) is *not* locally ambiguous as far as the Sausage Machine is concerned; all information about the sentence is available. Given the crucial six-word capacity of the Sausage Machine, any sentence of shorter length simply cannot be a garden path as the parser should make no error in the first place. A range of structures demonstrate that this is simply incorrect:

(108)   ¿While John sang a song played.
        (While John sang, there played a song.)
        (cf. While John coughed a song played.)

(109)   ¿Without her resistance is useless.
        (Without her, it is useless to resist.)
        (cf. Without him resistance is useless.)

(110)   ¿After I ran over Bob died.
        (Bob died after I ran over.)
        (cf. After I ran over he died.)

(111)   ¿Susan told her uncle died.
        (Susan told her that uncle died.)
        (cf. Susan told him uncle died.)

(112)   ¿Below the stairs collapsed.
        (The stairs collapsed below.)
        (cf. Earlier the stairs collapsed.)

(113)   ¿Greg tells students he intrigues to stay.
        (Greg tells students whom he intrigues to stay.)
        (cf. Greg expects students he intrigues to stay.)

In each of the first five examples, every lexical item should be visible to the PPP, circumventing any errors since there is consequently no local ambiguity as far as this model is concerned. In the last, although the final word, *stay,* is not visible, the presence of infinitival *to* should provide sufficient disambiguating information, in contrast to (105) above. Nevertheless, all of these sentences result in severe GP effects. Quite simply, the Sausage Machine's length-based approach which allowed the simplification of Kimball's principles seems impossible to maintain since garden path effects are severely underpredicted. Crucially, it appears that the *same syntactic structures* consistently lead to processing breakdown regardless of their length—exactly contra the predictions of the Sausage Machine.

The following contrast reveals even more strikingly the impossibility of maintaining a length-dependent account of parsing breakdown:

(114)   Rex knew Todd would die.

(115)   ¿Rex warned Todd would die.
         (Rex warned that Todd would die.)
         (cf. Rex warned he would die.)

Both sentences should fit entirely within the PPP's window and no reanalysis
should be necessary. Yet, the first is entirely unproblematic and the second a
garden path. Why there should be such severe reprocessing difficulties in one
case and not the other is completely unclear. Conversely, a sentence such as

(116)   Rex saw the little red train drive off the track.

is not at all problematic even though *Rex saw the little red train* should mistakenly be closed as an S and require reanalysis similar to that in (108)–(113).

   Counterexamples to Frazier and Fodor's length-based approach are not
restricted to garden path effects. Wanner (1980) presents various other types
of examples which cast doubt upon the relevance of length effects with respect
to Right- and Minimal Attachment:

(117)   The patient said that the doctor had [$_{VP}$ taken his appendix out
         yesterday].
(118)   John said Carol [$_{VP}$ died yesterday].

According to Wanner, there is no less a tendency for Right Attachment of the
adverbial in the short (118) than in the long (117), but the effect is only predicted with respect to the first sentence since both VPs will be visible to the
PPP in the second. As with examples in (108)–(113), the predicted length
effects do not appear to be well justified.[38]

   The garden path data above all very strongly suggest that it is something
about their particular structural configurations per se, as opposed to some accidental performance factor, that thwarts the normal operation of the human
sentence processor. Nevertheless, length-based approaches have remained
relatively common and deficiencies of other windowing and look-ahead models, similar in some respects to the Sausage Machine, are further discussed in
§2.1.2. In sum, there are two broad types of criticism to be levelled at Frazier
and Fodor's model. First and most obviously, it simply fails to account for the
presence of any GP effect in numerous cases. Second, in those instances
where processing problems are predicted, the model makes no discriminations
concerning the relative degree of difficulty and is thus completely incapable of
distinguishing problematic and unproblematic local ambiguity. It is this latter
failing that the next model to be considered attempts to address—a model that
continues to assume both RA and MA as independent principles.

2.0.4 Steal-NP

   Frazier and Rayner (1982) attempt to address the fact, which has been
repeatedly demonstrated in the discussion so far, that there are certain local
ambiguities which are unproblematic regardless of how they are globally re-

solved. They acknowledge that although parsing strategies originally proposed in Frazier (1978) (specifically Late Closure and Minimal Attachment) correctly appear to lead the processor down the garden path in a variety of cases, not all of the sentences which are initially misanalyzed yield a comparable degree of processing difficulty. They consequently endeavor to characterize reanalysis principles which would allow the parser to recover from an error in certain instances but not in others. (Their version of the theory does not assume the Sausage Machine architecture discussed in the previous section, and both LC and MA are taken to be independent principles.)

Of the two fundamental parsing strategies the authors posit, Minimal Attachment has been defined and exemplified in the preceding section. This must be supplemented with the additional stipulated principle of Late Closure (LC), essentially Right Association, which functions to admit newly encountered lexical items as members of the phrase being *currently* processed (where grammatically possible given the particular phrase structure rules assumed). For example, in a string such as

(119)   After Susan sang a song . . .

even though *after Susan sang* could itself be closed as a clause this principle maintains that there will be a preference to keep the VP (and S) open and admit the subsequent NP, *a song,* as a constituent of the current phrase à la Right Association. It is necessary to invoke LC in such cases since the matrix S to which the NP could attach as subject will already have been constructed given the top-down approach necessary for the operation of MA in general. Consequently, the subject attachment to S is as minimal as the VP object attachment internal to the adjunct. Since, unlike MA, LC is not easily attributable to any cognitively motivated desire for structural simplicity, it constitutes a fundamental weakness in the theory, as further discussed in §5.1. The Sausage Machine model discussed above represented an explicit attempt to eliminate LC, but was unsuccessful for the reasons considered.

Nevertheless, together these two principles do make certain desirable predictions. For example, canonical matrix-relative garden path sentences such as (15) are accounted for along the lines sketched in the discussion of the Sausage Machine. Prior to the occurrence of *fall,* a main clause rather than a relative NP analysis will be pursued since the former alternative requires that fewer nodes be posited but also ultimately requires reanalysis, predicting the difficulty. Contrast, however, the following pair of sentences:

(120)   The city argued the mayor's position forcefully.
(121)   The city argued the mayor's position was incorrect.

In both cases, Minimal Attachment and Late Closure predict that the post verbal NP will be attached as a verbal complement—the VP is kept open by Late Closure and the object is taken to be a bare NP rather than an NP dominated

by S via Minimal Attachment. However, neither the NP nor the S′ complement analysis yields difficulty. Similarly misanalyzed but unproblematic examples include the authors' own

(122) The linguists knew the solution to the problem would not be easy.

or additional examples with short or long ambiguous NPs:

(123)   a.   The Cincinnati Reds suspect Oakland cheats.
         b.   I believe the man who Ron says he met yesterday while riding on
               the T from Harvard to MIT will get off at Park Street.

It is quite obvious, as Frazier and Rayner note, that such sentences do not lead
to conscious processing problems, strongly suggesting that the simple necessity of reanalysis cannot be the source of the difficulty in garden path sentences, a point repeatedly demonstrated above.   (1982)
      Confronting these apparent mispredictions, Frazier and Rayner propose
that some independent principle or principles of selective reanalysis must be
available to license recovery in certain instances, though not in others. What
they informally hypothesize is that the availability of a previously parsed
"nominal constituent" to serve as the subject of the subsequently encountered
clause facilitates recovery, rendering it unproblematic. Borrowing a term
from Abney (1986), who adopts a similar strategy, this may be referred to as
STEAL-NP (though Frazier and Rayner apparently do not require that it be a
maximal projection, see below). The authors claim that this strategy is reasonable as it is constrained in both the degree and type of backtracking required:
the source of the error is quite locally identified by the appearance of a "sub-
jectless" verb, and a preprocessed (albeit attached) nominal is available to fill
that subject position. This contrasts strongly with the situation involving
canonical garden path sentences. In such cases, when the final verb is processed, backtracking will be required to return to the start of the clause and,
even at that point, there will be no available subject NP since Late Closure and
Minimal Attachment have provided a main clause rather than a relative NP
analysis. Notice that this is an extremely performance-oriented approach as
there is nothing about the syntactic structures involved per se which leads to
the parsing failure—rather it is the surface cues available and the string length
traversed in backtracking that are (loosely) hypothesized to be relevant.
      Frazier and Rayner's model is particularly important in being one of the
first perceptual theories to posit an explicit recovery procedure. Unfortunately, upon closer examination the proposed reanalysis strategy clearly
proves to be empirically inadequate. Consider the following:

(124)   Since Jay always jogs a mile this seems like a short distance to him.
(125)   ¿Since Jay always jogs a mile seems like a short distance to him.
         (Since Jay jogs always a mile seems like a short distance to him.)
         (cf. Since Jay never sweats a mile seems like a short distance to him.)

Frazier and Rayner note that Late Closure and Minimal Attachment correctly predict the post-verbal NP *a mile* to be interpreted as the object of the verb *jog* in both sentences. In sentence (125) of course, this proves to be a globally incorrect analysis, a fact which would appear to properly account for the resulting processing difficulty. In contrast, example (124) proves unproblematic since the object attachment consistent with Late Closure leads to the proper parse, the true subject is forthcoming. However, the situation is not so simple. The Steal-NP strategy previously motivated straightforwardly maintains that the availability of an NP to serve as the subject of the subsequently encountered clause should render reanalysis <u>unproblematic</u>. In this regard, sentences like (121) and (125) contrast strikingly. Each involves an obviously parallel misanalysis of a subject as an object over a very short distance across the terminal string, but only in one case is this misanalysis recoverable via Steal-NP as predicted, a quite unexpected result. Frazier and Fodor's theory encounters a double bind. Without the Steal-NP recovery strategy, examples such as (125) are correctly predicted to lead to processing breakdown, but so, unfortunately, are sentences such as (121). On the other hand, given the recovery strategy, the theory no longer mispredicts processing breakdown in (121), but completely fails to predict the striking garden path effect associated with sentences such as (125). Minimal Attachment and Late Closure coupled with Steal-NP fail to predict recovery in certain unproblematic instances as well as incorrectly predict unproblematic reanalysis in cases where severe GP effects do actually occur. There is an irreconcilable contradiction.

Furthermore, the problem is only exacerbated when a broader range of GP effects are investigated. Again, contrast the unproblematic examples in (121)–(123) with the following severe garden paths:

(126)   ¿While Malcolm sewed a sock fell on the floor.
        (A sock fell on the floor while Malcolm sewed.)
        (cf. While Malcolm belched a sock fell on the floor.)
(127)   ¿Without her contributions would be impossible.
        (Without her, obtaining contributions would be impossible.)
        (cf. Without him contributions would be impossible.)
(128)   ¿Katrina warned the professor was planning a murder.
        (Katrina warned that the professor was planning a murder.)
        (cf. Katrina suspected the professor was planning a murder.)

The structural equivalents of all of these sentences will be initially misanalyzed according to Frazier and Rayner's principles. Sentence (126) is an additional example structurally identical to (125). Example (127) is slightly different. In that sentences, *contributions* will be attached within the previously constructed NP which dominates *her,* via Late Closure. And, in (128), exactly analogous to the unproblematic (121)–(123), MA predicts the local attachment of *the professor* as object of the verb rather than as subject of a potential complement clause. However, in every single instance here, Frazier and Rayner's reanalysis strategy also predicts successful recovery from these attachments, just as it must do in (121)–(123). In (128) the NP object of *warn* should be transparently available to serve as a complement subject, precisely as *the solution to the problem* was available in (122) or *Oakland* and *the man who Ron says he met yesterday while riding on the T from Harvard to MIT* in (123). Similarly, in (127), *contributions* will have been parsed as a nominal projection and by hypothesis able to serve as the subject of the subsequent clause, whether its structure is

(129)   [$_{NP}$ [$_{NP}$ her] [$_{N'}$ contributions]]

as assumed by Frazier in other contexts, or

(130)   [$_{DP}$ [$_{D}$ her] [$_{NP}$ contributions]]

as assumed in certain alternative analyses (cf. Abney 1987).[39] (Note that Frazier and Rayner say nothing at all about the earlier reanalysis of the NP *her* from a head to a determiner.) All of these examples involve an initial misanalysis of an NP as a verbal complement which may be subsequently reanalyzed as subject via Steal-NP, but the processing difficulty is severe in stark contrast to the earlier unproblematic examples Frazier and Rayner intended to account for. It is apparent that by ignoring the grammatical differences between problematic and unproblematic structures, the authors' very surface-oriented recovery strategy simply fails and the need to develop a constrained theory of reanalysis remains crucial.

All perceptual models so far investigated have proven incapable of discriminating between instances of problematic and unproblematic processing ambiguity and have in general provided an account of only a single GP structure, the paradigmatic matrix–relative clause ambiguities, leaving the far broader range of problematic structures completely unaccounted for. As shown, given local ambiguity, any processing strategy will make incorrect attachments in certain instances, and there has been little success in developing constrained theories of backtracking. Several of the models to be considered in the next section attempt to deal with the problem of constructing a predictive theory of backtracking via an initial avoidance of local errors which obviates the need for reanalysis of any sort. This approach too differs quite dramatically from that to be developed in chapters 3 through 5 where the garden path phenomenon, and by extension human language processing in general, will be argued to be essentially grammatical in nature and therefore inexplicable purely in terms of any notions of performance.

2.1 Computational Approaches

To classify a model as computational rather than perceptual is not to imply that it lacks aspirations toward psychological reality but simply that it has a functional motivation strongly rooted in concerns of efficient and practical implementation, often as a proof by existence of the plausibility of a certain approach.[40] As computational models of human processing may appeal to putative human cognitive constraints, distinguishing them from perceptual models is somewhat arbitrary, though nevertheless expositorily useful. These dual concerns of psychological and computational plausibility are clearly reflected in the most influential concept to arise from computational approaches to natural language processing, the *determinism hypothesis*. Though derived rather directly from work in artificial language parsing, determinism is also frequently justified via an appeal to human cognitive limitations. It should therefore be borne in mind that the distinction between perceptual and computational accounts is by no means a rigid one since all psycholinguistic models by their very nature share fundamental goals and assumptions.

2.1.1 Augmented Transition Networks

A good example of the lack of clear distinction between perceptual and computational approaches is exemplified by work of Wanner, Kaplan, and Shiner (1975). The authors propose a general Augmented Transition Network (ATN, cf. Woods 1970) model of clause processing which they maintain is capable of accounting for classical garden paths of the familiar *The girl pushed through the window cried* variety. Like other Canonical Sentoid Strategy type approaches, it fails to account for the range of occurring GP effects, but within that realm it makes some rather sophisticated predictions which are well worth considering. Their fundamental hypothesis is that declarative and relative clauses may be parsed by precisely the same mechanism. The particular ATN they assume operates top-down, parsing each clause as if it were an independent declarative. This strategy breaks down, of course, in relative clause constructions where NPs may fail to occupy their expected deep structure positions. This resulting breakdown is, by hypothesis, taken as the sole cue to the nature of the clause, whether declarative or relative—a *wh*-word does not initiate some special relative clause–parsing strategy. Whenever the parser anticipates a noun phrase, it activates a SEEK NP arc which may be satisfied by either the appearance of an overt NP or the hypothesis of an empty noun phrase. Consequently, the failure to locate an overt NP need not be fatal since a gap may instead be associated with a *wh*-operator, allowing a relative clause to be parsed via the declarative clause mechanism.

Consider a simple transitive sentence:

(131)   Louis slugged the little boy.

When *slugged,* which requires an object, is encountered the SEEK NP arc is activated and subsequently the phrase *the little boy* is be processed and admitted as object. Similarly, in a relative clause:

(132)   I saw the little boy (who) Louis slugged on the arm.

the SEEK NP arc will again be activated. No NP follows *slug,* but an NP gap may be hypothesized and associated with the operator. In the case of a verb displaying a surface transitive-intransitive alternation, the situation is slightly more complicated. Wanner and his associates maintain that sentences such as

(133)   The dog I walked down the street was black.

are more difficult than

(134)   The book Katy read in the garden was blue.

This is attributed to the fact that *walk* is putatively more often intransitive than *read* and thus an object is somehow less anticipated in the former case. The authors account for this by stipulating the ranking of alternative subcategorization frames for verbs. For instance, since *walk* is held to be more typically intransitive, it receives the stipulated ranking $\binom{\varnothing}{NP}$, while the more frequently transitive *read* has the frame $\binom{NP}{\varnothing}$, where the order of NP and $\varnothing$ reflects expectations on the part of the processor. Since the routine which postulates an empty NP is the same as that which admits overt NPs, verbs may only be ranked as preferentially transitive $\binom{NP}{\varnothing}$ or intransitive $\binom{\varnothing}{NP}$. A logically conceivable ranking such as $\binom{GAP\ \varnothing}{NP}$ is not possible since GAPs and NPs are identical. Though a seemingly uncontroversial notion, at a time before the concept of empty categories was widely accepted this represented a theoretically appealing attempt to deal with transformed sentences (as did the ATN architecture in general).

It is easy to see in broad terms how this approach is intended to account for certain classical garden path sentences, such as (15) repeated here:

(135)   The horse raced past the barn fell.

Since *race* exhibits a transitivity alternation (and is presumably preferentially ranked as intransitive), the entire string prior to *fall* may be parsed as a main clause. In this fashion the model fairly transparently reflects the Canonical Sentoid Strategy discussed in §2.0.1 and is subject to a similar critique. The most interesting feature of this model is doubtless its more sophisticated prediction that canonical garden path structures may differ in acceptability depending on verb valency. Most strikingly, obligatorily transitive verbs should not lead to processing breakdown at all since the gap should be postulated and construed with an operator as soon as an overt NP is found to be missing. Quite interestingly, there is clear evidence that this is the case:

(136)   The bird bought yesterday died.
(137)   The man hit in the head fainted.

Though syntactically parallel to canonical garden path sentences, these examples fail to display the otherwise expected effects, something not predicted by any model previously considered, most of which have tacitly assumed lexically blind operation. However, the situation is not quite so simple as Wanner,

Kaplan, and Shiner's model would suggest. The contrast between the above two sentences and the following is not accounted for:

(138)   ¿The bird bought died.
        (The bird which was bought died.)
(139)   ¿The man hit fainted.
        (The man who was hit fainted.)

In these examples, a gap should be postulated just as in (136) and (137), but processing difficulty does occur here. Although, extremely light relative clauses of this sort are marginal in English, these sentences are unarguably far more difficult to process than the following:

(140)   ??The bird eaten died.
(141)   ??The man beaten fainted.

That processing breakdown in (certain) canonical garden path structures appears to depend in part on the valency of the verb is an interesting syntactic fact, and one which any complete theory must ultimately address.

Relatedly, given ranked subcategorization frames, this model also predicts that preferred intransitives should be more likely to garden path than preferred transitives in those cases where alternations are possible. Despite this prediction, at a conscious level both preferred intransitives like (142) and preferred transitives such as (143) yield equivalent processing breakdown:

(142)   ¿The dog walked past the hydrant sniffed.
        (The dog which was walked past the hydrant sniffed.)
        (cf. The dog run past the hydrant sniffed.)
(143)   ¿The boy kicked repeatedly fainted.
        (The boy who was kicked repeatedly fainted.)
        (cf. The boy beaten repeatedly fainted.)

Consequently, it appears that it is the existence of a transitivity alternation (a syntactic fact) rather than mere internal preferences (arguably a contextual or statistical effect) which is directly relevant in predicting the presence of the GP.

Finally, there is a surprising class of problematic structures that this model appears to provide an account for:

(144)   ¿Susan gave the boy the dog bit a bandage.
        (Susan gave a bandage to the boy whom the dog bit.)

What is perhaps unexpected about such examples, is that the same effect occurs even when there is an overt *wh*-word:

(145)   ¿Susan gave the boy whom the dog bit a bandage.

Its presence apparently does not allow breakdown to be circumvented as *bandage* appears to be construed as the complement of *bite* regardless of that cue.

Impressively, both cases appear to be straightforwardly predicted by Wanner, Kaplan, and Shiner's model which may parse the string *the dog bit a bandage* as a simple declarative. To convincingly extend their model to such examples would require a fuller understanding of how double object constructions are handled, but the account is suggestive, although one potential problem results from the fact that in many other cases, overt relative pronouns clearly do facilitate processing:

(146)   ¿The patient persuaded the doctor he feared to leave.
(147)   The patient persuaded the doctor whom he feared to leave.

This model, which ignores such cues, does not obviously explain the contrast, and such questions are explored in more detail in §4.0.4.

By far the most important issue raised here is one which will become increasingly important as investigation of GP effects continues—specifically, what is the role of verbal subcategorization in accounting for processing breakdown? This issue is next taken up in detail in §2.2.1.

2.1.2 Deterministic Parsing and Look-Ahead

In light of the widespread existence of linguistic ambiguity as exemplified in the previous sections of this chapter, it has generally been assumed that humans parse natural language through (simulated) nondeterminism via backtracking or parallelism, an assumption made explicit by Marcus (1980). The fundamental psycholinguistic data concerning preferred interpretations of ambiguous sentences and processing breakdown initially seem to provide clear evidence that the human sentence processor is of the serial-backtracking sort since parallel processing models, which build and maintain all legitimate syntactic structures associated with a string, appear by their very nature to be incapable of explaining such effects, predicting no contrasts.[41] While it is obvious that unconstrained parallelism is psycholinguistically unrealistic, even somewhat constrained backtracking models, as demonstrated, have fared little better in accounting for the primary cognitive data, conversely predicting rampant difficulty where a parallel processor might predict none. Ultimately, however, the distinction between parallel and serial models may not be nearly as great as it superficially appears and is largely interesting only to the degree that contrasting empirical predictions are made, something which is attributable to the constraints on the mechanisms, rather than the mechanisms themselves. Recognizing this, Marcus (1980) makes a far more radical proposal, rejecting both serial and parallel forms of nondeterminism altogether.

What Marcus hypothesized was that natural language could instead be parsed deterministically (temporally) from left to right—in other words that a single choice could be made at every locally ambiguous point (i.e., no parallelism) and that a structural decision, once made, could never be altered (i.e., no backtracking).[42] He maintained, in other words, that each move made by the processor was always fully determined—that its path was always unambiguous.[43] The primary computational motivations for favoring determinism are based on the memory and processing load imposed by parallelism and backtracking as well as the fact that deterministically processable languages form a proper subset of nondeterministically processable ones. Of far greater psycholinguistic relevance is the fact that Marcus's primary empirical motivation for the determination hypothesis was its putative ability to provide an account of garden path phenomena.

Marcus argues that for deterministic parsing to be feasible

   i. it must be partially data driven:
     a. Lobo hit Jason with a stick.
     b. Did Lobo hit Jason with a stick?
  ii. it must reflect expectations:
     a. I promised Kal [to make Guy feel better].
     b. I expected [Kal to make Guy feel better].
 iii. it must have some sort of look-ahead:
     a. Have the boys devoured their food?
     b. Have the boys devoured by the cannibals!

Broadly, a data driven (bottom up) parser contrasts with one which is hypothesis driven (top down), though of course in practice mixed strategies are often employed. A purely hypothesis driven parser simply cannot be deterministic, as it is impossible for its starting hypotheses to be correct in every instance, even in the absence of ambiguity. For example, if the deterministic parser always began its operation top down by postulating a declarative sentence via a rule such as S → NP AUX VP, it would commit an unrecoverable error whenever a question was encountered as it must instead match a rule such as S → AUX NP VP. Consequently, such a parser must be at least partially data driven. Nevertheless, it is still not sufficient for a deterministic parser to take only gross category information into account, as the examples in (ii) reveal. Without access to lexical information concerning verb complement structures, is entirely unclear how to analyze the string *Kal to make Guy feel better* in each example. Categorical information alone is insufficient as each sentence consists of a sequence of NP V NP AUX V NP V AP and consequently subcategory information must also be available on-line, something which sets deterministic processors apart from the blind phrase structure parsers heretofore considered. Finally, the parser must have some sort of look-ahead to replace the search capability—it cannot operate strictly left to right, precisely because there exists unproblematic bidirectional local ambiguity in language as exemplified in (iii) and repeatedly demonstrated previously.

It is this last mechanism (realistically implemented as some form of decision delay) which actually makes deterministic parsing feasible and sets Marcus's approach apart.[44] Furthermore, as Marcus quite clearly recognized, it is crucial that this look-ahead be constrained in some fashion, for otherwise, were the parser capable of looking ahead to the end of the sentence, there would simply be no content to the notion of determinism. That is, if all lexical information were available simultaneously, the ambiguity problem would be greatly reduced or eliminated, but the parsing process would bear little apparent relation to human real-time parsing. Even more importantly however, Marcus proposes not simply that the parser incorporates a look-ahead capability, but that the size of this look-ahead buffer is defined in terms of linguistic constituents rather than absolute elements. This is radically different from previous uses of look-ahead, where the size is typically defined in terms of words or characters, and it is this distinction which is responsible for most of the predictions made by the model.

Upon first inspection, it would appear that the mere existence of garden path sentences indicates that people do *not* parse natural language deterministically simply because such sentences may be consciously *re*analyzed. What Marcus suggests is that sentences that require such deliberate effort are actually not being parsed deterministically, which accounts for their extreme difficulty. Therefore, the existence of garden path phenomena may be taken to provide an argument for rather than against the determinism hypothesis. (Notice however that this hypothesis does not actually depend on determinism per se but simply the notion that the normal operation of the parser is somehow thwarted. It would therefore be more correct to say that the existence of garden path sentences is consistent with the determinism hypothesis, which provides one particular account of the phenomenon.) Furthermore, Marcus claims that the form of actually occurring garden path structures constitutes evidence for his particular model with a look-ahead buffer of a fixed (albeit variable) size. Put simply, Marcus hypothesizes that garden paths are sentences which cannot be parsed deterministically with a constituent buffer of *three* elements[45] and claims that his implementation of such a parser, PARSIFAL, fails to parse in GP contexts just as people do, providing evidence for PARSIFAL's psychological reality. Although, as will be seen, this particular implementation of the determinism hypothesis ultimately fails to account for the range of human processing breakdown, it is noteworthy both in its explicit recognition of a coherent class of data characterized by the need for conscious reanalysis and as an explicit attempt to account directly for the phenomenon with an interesting and predictive hypothesis.

Because Marcus hypothesizes that each grammar rule can only examine the first three constituents in the buffer, this model, like the Sausage Machine with its six-element window, predicts length effects in processing. However PARSIFAL is quite a bit more sophisticated than the Sausage Machine, which defines the buffer in terms of absolute elements, words, rather than variable length constituents. As a result of this variable buffer size, certain locally ambiguous structures which are sometimes associated with processing breakdown should fail to yield garden path effects in those cases where the resolution of the ambiguity is visible within the limitations of the three-constituent window. Indeed, Marcus's approach essentially maintains that there are no specific garden path structures at all, but only local ambiguities whose resolution may or may not lie within the scope of the look-ahead. This potentially allows for garden path effects to occur in more than one direction, for example, at times favoring the interpretation of an S' as an adjoined relative clause and at other times as a complement, as in examples such as (146).[46]

Consider how the processing breakdown associated with paradigmatic garden paths occurs within PARSIFAL. In a sentence such as *The boat floated down the river sank,* once the subject NP has been processed and attached under S, the buffer will hold a verb, preposition, and NP:

(148)   ❮floated❯$_V$ ❮down❯$_P$ ❮the river❯$_{NP}$

The final verb, *fall,* is not visible at this point and the matrix S rule is most directly matched. However, when the final verb appears, the preceding analysis is proven to be incorrect, and, since structure once built cannot be abandoned, nondeterministic and hence conscious reprocessing is required. Certain odd assumptions are involved even in this example, however. First, why does *down the river* does not enter the buffer as a PP in the same way that *the boat* enters as an NP?[47] Marcus's motivation for this actually seems to have been to account for the GP effect in these instances. He maintains that NPs enter the buffer as NPs because their "leading edges" are usually clearly defined by determiners, but this argument would seem to apply even more strongly to PPs, which always begin with one of the small closed class of prepositions whereas NPs may begin with members of the open class of nouns. If the account of GP effects were otherwise unproblematic, this might not be particularly disturbing, but consider a variation of the above sentence:

(149)   ¿The boated floated quickly sank.

Again, after the subject NP has been processed, the buffer will contain:

(150)   ❮floated❯$_V$ ❮quickly❯$_{ADV}$ ❮sank❯$_V$

In this instance, the disambiguating verb clearly lies within the range of PARSIFAL's look-ahead capability since the adverb doubtless occupies only a single buffer cell. Nevertheless, the garden path effect is just as severe in such examples as in those involving PPs. Similarly, modulo the previous caveats concerning extremely light relative clauses, there are even shorter garden path sentences

(151)   ¿Boys hit cry.
        Boys who are hit cry.
        (cf. Boys beaten cry.)

in which every word of the sentence would clearly fit within the buffer and therefore all global syntactic information would be available.

Additionally, a garden path sentence of a completely distinct structural type makes an identical point:

(152)   ¿Without ⟨her⟩$_{NP}$ ⟨money⟩$_{NP}$ ⟨would⟩$_{AUX}$ be hard to come by.

In (152), after *without* unambiguously matches a PP rule, *would* is visible within the buffer which views the next three elements, clearly revealing the need for a subject so that the initial error should not be made. Furthermore, the now familiar contrast between the following sorts of sentences cannot obviously be accounted for:

(153)   I suspected the boy from Spain would run away.
(154)   ¿I warned the boy from Spain would run away.

However the NP attachment ambiguity is ultimately resolved by PARSIFAL in such sentences, why only the latter case is problematic remains completely puzzling (as Marcus admits and as discussed in the following section, PARSIFAL mistakenly garden paths on all such ambiguities including (153)). It is therefore quite clear that Marcus's model cannot account comprehensively for garden path phenomena.[48] Most damagingly, it cannot account even for short canonical GPs which fail to display the expected length effects. Given that there are GPs which should be deterministically parsable by PARSIFAL but which nevertheless lead to processing breakdown, then at least this version of the determinism hypothesis is severely undermined.[49] In subsequent work, motivated at least in part in response to counterexamples such as these, Marcus developed a rather different and more sophisticated version of the determinism hypothesis which may now be considered.

2.1.3 Deterministic Parsing and Minimal Commitment

Building on the framework of Marcus (1980), Marcus, Hindle, and Fleck (1983), and Marcus (1987) outline a substantially revised model of deterministic parsing known as Description-theory (D-theory). As the name suggests, the on-line syntactic analysis of a sentence in this model consists not of a phrase marker but rather of a syntactic description, which has the crucial property of (possibly) locally encoding less information than a tree. Put simply, the parser describes structure on-line in terms of dominance, but not direct dominance, relations (hence D-theory is also sometimes referred to as Dominance-theory). Since descriptions founded on the predicate *dominates* (D) encode constituency, but not necessarily immediate constituency, D-theory parsers may be thought of as "minimal commitment" models (cf. Gorrel 1991; Weinberg 1990). The possibility of minimal commitment is obviously quite appropriate for a deterministic model. Since phrase structure descriptions may be locally underspecified, there is consequently less opportunity for the parser to commit irrevocable errors while building a representation. In other words, a local parsing decision that α dominates β is simply less likely to be false than a decision that α directly dominates β since the latter entails the former and is hence compatible with a wider range of structures. As a result, on-line underspecification is less likely to lead to processing breakdown.

Consider an example discussed by Marcus et al.:

(155)   I drove my aunt from Peoria's car.

Marcus notes that PARSIFAL is inappropriately led down the garden path on such examples and attaches the post-verbal NP *my aunt* directly as the complement, an analysis which is proven incorrect when the genitive *'s* is encountered. The local ambiguity is precisely parallel to that found in an example such as

(156)   I drove her car.

where *her* is ambiguous as between a head and a determiner. In Marcus's terms, such sentences contain a misleading edge, an initial left-embedded subconstituent (*my aunt, her*) which could wrongly be interpreted as the direct object of the prior verb rather than as a determiner. PARSIFAL itself errs in this fashion, mispredicting a garden path. Since such sentences are completely acceptable, this is quite problematic for that deterministic model. For precisely parallel reasons, PARSIFAL also incorrectly breaks down on unproblematic examples such as

(157)   I discovered the boy from Bethesda liked to run.

as briefly alluded to in the previous section.[50] An impressive advancement of the D-theory approach over PARSIFAL is its ability to handle such ambiguous object attachment cases which certainly present no difficulty for humans. Marcus notes that the problem with sentences of this sort is neither that PARSIFAL incorrectly processes a constituent as "a structure of the wrong kind," (since it is correctly parsed as an NP) nor that the constituent is attached to some node which does not dominate it (since the ambiguous NP is globally a constituent of the VP in either case). Rather, the source of the difficulty for PARSIFAL stems from the fact that the NP is structurally attached too high, directly as a complement rather than as a determiner or subject of the complement.

As is doubtless evident, this is no longer a problem within the D-theory model since only dominance, not direct dominance, is locally encoded. When such structures are initially parsed, only the information that the ambiguous NP is dominated by the local VP will be directly represented, direct dominance will not be indicated. As further material is processed, additional dominance statements are added and ultimately the NP's precise locus of attachment may be globally calculated from the sum total of these statements. This is the essence of the D-theory parser:

(158)   D-theory allows nodes to be attached initially by a parser to some point which will turn out to be higher than its lowest point of attachment . . . without such initial states causing the parser to garden path. Because of the nature of "D" the parser can in this sense "lower" a constituent without falsifying a previous prediction. The earlier predication remains indelible. (Marcus, Hindle, and Fleck 1983, 131)

In an example like (155), what is first encoded is only that the VP dominates the NP, *my aunt*. Later the additional dominance statements that another NP dominates a Det which dominates the original NP, etc., may be added without falsifying the initial dominance predicate and consequently without altering the structure. Similarly, in (157), speaking loosely, it will first be specified simply that the VP dominates *the boy from Bethesda,* and only subsequently is the information added that this VP dominates an S which itself dominates *the boy from Bethesda,* circumventing processing breakdown.

As shown, Marcus emphasizes the fact that a D-theory parser can "recover" from structures which would lead a deterministic tree-building parser down the garden path. However, as was demonstrated in the previous section, a primary failure of PARSIFAL was conversely the underprediction rather than the overprediction of GPs. This remains true of the D-theory parser, which is less, rather than more likely to fail than PARSIFAL.[51] Consider again the familiar contrast:

(159)   I discovered my aunt from Peoria had left.
(160)   ¿I warned my aunt from Peoria was wielding a knife.

As with (157) or (159), D-theory does not predict the structure in (160) to yield a garden path, initially specifying only that the post-verbal NP is dominated by VP. This remains true even in light of later information that that NP is the subject of an S which is dominated by a VP, just as in the example involving *discover.* The initial description is never undone in such examples, but processing breakdown nevertheless results.[52] Again, the structure built is neither of the wrong kind nor attached to material which does not dominate it. It is crucial to recall that parallel examples are fully grammatical:

(161)   President Gorbachev warned there would be severe food shortages.

Although the class of verbs which allow both the first internal argument and the complementizer to be dropped is limited, there are further examples:

(162)   ¿I promised my friend from Aruba would go skiing.
           (I promised that my friend from Aruba would go skiing.)
           (I promised we would go skiing.)

The same problem also arises with respect to paradigmatic garden paths such as (149) in a D-theory parser. Initially, the processor ought to specify only that the NP *the boat* is dominated by an S node which also dominates *floated* and *quickly*, which are further dominated by VP. This, however, remains true in the globally required relative clause structure as well.[53] D-theory is also unable to account for the garden path effect descriptively attributable to a preference for complement over relative clause:

(163)   ¿The doctor persuaded the patient that he was having trouble with to leave.

The S′ following the NP should initially be analyzed simply as a VP-dominated constituent. Subsequently, additional statements will be required specifying that a higher NP dominates both the NP and the S′, but previous dominance statements remain indelible. Recovery should not be problematic, but indeed is. Furthermore, the contrast of (163) with examples like:

(164)   a.   John gave the boys gifts.
        b.   John gave the boys' gifts to Mike.

where a similar indeterminacy *is* completely unproblematic simply cannot be accounted for. Clearly, D-theory, a more tolerant model, does not correct the primary problem associated with PARSIFAL, the underprediction of GP effects.

It appears then that, whatever their other virtues, the two particular implementations of the determinism hypothesis exemplified by PARSIFAL and D-theory fare little better than nondeterministic models in accounting for the range of unprocessable structures, and the contrast between problematic and unproblematic local ambiguity remains unexplained. As with all of the other processing models discussed so far, Marcus simply assumes that GP effects are to be accounted for in terms of the parsing architecture per se (perhaps as determined by human cognitive limitations) and consequently fully ignores the possibility that there may actually be something about the syntactic structures of the local ambiguities themselves which is crucial to the presence or absence of the garden path effect. In other words, each approach considered tacitly adopts the standard assumption that processing effects are pure performance phenomena, independent of grammatical theory. Ford, Bresnan, and Kaplan's lexical approach to processing outlined in the next section takes some tentative steps away from this assumption, however.

2.2 Lexical Approaches

Each of the theories of human natural language parsing heretofore considered characterizes processing difficulty directly in terms of errors of syntactic construction and the resulting need for reanalysis. Furthermore, most have focused on purely structural ambiguities and have had little explicit to say about lexical ambiguity, despite the fact that it may itself directly lead to structural ambiguity:

(165)   Japanese push bottles up Chinese.
   a. $[_{IP}$ $[_{NP}$ Japanese] $[_{VP}$ $[_V$ push] $[_{NP}$ bottles] $[_{PP}$ up Chinese]]]
   b. $[_{IP}$ $[_{NP}$ Japanese push] $[_{VP}$ $[_V$ bottles up] $[_{NP}$ Chinese]]]

However, given the fact that lexical ambiguity is neither a sufficient condition

(166)   a.   The construction workers $\left\{ \begin{array}{l} \text{raised} \\ \text{razed} \end{array} \right\}$ the building.
   b.   Ron visited the *bank*.

nor a necessary condition

(167)   The chicken is ready to eat.
   a. $[_{IP}$ $[_{NP}$ The chicken$_i$] $[_{I'}$ $[_I$ is] $[_{AP}$ $[_A$ ready] $[_{CP}$ $[_{IP}$ $[_{NP}$ PRO$_i$] $[_{I'}$ $[_I$ to] $[_{VP}$ eat]]]]]]]]
   b. $[_{IP}$ $[_{NP}$ The chicken$_j$] $[_{I'}$ $[_I$ is] $[_{AP}$ $[_A$ ready] $[_{CP}$ O_i^j $[_{IP}$ $[_{NP}$ PRO] $[_{I'}$ $[_I$ to] $[_{VP}$ $[_V$ eat] $[_{NP}$ e_i]]]]]]]]]

for structural ambiguity, the former has typically been ignored or treated as a distinct subclass, subject to independent (albeit generally unspecified) principles.[54]

Clearly, the theoretical and empirical relationship between lexical and structural ambiguity is not a priori obvious and several conceivable perspectives are open. One extreme but logically possible position would be that all apparently structural processing effects are actually to be attributed directly to lexical effects. Paradigmatic garden path structures upon this conception would most clearly be represented by sentences such as (168), which exhibit (at least) a noun-verb ambiguity with respect to the categorial identity of *train*.

(168)   ¿The old train the next generation.

The diametrically opposed position that it is only the structural ramifications of lexical ambiguity which are relevant will be argued in §4.1, but it will prove useful to consider the alternative view in some detail first.

2.2.1 Lexical Functional Grammar

The radical approach to ambiguity outlined above is developed in detail by Ford, Bresnan, and Kaplan (1982) within the framework of Lexical Functional Grammar (though it is not obviously dependent on any particular theoretical constructs of that approach). The authors argue that there is no a priori reason to believe that on-line reanalysis per se should be costly and hypothesize, contra the assumptions of every relevant model heretofore considered, that the need for backtracking when a local structural ambiguity must be resolved in a fashion inconsistent with the primary attachment strategies employed by the parser will not be problematic:

(169)   Reanalysis of phrasal structure without the need to recategorize a word may increase the complexity of local parsing decisions as measured by reactions times, but without perception of a garden path. (Ford, Bresnan, and Kaplan 1982, 763)

Instead, what they suggest is that a garden path results only when the stronger form of a lexical item must be rejected in favor of a weaker form in order to satisfy the functional compatibility requirements of the grammar with respect to the input string. This characterization is founded on the hypothesis that, "the various lexical forms of a given verb have different 'strengths' or 'saliencies,' and that the strongest form somehow determines the preferred syntactic analysis" (Ford, Bresnan, and Kaplan 1982, p. 745):

(170)   [R]eanalysis which requires a new morphosyntactic analysis of a word within the functional structure of a completed constituent may cause a conscious garden path. (Ford, Bresnan, and Kaplan 1982, 763)

In other words, GPs result from certain forms of lexical (morphosyntactic) ambiguity rather than from structural ambiguity in and of itself.[55] This tack is the fundamental opposite of that taken by Frazier and Rayner (1982), who assumed all backtracking to be costly modulo a specific reanalysis strategy (Steal-NP). In contrast, Ford, Bresnan, and Kaplan maintain that what is difficult is only lexical reanalysis. Since lexical information is indisputably grammatical information, it is in this sense, according to the authors, that the model is more competence based than alternative frameworks. However, in absolute contrast to the theory to be developed in chapters 3 through 5, their model is in no way conceptually derived from grammatical theory, but simply appeals to very idiosyncratic aspects of word knowledge. Furthermore, neither Ford, Bresnan, and Kaplan's nor Frazier and Rayner's approach recognizes the paramount importance of structural factors in accounting for human parsing performance.

Consider what Ford, Bresnan, and Kaplan consider to be a motivating example:

(171)   ¿The boy got fat melted.

The initial functional structure is built (by stipulation) based on *fat* as an adjective rather than a noun. The necessary recategorization as a nominal subsequently results in the GP effect. The account of paradigmatic garden paths of the *The boat floated down the river sank* variety is similar. The verb is first categorized as *active intransitive* and *tensed* (again by stipulation), which must subsequently be rejected in favor of a new morphosyntactic analysis as a *passive participle*. The garden path effect is considered a *direct* result of this lexical recategorization and not its structural ramifications. Ford, Bresnan, and Kaplan's claim, then, is that reanalysis only results in a conscious garden path when lexical recategorization of a word is necessary, though it should be noted that the requisite notion of "recategorization" is quite broad and need involve no major category shift.

Although this theory is appealingly simple on the surface, there are numerous empirical problems. On the one hand, in several instances it overpredicts high processing cost. For example, the following sentences are clear counterexamples to (170):

(172)   a.   The bird bought yesterday sold.
        b.   The tank blown up in the battle was removed from service.

Although they appear to conform to the canonical GP pattern, and the lexical recategorization required is precisely the same as that necessitated in canonical GP structures, the sentences are not difficult to process. Even more simply, it is not clear why one of the following is not a garden path sentence

(173)   a.   I like green very much.
        b.   I like green M&Ms.

since whatever the stronger lexical form of *green,* the choice will be wrong in one instance.[56]

On the other hand, high processing cost is also severely underpredicted within this model:

(174)   ¿The cotton fields produce makes warm clothing.
        (The cotton which fields produce makes warm clothing.)
        (cf. The plants fields produce make warm clothing.)
(175)   ¿I warned the new professor failed many students.
        (I warned that the new professor failed many students.)
        (cf. I warned he failed many students.)
(176)   ¿While Ron was sewing the shirt slipped to the floor.
        (The shirt slipped to the floor while Ron was sewing.)
        (cf. While Ron was sewing he fell to the floor.)
(177)   ¿The patient persuaded the doctor that he was having trouble with to
        leave.
        (The patient persuaded the doctor with whom he was having trouble
        to leave.)
        (cf. The patient expected the doctor that he was having trouble with
        to leave.)

There is no lexical recategorization required in any of these sentences, which are, nevertheless, extremely problematic. In other words, purely structural garden path sentences clearly exist. For example, in (175) and (176) the NPs remain NPs and it is simply their locus of attachment which is reanalyzed, while in example (177) it is only the attachment of the S' which is in question. Example (174) is particularly interesting as it is an object relative variation on the canonical garden path pattern and cannot be accounted for in terms of any obvious categorial ambiguity. Both locally and globally, *produce* is clearly a verb not a passive participle, and *cotton* and *fields* each remain nominal in both the mistaken compound reading and the correct relativized NP interpretation.

However, one might imagine that at least (175)–(177) could be explained were each instance of a lexical item with a distinct complement structure classified as an independent morphosyntactic form. In that case it might be argued that a lexical recategorization of the *verb* does take place. Such a move would be virtually identical to extending the authors' general account of structural attachment heuristics to GP effects, something Ford, Bresnan, and Kaplan explicitly reject. Nevertheless, it is useful to consider whether such an analysis could be successfully developed. For example, ignoring the numerous theoretical objections which might be raised, distinct subcategorizations of verbs, such as *sew* (<(SUBJ), (OBJ)>, <(SUBJ), ∅>) or *warn* (<(SUBJ), (OBJ)>, <(SUBJ), (OBJ2), (SCOMP)>) might be considered independent morphosyntactic forms. Additionally, it would be necessary to stipulate a preferred subcategorization pattern, just as it is necessary to stipulate that the active intransitive interpretation of the verb *raced* is preferred to the passive participle reading. Granting these assumptions, recategorization which requires a change in complement structure would be predicted to be equally as problematic as, for example, the recategorization of an active intransitive as a passive participle. The authors do actually maintain that the various lexical forms of verbs have different saliencies and that it is the strongest form which steers attachment. As noted, however, they do not hold that these constitute different morphosyntactic forms[57] and hence rejection of one in favor of another does not constitute lexical reanalysis upon their account.

For example, the verb *want* putatively favors the complement structure <(SUBJ), (OBJ)> over <(SUBJ), (OBJ), (PCOMP)> while in the case of *position* the situation is just the reverse:

(178)   The woman wanted [NP the dress [PP on the rack]].

(179)   The woman positioned [NP the dress] [PP on the rack].

And it is through the interaction of the following two principles, that the parser attempts to satisfy such lexical tendencies:

(180)   *Lexical Preferences*
         If a set of alternatives has been reached in the expansion of a phrase structure rule, give priority to the alternatives that are coherent with the strongest lexical form of the predicate. (Ford, Bresnan, and Kaplan 1982, 747)

(181)   *Final Arguments*
         Give low priority to attaching to a phrase the final argument of the
         strongest lexical form of that phrase and to attaching any elements
         subsequent to the final argument. Low priority is defined here with
         respect to other options that arise at the end position of the element
         whose attachment is to be delayed. (Ford, Bresnan, and Kaplan
         1982, 752)

Together, the effect of the above is to hold the final argument (the rightmost
argument specified in a lexical form) of the strong form of a lexical item open
and to delay that argument's own higher attachment, while closing nonfinal
arguments early. The effects will vary item by item since Lexical Preferences
forces the priority of the form which is simply stipulated to be the strongest.
For example, in (178), Lexical Preferences operate on the strong form of
want, hypothesized to be <(SUBJ), (OBJ)>. The Final Arguments strategy
will both delay the attachment of *the dress* to VP and attach *on the rack* to the
NP. In the case of *position,* <(SUBJ), (OBJ), (PCOMP)> is preferred and therefore in (179) *the dress* is closed early as a nonfinal argument and *on the rack*
is attached to VP rather than NP.

    There are a number of undesirable aspects of this approach, both theoreti-
cal and empirical. First, on general theoretical grounds, while any grammatical framework must of course encode the argument structure possibilities
associated with individual heads, data concerning the preferred interpretations
of lexical items is not something obviously necessary for any *syntactic* theory.
Not only will favored complement structures have to be stipulated, but completely independent lexical information will be needed to ensure putative
categorial preferences (e.g., prefer *fat* as an adjective rather than a noun).
Furthermore, since these facts are specific to particular lexical items and apparently independent of their syntax or semantics, they must presumably be
learned individually. The amount of information required is far from trivial.

    Since there is no apparent grammatical justification for the inclusion of
such information, the issue hinges entirely upon empirical issues of performance. However, encumbering the Lexicon with a very large amount of
idiosyncratic information has the effect of making the approach extremely un-
predictive, and indeed, it even becomes difficult to explain why garden path
effects do not vary wildly from individual to individual depending on their
personal histories with specific words. The fundamental empirical basis is
undermined from the start. Far more importantly, however, there are numerous specific problems with the approach. Consider the authors' example:

(182)   The saleslady wanted [NP the dress] [PP on the rack].

Here the weaker interpretation <(SUBJ), (OBJ), (PCOMP)> arguably comes to
be favored simply because of a trivial change in lexical item from *woman* to

saleslady, raising considerable doubt as to the reality of the original "preference." Similarly contrast:

(183) a. The tourists [$_{VP}$ signaled [$_{PP}$ to the guide] [$_{S'}$ that they couldn't hear]].
<(SUBJ), (TO OBJ), (SCOMP)>

b. The tourists [$_{VP}$ signaled [$_{PP}$ to [$_{NP}$ the guide [$_{S'}$ that they couldn't hear]]]].
<(SUBJ), (TO OBJ)>

(184) a. The tourists [$_{VP}$ objected [$_{PP}$ to [$_{NP}$ the guide [$_{S'}$ that they couldn't hear]]]].
<(SUBJ), (TO OBJ)>

b. The tourists [$_{VP}$ objected [$_{PP}$ to the guide] [$_{S'}$ that they couldn't hear]].
<(SUBJ), (TO OBJ), (SCOMP)>

Ford, Bresnan, and Kaplan claim that the strongest form of *signal* is <(SUBJ), (TO OBJ), (SCOMP)> and of *object,* <(SUBJ), (TO OBJ)>. This accounts for what they consider to be the preferred interpretations of the globally ambiguous sentences in (183) and (184). However, since they explicitly state that rejection of the strong form of a lexical item without the need for morphosyntactic reanalysis does not lead to garden path effects, the following contrast is unexplained:

(185) ¿The tourists [$_{VP}$ signaled [$_{PP}$ to [$_{NP}$ the guide [$_{S'}$ that they disliked]]]].
<(SUBJ), (TO OBJ)>

(186) The tourists [$_{VP}$ objected [$_{PP}$ to the guide] [$_{S'}$ that they couldn't hear him]].
<(SUBJ), (TO OBJ), (SCOMP)>

In (185) a weaker form of *signal* as a <(SUBJ), (TO OBJ)> verb is required and the garden path effect results, while in (186) a weaker form of *object* as a <(SUBJ), (TO OBJ), (SCOMP)> verb is required, and no processing difficulty arises. If it is held that reanalysis without the need for morphosyntactic re-categorization is not costly, then the GP status of sentence (185) is unexplained. On the other hand, if the general parsing model is extended to GP effects and such reanalysis is in fact predicted to be difficult, the lack of GP effects in (186) is unaccounted for. Furthermore, an example such as

(187) ¿The tourists objected to the guide that they disliked that they should leave.

should require no reanalysis at all since the globally correct relative NP interpretation should initially be favored, yet it is nevertheless a clear garden path.

There are numerous additional examples which reinforce this same point that rejection of a stronger form in favor of a weaker form cannot be equated with morphosyntactic reanalysis—i.e., that Ford, Bresnan, and Kaplan's general account of closure effects cannot be extended to garden path sentences. Recall the sentences of (175)–(176). Given the processing effects displayed, *warn* <(SUBJ), (SCOMP)> and *sew* <(SUBJ), ∅> must be considered weak frames since the alternative forms are processed quite easily. This, however, will incorrectly predict the following sentences to be garden paths:

(188)   I warned that he was coming to collect the rent.

(189)   Ron sewed for hours last Tuesday.

Notice similarly that, strictly interpreted, sentences such as

(190)   The boy obtained fat.

should be GPs, since *fat* is stipulated to have an adjectival strong form which must be recategorized as a noun.[58]

In the above examples, a certain reading of Ford, Bresnan, and Kaplan's principles drastically overpredicts GP effects. However, there are additional examples in which strict adherence to their syntactic processing principles in contrast fails to predict occurring GP effects. Consider the sentence:

(191)   ¿I warned her mother was wielding an axe.

On the quite defensible assumption that the strongest form of *warn* is <(SUBJ), (OBJ2), (SCOMP)> as in the perfectly acceptable

(192)   I warned my brother his teacher was out to get him.

sentence (191) should be processed without difficulty according to Ford, Bresnan, and Kaplan's established principles. Lexical Preferences maintains that a parse consistent with the above frame is to be pursued and in combination with Final Arguments should insure the early closure of (OBJ2) and the early building of the final argument (SCOMP). When *mother* is encountered and its ambiguous attachment possibilities noted, the strategies predict the closure of *her* and the attachment of *mother* as a constituent of (SCOMP), precisely the interpretation which people do *not* easily obtain. The correct parse should follow automatically from the authors' principles and consequently, they wrongly predict that such sentences are not garden paths.

However, if their principles were altered and the (OBJ2) constituent closed late, explaining the incorrect inclusion of *mother* above, sentences such as

(193)   ¿The patient warned the doctor he was having trouble with he should leave.

could not be explained. Again, if *warn* has a strong form <(SUBJ), (OBJ2), (SCOMP)>, then the garden path is only predicted if *the doctor* is closed early and *he was having* parsed as an (SCOMP) rather than as a constituent of the NP, precisely as should have been done to predict the garden path in (191). In

(193) the (OBJ2) of *warn* should be closed early if the GP effect is to be pre-dicted, while in (191) it must be closed late in order to account for the pro-cessing difficulty. This contrast cannot be handled by this approach and hence even when sentences are consistent with putative strong forms, parsing in ac-cord with Ford, Bresnan, and Kaplan's syntactic strategies remains incapable of accounting for the data.

In light of the above discussion and the numerous counterexamples, there seems to be no coherent way of attributing the range of GP effects solely to lexical ambiguity no matter how broadly that term is construed. This point has been made in somewhat exhaustive detail since informal versions of this claim are commonly put forward based on the finite-participial ambiguity in the canonical garden path structure, and it is important to recognize that even an extremely sophisticated approach along such lines closely tied to a well-developed grammatical theory is nevertheless destined to fail. The above dis-cussion leaves open the converse question of whether the processing difficulty associated with lexical ambiguity can be wholly characterized in terms of its structural ramifications or must be considered an independent phenomenon, as is traditionally if tacitly assumed; the former view is defended in detail in §4.1. Note finally that it is crucial not to confuse the authors' use of the term "competence based" to refer to a parser which makes use of quasi-semantic item-dependent subcategorization information with a fully grammar-derived parsing theory as foreshadowed in chapter 1.

2.3 Semantic Approaches

This section of the chapter examines two models in which semantic fac-tors are held to be of primary relevance to an account of human natural parsing, but which differ significantly with respect to the role they play. One attributes a range of processing effects directly to semantic interpretation, ar-guing that once linguistic material is interpreted its internal structure is no longer syntactically accessible, while the other rather conversely argues that semantic factors instead facilitate error recovery. It is important to recognize that both approaches continue to assume that the fundamental processing strategies employed by the parser are themselves syntactic[59] and that its output includes a syntactic representation of the input string, with semantics playing a role primarily with respect to reanalysis.[60]

2.3.1 Interpretive Islands

Frazier (1985) presents an analysis of processing complexity which ap-peals to certain aspects of semantic interpretation as well as to syntax, and, although she herself does not do so explicitly, it is natural to attempt to extend the approach to garden path phenomena. Quite simply, Frazier hypothesizes that in order to reduce processing load, nonsemantic (i.e., syntactic, lexical, and phonological) information will be forgotten as soon as it is no longer required for understanding. Specifically, she suggests that this occurs as soon as a *complete minimal governing category* (CMGC) is processed. For the purposes of discussion here, a CMGC may be taken as equivalent to a simple governing category upon the following definition:

(194)   *Governing Category*
          . . . the minimal NP or S containing both a governor and governed
          material (where tense governs the subject, verbs and prepositions
          govern their objects, and nouns govern their complements). (Frazier
          1985, 173)

For example, consider the following:

(195)   a.   The students tried [PRO to learn]$_{S \neq CMGC}$
          b.   The students tried [PRO to learn phonetics]$_{S=CMGC}$
          c.   The students expected [John to think about shoes]$_{S=CMGC}$

By this definition, the embedded S in sentence (195a) does not constitute a governing category because PRO is ungoverned and *learn* has no object. In (b) in contrast, *phonetics* is governed by *learn* and the lower clause is a CMGC as it is in (c), where the preposition *about* governs *shoes*.

Frazier's fundamental claim that these complete minimal governing categories constitute semantic replacement units which license the "forgetting of non-semantic information" on-line is quite transparently reminiscent of Kimball's sixth (Fixed Structure) and seventh (Processing) principles recast in more contemporary theoretical argot. It is also necessary for her to stipulate that only those CMGCs which lie off the main projection path (roughly subjects and adjuncts) may undergo semantic replacement. Those on the path do not yield all grammatical information necessary for interpretation until the termination of the entire matrix S, even though their status as CMGCs may be detected much sooner. Recall from §2.0.2 that Kimball too was forced to introduce a similar condition into his definition of a closed phrase in order to avoid equating left- and right-branching structures with center-embeddings. (See Stabler 1991 for a discussion of some bizarre aspects of related assumptions, however.) As a result, Frazier claims, subjects and adjuncts are natural interpretive islands since their grammatical content may be forgotten on-line, or, in Kimball's terms, "cleared from short-term memory." Notice that this approach simply assumes that it is less costly to store semantic as opposed to grammatical information.

Frazier applies this theory primarily to certain referential dependencies resulting from leftward or rightward movement out of CMGCs in an effort to provide a perceptual rather than a grammatical account of certain transformational constraints, issues not of direct concern here. However, although she does not attempt to extend this analysis to garden path phenomena, it is reasonable to do so since, as this article itself demonstrates, the notion of semantic replacement has tended to resurface. Consider then certain garden path examples which the CMGC hypothesis does appear capable of predicting:

(196) ¿While John painted the portrait dropped off the tripod.
(While John painted it, the portrait dropped off the tripod.)
(cf. While John slept, the portrait dropped off the tripod.)

In (196), as soon as *the portrait* is encountered, a CMGC off of the main projection path is established, since the adjunct clause is not an argument and *paint* governs *the portrait*. Consequently, this clause should be able to serve as a semantic replacement unit and its internal syntax forgotten. The subsequent appearance of *drop* reveals this to be incorrect and necessitates the syntactic reanalysis of a constituent whose grammatical structure may have been forgotten, thus apparently correctly predicting the garden path effect. Consider an even simpler example involving canonical GPs:

(197) ¿The little boy painted on the canvas was asleep.
(The little boy who was painted on the canvas was asleep.)
(cf. The little boy drawn on the canvas was asleep.)

Minimal Attachment and Late Closure provide a main clause analysis before the matrix element *was* is encountered, and the parser will at this point hypothesize that it has completed parsing the main clause and reached the end of the main projection path, shunting the clause to some semantic interpreter. The subsequent appearance of *was asleep,* however, will force reanalysis, which is problematic since previous syntactic structure is no longer available, accounting for the difficulty (again compare Kimball's seventh principle).

Despite the CMGC hypothesis's apparent success in accounting for these two garden path structures, numerous questions arise even with respect to these examples. Why, for instance, in (196) does the parser not hypothesize *While John painted* to be a CMGC, since it contains a tensed INFL which governs *John*?[61] Were syntactic forgetting licensed at this point, the correct reading would be predicted unproblematic since the adjunct internal syntax would be forgotten before the subsequent appearance of *the portrait*, which would then be available to serve as subject.

Likewise, the GP effects in (198) and (199) and their complementary absence in (200) are completely unaccounted for:

(198) ¿The doctor told the patient that he was having trouble with to leave.
(199) ¿The doctor told the patient that he was having trouble with.
(The doctor told the patient with whom he was having trouble.)
(cf. The doctor awaited the patient he was having trouble with.)
(200) The doctor told the patient that he was having trouble with his bill.

According to Frazier, a complement clause lies along the main projection path whereas a complex relative NP does not. Since it behooves the parser to perform semantic interpretation as quickly as possible in order to reduce processing load, this would appear to predict a preference for the relative clause structure which could be interpreted and cleared from memory—but this is of course precisely the analysis which is disfavored.

Additionally, there are numerous garden path structures which this analysis simply has no hope of handling since the effects lie along the main projection path:

(201)   ¿Susan persuaded her demons were out to get her.
        (Susan persuaded her that demons were out to get her.)
        (cf. Susan persuaded him demons were out to get him.)
(202)   The warlock discovered the witch was out to get him.
(203)   ¿Theresa warned Zeny liked to kiss cats.
        (Theresa warned that Zeny liked to kiss cats.)
        (cf. Theresa warned she liked to kiss cats.)

However, even if this assumption were somehow abandoned (ignoring obvious complications) and closure assumed to occur whenever a CMGC was encountered, the wrong predictions would still be made. Even disregarding INFL, in (201) a CMGC exists as soon as *her* is processed, falsely predicting that *demons* should be available to serve as subject. Though an account of (203) would become available, the same assumptions would falsely predict (202) to be costly to process, failing to account for the contrast.

Unfortunately then, it seems that despite the appeal of a model which makes a relatively explicit claim as to the realm in which syntactic reanalysis is problematic, the specified domain simply appears irrelevant to garden path effects under any consistent interpretation. Again, it is important to recall that Frazier herself does not present the interpretive island hypothesis as a model of ambiguity effects, and the discussion above has necessarily extrapolated from her model somewhat. However, given the historical importance of similar notions, it is nevertheless vital to recognize that this and related approaches appear to fail as accounts of on-line processing effects.

2.3.2 Semantic Reanalysis Strategies

In contrast to Frazier, who ascribes certain aspects of processing difficulty to the loss of grammatical information which purportedly occurs upon semantic interpretation, Carlson and Tanenhaus (1988) hypothesize that (lexical) semantics may aid rather than hinder the processor's recovery. The authors focus their attention on two types of intracategorial verbal ambiguity, which they distinguish as "sense" versus "thematic." Sense ambiguities are those which exist between verbs with truly distinct core meanings, that is, between verbs which are simply either homophonous or polysemous. For instance, according to the authors the verb *set* may mean, roughly, "to place" or "to adjust": [62]

(204)   John set the vase on the table.
(205)   John set the clock to noon.

Carlson and Tanenhaus contrast such sense ambiguities with the thematic ambiguities which arise when multiple argument structures are associated with the same core predicate. For example, the verb *slice* appears in at least two surface patterns, one in which it assigns the AGENT role to its subject, THEME to its direct object, and INSTRUMENT to a PP headed by *with*:

(206)   Rex sliced the salami with a knife.

and another where the THEME continues to be realized as direct object but where the INSTRUMENT role is assigned to subject and no AGENT is expressible:

(207)   A sharp knife sliced Rex's salami (*by John).

Based on work of Simpson (1984), the authors hypothesize the processor initially recovers all distinct "senses" of an ambiguous item as well as all of the sets of thematic roles associated with each sense. The choice between verb senses, and subsequently between thematic grids, is then made based on contextual information. [63] Alternative senses, and apparently alternative grids, are discarded, but crucially:

(208)   Any thematic roles on an active grid not assigned to an argument remain active as open thematic roles in the discourse model, appearing as free variables or unspecified "addresses" in the model. (Carlson and Tanenhaus 1988, 264)

Though Carlson and Tanenhaus neither attempt to characterize garden path environments nor the distinction between problematic and unproblematic syntactic reanalysis, they do employ (208) to explain why certain garden paths of the canonical type are putatively easier than others to recover from:

(209)   a.   (¿)The girl sent the note didn't respond.
                (The girl who was sent the note didn't respond.)
                (cf. The girl given the note didn't respond.)
         b.   (¿)The man served the rare steak complained.
                (The man who was served the rare steak complained.)
                (cf. The man given the rare steak complained.)
(210)   a.   ¿The child hurried out the front door slipped.
                (The child who was hurried out the front door slipped.)
                (cf. The child thrown out the front door slipped.)

b.   ¿The athlete trained at the gym lost the fight.
(The athlete who was trained at the gym lost the fight.)
(cf. The athlete beaten at the gym lost the fight.)

The authors maintain that there is a contrast between the sentences of (209) and (210) with the former examples displaying milder GP effects than the latter. This they equate with the availability of an "open thematic role" in the theta grid of the former. By hypothesis, this facilitates recovery by providing feedback to the processor and suggesting an alternative thematic analysis with respect to the same thematic grid already selected. For example, the semantic roles assigned by *send* are <AGENT, THEME, GOAL>. In (209a), *the girl* is initially marked as AGENT and *the note* as THEME, since that reading is presumably the most contextually appropriate. When this analysis proves incorrect, the unassigned GOAL role is available for association with *the girl,* which facilitates reanalysis, though how this is syntactically accomplished is unclear. On the other hand, consider the situation involving a paradigmatic garden path, such as those in (210). On the initially pursued unaccusative reading of *hurry, the child* is assigned a THEME role, and, upon reanalysis as passive, *the child* continues to receive that same role. Because the role assignments do not change from one sentence to the next, reprocessing is in no way facilitated. No alternative thematic assignments are possible given the active theta grid, accounting for the difficulty. Even given its modest goal of characterizing degrees of difficulty among paradigmatic GPs, the account requires some extremely puzzling assumptions.

Consider for example, (210a). Verbs like *hurry* occur in two surface argument structure patterns which the authors would associate with distinct thematic grids (one associates a THEME role with the subject position, and another links AGENT with subject and THEME with complement):

(211)   a.   The child$_{\text{THEME}}$ hurried out the door.
b.   The child$_{\text{AGENT}}$ hurried the dog$_{\text{THEME}}$ out the door.

In order to account for the lack of facilitation effects, Carlson and Tanenhaus must assume that it is the unaccusative analysis of (211a) which is initially pursued in such cases, but there is simply no justification provided for this assumption. Suppose instead that the agentive interpretation were initially postulated and the NP *the child* in (210a) assigned the AGENT role (animate subjects are certainly no less likely as AGENTS than THEMES), paralleling an example such as (211b). When this analysis becomes untenable, the open THEME role will be available to aid in reanalysis. In fact, the authors maintain that something very similar does account for the putative improvement of sentences such as

(212)   (¿)The cat watched in the pet shop ran away.

which involve not a transitive-unaccusative alternation (like *hurry*) but a transitive-unergative alternation. The verb *watch* assignes a PERCEIVER role to its (nonpassive) subject, regardless, and a THEME role to its optional complement. In (212) *the cat* will initially be misassigned a PERCEIVER role but reanalysis is facilitated by the open THEME role, according to the authors. What Carlson and Tanenhaus fail to recognize is that something very similar should be available to facilitate reanalysis in the case of *hurry*. Those verbs also display an alternation, and when considering just the local subject-verb sequence it will be impossible to discern which analysis to pursue. Consequently, to account for the contrast between the two classes of verbs it is absolutely crucial to insure that the subject of unaccusatives always be initially assigned the role associated with the complement in its transitive alternation. Otherwise, an open role will be available falsely predicting ease of recovery. If true, however, this is surely a syntactic fact par excellence and remains entirely a stipulation within their contextual model.

It should furthermore be quite evident that their framework cannot directly account for the impossibility of recovery from a wider range of garden path effects than the canonical sort considered GPs as discussed throughout this chapter. In each individual case (including *warn, persuade, sew,* and *convince* type examples), the verb which forces reanalysis will have available an open role, incorrectly predicting easy reanalysis precisely in those cases where it is highly costly.

Finally, there are several rather unclear and seemingly inconsistent aspects of the approach. As noted, the authors maintain that their notion of theta roles is purely conceptual, not configurational, and they essentially ignore both transformational and lexical-semantic accounts of thematic alternations. However, this raises the significant question of how the presence of an open role can aid in structural reanalysis when thematic roles are divorced from structure. It cannot be the case that Carlson and Tanenhaus would wish to maintain that it is thematic rather than structural reanalysis per se which is the source of the difficulty, as it is precisely in those cases where *no* such thematic reanalysis can occur that canonical GP effects are most difficult to recover from according to their own analysis. The fact that reanalysis is costly although *the child* remains THEME in both the unaccusative and passive interpretations of the canonical GP strongly suggests that the relevant factors are syntactic since no purely semantic reanalysis is involved at all. Furthermore, as the authors themselves recognize, the simple necessity of switching within and between thematic grids (and apparently between distinct verb senses) does not lead to significant processing difficulty. For example the following pair of unproblematic sentences are both thematically ambiguous through the occurrence of the NP *the truck*:

(213)   J.B.$_{AGENT}$ loaded the truck$_{GOAL}$ with bananas$_{THEME}$.
(214)   J.B.$_{AGENT}$ loaded the truck$_{THEME}$ onto the boat$_{GOAL}$.

Finally, it is a significant shortcoming of their approach that the notion "open role" is so poorly defined. At times it is identified with a true implicit argument, such as the AGENT of *by*-less passives, which, as is well known, has overt syntactic properties, such as the ability to control the empty subject of purposive clauses (cf. Keyser and Roeper 1984):

(215)   The boat was sunk to collect the insurance.

At other times, it simply appears to be identified with any unexpressed roles associated with a verb, such as the GOAL role in a sentence such as (216b):

(216)   a.   Susan lectured Malcolm about belching.
        b.   Susan lectured about belching.

which, in contrast to the AGENT in (215), does not behave as if it were syntactically present:

(217)   a.   Susan lectured Malcolm$_i$ about himself$_i$.
        b.   *Susan lectured about himself.
             ($\neq$Susan lectured someone$_i$ about himself$_i$.)

The great number of these problems may be ascribed directly to Carlson and Tanenhaus's unmotivated assumption that thematic roles are purely conceptual rather than structural. Consequently, the approach neither serves as a general theory of sentence processing nor has significant success even within its rather narrow domain.

2.4 Summary

Although the perceptual, computational, lexical, and semantic models of human natural language processing reviewed above have distinct functional motivations, all share a common underlying assumption. In each, both the strategies for ambiguity resolution as well as the constraints on "reanalysis" are attributed in some fashion to limitations inherent in the architecture of the parser. Broadly, perceptual and computational models cast these restrictions in terms of cognitive resources, while lexical and semantic frameworks assume a fundamental dichotomy in the availability of different types of information during the time course of the parse. As a means toward establishing the fundamental psycholinguistic data as well as the theoretical issues they raise, this chapter has tested the predictions of representative approaches of each type against facts concerning human processing breakdown. The robustness of the garden path phenomenon—the inability of the parser to assign a globally grammatical interpretation to the well-formed input string because of a severe misanalysis—makes it a particularly valuable class of data capable of serving a role parallel to that of ungrammaticality within linguistic theory.

By definition, any cognitively valid model of human sentence parsing must predict breakdown in precisely those instances where it is actually experienced by humans. Of course, any model founded upon such data will necessarily distinguish costly reanalysis from cost-free reanalysis from nonreanalysis, naturally yielding a general theory of human natural language processing. This is of course the only reasonable goal, and it is important not to allow the fact that the primary data derive from processing breakdown to lead one to the patently false conclusion that what is being developed is a theory of garden path phenomena per se. Clearly, this is no more true than it is to say that linguistics is a theory of ungrammatical utterances, but because the methodology employed here is more typical of linguistics and less typical of experimental psycholinguistics, the danger is perhaps more real.[64]

Recall the following descriptive taxonomy presented in chapter 1 and discussed throughout chapter 2:

(218)   *Taxonomic classification of local ambiguity*
   i. Main Clause–Relative NP Ambiguity is resolved in favor of a main clause analysis, with relative clauses yielding GP effects.
   ii. Complement Clause–Relative Clause Ambiguity is resolved in favor of a complement clause analysis, with relative clauses yielding GP effects.
   iii. Object-Subject Ambiguity appears to be resolved in favor of objects, with only certain subjects yielding GP effects.
   iv. Double Object Ambiguity appears to be resolved variously, sometimes yielding GP effects.[65]
   v. Lexical Categorial Ambiguity appears to be resolved variously, sometimes yielding GP effects.

As repeatedly demonstrated, no consistent interpretation of attachment preferences alone can possibly account for these distinctions between problematic and unproblematic local ambiguity and there does not exist any empirically adequate theory of syntactic "recovery." Consequently, this list remains purely descriptive, and the questions posed at the beginning of chapter 1 remain unanswered:
   i. How is it that humans are able to (rapidly and automatically) assign grammatically licit structure to incoming strings of words?
   ii. What is the relationship between the parser and the grammar that makes this possible?
The next three chapters provide an answer in terms of grammatical theory.

CHAPTER THREE

A Grammatical Theory of Processing

3.0 Starting Assumptions

In the introductory chapter, it was suggested that there was a single answer to the two primary questions posed there and repeated at the end of chapter 2:

    iii. The core of syntactic parsing consists of the local application of global grammatical principles.

This chapter argues in detail for such a grammar-derived theory of human natural language processing, demonstrating that unlike the alternatives discussed previously, such a model provides a natural account of established processing phenomena. Initially, the analysis is cast in terms of concepts common to all major grammatical theories (though in the vocabulary of modern transformational grammar), but it comes to rely increasingly on notions specific to the Government and Binding (a.k.a. Principles and Parameters) framework. As noted in chapter 1, the shift away from specific rules to constraints on representation has permeated virtually all syntactic theories, but has been the most pervasive within GB. Consequently, the adoption of Government and Binding as the ultimate grammatical basis of the derived parsing theory is by no means an arbitrary decision. Only a principle-based model of grammar readily lends itself to the requisite form of local application without substantial reinterpretation of the grammatical theory itself, and it is only GB that provides the theoretical apparatus necessary for the construction of the proper processing theory.[66]

In order to motivate the grammar-based theory as directly as possible, it is useful to analyze the data considered throughout chapter 2 while attending to but a single syntactic principle, the theta criterion, applied locally in the form of theta attachment, as partially undertaken in chapter 1. Recall then the following principles of attachment and reanalysis:

(219)   **Theta Attachment:** The theta criterion attempts to be satisfied at every point during processing given the maximal theta grid.

(220)   **Theta Reanalysis Constraint (TRC):** Syntactic reanalysis which re-

interprets a theta-marked constituent as outside of its current theta domain is costly. [Version 1]

(221)   **Theta Domain:** α is in the γ theta domain of β iff α receives the γ theta role from β or α is dominated by a constituent that receives the γ theta role from β.

The definition of theta domain appeals to two well-established grammatical notions, *dominance* and *thematic role*. As in the Government and Binding framework itself, thematic roles are held to be purely configurational rather than conceptual phenomena (at the level of the syntax) and consequently what is relevant is structural *position* rather than role content. However, use of thematic role labels (e.g., AGENT, THEME, PROPOSITION, etc.) is initially helpful for expository purposes. (See §1.6 for an expanded discussion of the motivations behind these assumptions.) Notice that neither (219) nor (220) is functionally motivated in terms of the inherent architecture of the parser but rather in terms of grammatical theory.

3.0.1 An Unambiguous Example

Before turning to the primary issue of ambiguity resolution, an extremely simple example may provide a useful introduction to the fundamental operation of the parsing model:

(222)   The vampire bit a child.

a. **The vampire:** Once this string is projected as an NP,[67] the sole attachment strategy so far postulated, theta attachment,[68] attempts to apply. However, since no theta assigner has been encountered and hence no theta role is available, the theta criterion cannot be locally satisfied. Consequently, the parser at this stage will contain only a single unattached NP, $[_{NP}$ *the vampire]*, with no attachment to a higher S postulated. Recall from chapter 1 that this is not predicted to be problematic as theta attachment is a hypothesis about structure building and ambiguity resolution while the TRC concerns processing cost.

b. **bit:** *Bite* is identified as a verb and its theta grid recovered: <AGENT, THEME> (following common convention, the external role, which is assigned to the d-structure subject, is indicated by underscoring). Theta attachment again attempts to apply and at this point may do so successfully since both a potential argument (*the vampire*) and a theta assigner (*bit*) are available. The appropriate X′ structure, including VP and (by virtue of its inflectional features) IP is projected, allowing the NP to be attached to a structural position where it may receive a role.[69] In this instance attachment is made into IP specifier (subject) position and as a result the parser will contain: $[_{IP}[_{I'}[_{NP}$ *the vampire]*$[_{VP}[_{V}$ *bit]]]]*.

c. **a child:** When this NP is identified, theta attachment once again attempts to apply in order to assure that *a child* is not left roleless if possible.

Since *bit* also assigns a THEME role to its direct object, this may be accomplished by attaching the NP as a sister of V, yielding the parse tree: *[$_{IP}$[$_{NP}$ the vampire][$_{I'}$[$_{VP}$[$_V$ bit][$_{NP}$ a child]]]]*.

That the parser proceeds word by word through the string attempting (minimally) to satisfy the theta criterion is fully compatible with the virtually uncontroversial hypothesis that human language comprehension proceeds incrementally. This seems particularly natural given that theta attachment may be viewed simply as one expression of the overriding grammatical principle of Full Interpretation (cf. Chomsky 1986b), which prohibits any linguistic element from being (globally) disregarded. Even with this limited introduction to the theory, significant questions concerning local ambiguity can be resolved.

3.1 Object-Subject Ambiguity

This section examines a variety of structurally distinct object-subject ambiguities whose contrasting processing loads have proven impossible for prior models to account for. Both the initial interpretations and the relative costs are explained quite directly within the theta attachment model.

3.1.1 Prepositional Object versus Clausal Subject

Consider first a sentence such as (223) where the relevant local ambiguity concerns the status of a nominal, here *donations*, as either the (head of the) object of the preposition or the subject of a forthcoming clause:

(223)   ¿Without her donations to the charity failed to appear.

The garden path status of (223) would seem to indicate that the former option is pursued and that processing breakdown results given the necessity of reinterpreting the object as a subject. However, recall that sentences such as

(224)   I suspected her donations to the charity would fail to appear.

reveal that the situation is not so easily characterized.

Though a similar example was considered in chapter 1 when the theory was first presented, it will prove insightful to examine both this example and other closely related structures in somewhat more detail. Consider then the course of the parse:

a. **without:** This is identified as a preposition and a PP with an associated theta grid, <THEME>[70] is projected: *[$_{PP}$[$_{P'}$[$_P$ without]]]*. However, since no potential target is available, the role cannot at this point be discharged.

b. **her:** This is identified as an NP, and, as a role and target are now available, it may be attached into the object position to which the preposition assigns its role, in local satisfaction of the theta criterion: *[$_{PP}$[$_P$ without] [$_{NP}$[$_N$ her]]]*. The possibility that *her* is attached as a determiner of NP is not pursued since this would result in an avoidable local violation of the theta criterion with *her* receiving and *without* assigning no role.[71] In other words, global grammatical principles, specifically the theta criterion, are maximally satisfied in the former configuration, which is consequently pursued.

c. **donations:** *Donations* is admitted as a noun and the relevant local ambiguity arises. At this point the processor could posit $[_{NP}$ *donations]* as a separate NP or could construct $[_{NP}[_{Det}$ *her][_{N'}[_{N}$ *donations]]]*. Since *without* assigns a single theta role, the latter configuration is selected by theta attachment, despite the fact that it requires reanalysis of the structure $[_{PP}[_{P}$ *without]* $[_{NP}[_{N'}[_{N}$ *her]]]]* as $[_{P}$ *without][_{NP}[_{Det}$ *her][_{N'}[_{N}$ *donations]]]]*. In the latter configuration, both *her* and *donations* may receive a theta role, and the role assigned by *without* may be discharged. (Recall that under common assumptions a genitive determiner receives the POSSESSOR role in this structural configuration under government by the lexical head, cf. Gruber 1976; Chomsky 1986b.) The alternative analysis would simply leave *donations* unmarked in local violation of the theta criterion. No attachment to a higher S could be made since the relevant theta assigner, the verb which licenses the subject, has not been encountered. Notice crucially that this restructuring does not violate the theta reanalysis constraint as *her* stays within its original theta domain. Even though that NP ceases to receive its theta role directly as a complement of the preposition *without*, it remains dominated by the NP which does receive that role and hence by hypothesis the reanalysis should be unproblematic.[72]

The fact that such cannot empirically be considered unacceptable is made even more strikingly by the absolute lack of conscious processing difficulty associated with sentences such as the following:

(225)   I hate her friends neighbors babies mewling.

Multiple syntactic reanalyses involving ambiguous specifiers and heads are required throughout the parse but in no way yield a conscious garden path (and the singular-plural indeterminacy associated with the specifier also provides unproblematic). This is elaborated in §3.1.2.3 below.

d. **to the charity:** This is admitted as a PP, with *the charity* receiving a theta role from *to* in the expected fashion, and the PP attached as the complement of *donations* also in accord with theta attachment (the attachment of adjunct PPs is discussed in §5.1).[73] The parse to this point has thus yielded: $[_{PP}[_{P}$ *without][_{NP}[_{Det}$ *her][_{N'}[_{N}$ *donations][_{PP}[_{P}$ *to][_{NP}$ *the charity]]]]]*.

e. **failed:** This analysis is revealed to be incorrect when *fail* is encountered, however, since no unattached NP is available to serve as its obligatory subject, receiving the external theta role. The syntactic manipulation necessary to yield a globally licit structure must reinterpret *donations to the charity* as the subject of *fail*, leaving *her* to be reanalyzed as the prepositional object.[74] However, the NP *donations to the charity* must be reattached in a position outside of its current theta domain where it neither receives a theta role from *without* nor is dominated by a constituent which receives that role. This constitutes a straightforward violation of the theta reanalysis constraint and the result is a sentence which may only be processed with significant conscious effort:

(223′)

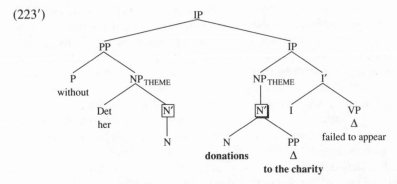

In (223′) and subsequent diagrams, as much of the final global representation as possible will be indicated, but the structures are of course slightly abstract since they are intended to demonstrate reanalyses, not final structure. The lexical material representing a reanalyzed constituent is indicated in **boldface;** the original attachment site of an element is indicated by a plain box and its final attachment site by a shadowed box; relevant theta domains are subscripted where appropriate. Aspects of the reanalysis irrelevant to the garden path effect will not generally be represented.

Of course, a parallel non–garden path sentence is correctly predicted to be completely unproblematic since the requisite local ambiguity never arises:

(226)   Without him donations to the charity failed to appear.

The parse proceeds precisely as in (223) through the attachment of *him* as the prepositional complement. Subsequently, when *donations* is admitted as an NP, theta attachment cannot apply since no additional role is available and there is no grammatical NP, *[*NP* him donations]*. Hence the constituent must remain roleless, a situation which has been seen to be unproblematic in itself. As a result, the NP will be left unattached and free to serve as the subject of the forthcoming verb. As the NP lacks a theta domain, there is no violation of the theta reanalysis constraint upon attachment of *donations* and the sentence is correctly predicted to be unproblematic. In other words, an unattached element appears free to attach anywhere within the limitations imposed by the grammar, a virtually self-evident hypothesis that will become relevant to certain reanalyses discussed in §3.3.2.

Quite similarly, a sentence such as (227) also presents no difficulty:

(227)   Without her donations to the charity Bob failed to appear.

The parse proceeds as in (224) through the processing of *her donations to the charity* and its attachment as the complement of *without*. However, since there is no way to incorporate *Bob* into an NP, *$*[_{NP}$ *her donations to the charity Bob]*,[75] the NP will remain roleless, unattached, and available for attachment as the subject of *fail*.

3.1.1.1 The TRC Revised: Impossible Reanalysis versus Failure

A potential complication is why a sentence such as the following does not yield the garden path effect:[76]

(228)   Without her contributions would it be impossible?

It might be expected that reanalysis should prematurely be attempted at *would*, reinterpreting *contributions* as outside its original theta domain in violation of the TRC and falsely predicting a garden path. It turns out that this problem is only apparent, however. The solution lies not in positing some sort of look-ahead or decision delay but in properly understanding the theta reanalysis constraint as a characterization of analyses which the parser itself simply cannot perform rather than operations which actively cause it to fail. Under this conception, the problematic restructuring does not take place at *would* simply because, as an impossible reanalysis, it can never occur. Rather, the parser continues its automatic operation and, in this instance, a pronoun appears which is capable of serving as the subject of *would* in an inversion construction, salvaging the parse. In (223) in contrast, the situation continues to deteriorate with no subject appearing and the relevant reanalysis not possible.[77]

Although it is useful to continue to speak informally as if parsing failure were actively and immediately caused by the actual operation of reinterpreting a constituent outside of its current theta domain, it is nevertheless important to recognize that the two interpretations are clearly, albeit subtly, distinct. In effect, the TRC limits the range of possible reanalyses the parser must consider, allowing it to ignore certain local attachment possibilities though at some risk of subsequent failure. A more accurate formulation of the TRC is therefore:

(229)   **Theta Reanalysis Constraint (TRC):** Syntactic reanalysis which reinterprets a theta marked constituent as outside of a current theta domain is impossible for the automatic human sentence processor. [Version 2]

This characterization of parsing failure does raise the important related questions of how structures which violate the TRC are ever interpreted and why there are distinct degrees of difficulty among garden path structures. A unified solution to both of these questions is discussed in §3.3.2.3.

Before turning to the contrasting class of unproblematic object-subject ambiguities, it is worthwhile to introduce a structurally distinct set of costly object-subject ambiguities which form more nearly minimal pairs with the crucial unproblematic sentences.

3.1.2 Verbal Complement versus Clausal Subject

This section considers an additional set of problematic object-subject ambiguities, these involving the direct dominance of some NP by either VP (as object) or by S (as subject). Consider first examples such as (230) which are minimally distinct from both preposed PP examples like (223) just considered and in situ S' complements as in (235) to be discussed below.

3.1.2.1 Fronted Clauses[78]

(230)   ¿After Todd drank the water proved to be poisoned.

a. **After Todd:** This string is built as a PP via theta attachment in the now familiar fashion.

b. **drank:** This is identified as a verb, its theta grid (<AGENT, THEME>) recovered, and *Todd* reanalyzed as a subject. In this fashion, the theta criterion is maximally satisfied locally with the clause receiving a role from the preposition *after* and the NP from *drink*.[79] Failure to reanalyze at this point would result in two local theta criterion violations—the clausal argument dominating *drink* would be roleless and *drink* itself would be unable to discharge its obligatory external role.

c. **the water:** This is identified as an NP and in accordance with theta attachment is incorporated as the object of *drink* in order that it may be assigned the THEME role.

d. **proved:** When *proved* is encountered, it forces reanalysis to allow its obligatory role to be discharged on a subject. This, however, requires the reinterpretation of the only available NP, *the water,* as outside of the THEME domain of *drink* since the subject position of *prove* obviously receives no role from *drink* and neither is it dominated by a constituent which receives such a role. Consequently, this is not a possible automatic reanalysis and conscious reprocessing must be invoked, yielding the GP effect:

(230')

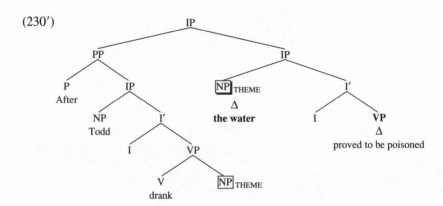

A closely related example demonstrates the importance of the clarification of the TRC given in (229) above, that it is not actually the case that problematic reanalysis occurs at *prove* but rather that the operation which is required to obtain the globally grammatical structure cannot be performed by the parser. This is clearly reflected in the fact that subsequent information may appear which saves an analysis:

(231)   After Todd drank the water proved to be poisoned he fainted.

Or, significantly better for those who do not prefer *proved* as a passive participle:

(232)   After Susan sang the music played on the radio she cried.

In each sentence, theta attachment will of course attach the post-verbal NP as object. Problematic reanalysis does not occur at *play* in order to provide a subject, causing failure, however, precisely because it is an impossible reanalysis. Additional input appears, confirming that the verbal complement is a complex NP within the THEME domain of *sing,* and the sentence continues to be parsed automatically to completion with no violation of the TRC. In (230), the processor also simply continues with its analysis, but ultimately fails when the globally ungrammatical structure results.

Now consider a structurally identical sentence which is clearly not a garden path:

(233)   After Todd arrived the water proved to be poisoned.

The analysis proceeds as in (230) through the processing of the lower verb. In contrast to that case, however, the post-verbal NP will not be theta attached as a complement for the simple reason that *arrive* has no additional theta role to assign. And, because *the water* has never been attached, it is consequently freely available for attachment as the subject of *prove,* circumventing the need for impossible reanalysis. Such examples provide striking evidence that the parser is indeed steered by specific lexical information, something which is not a priori necessary.[80]

Sentences such as (230) provide near minimal pairs with prepositional examples like (223), and serve to reiterate the important point that it is not the necessity of splitting a constituent such as *[NP her donations]* in the latter case which is the source of the difficulty. No such manipulation is necessary in the former instance, which begins with an initial clause rather than PP, yet the GP effect also results. In fact, parallel environments can be constructed using optionally intransitive PPs (cf. Emonds 1985 for this characterization of what may more traditionally be considered adverbs):

(234)   ¿Below the stairs collapsed.
            (The stairs collapsed below.)
            (cf. Below there was an explosion.)

Below the stairs is first parsed as a PP via theta attachment, and reanalysis of the NP as the subject of *collapse* exceeds the capabilities of the parser. (In fact, it appears easier for the processor to (ungrammatically) interpret the entire PP as subject, a reanalysis which avoids a TRC violation by allowing *the stairs* to remain in the theta domain of *below*.) It is merely an accidental fact, attributable to the general transitivity of (English) prepositions, which forces "NP splitting" in most cases involving initial PPs. Where such a split is necessary, a theta reanalysis constraint violation will result, but it is incorrect to consider the splitting per se problematic. Notice also that the contrast between prepositional (223) and clausal (230) further reveals that the processing difficulty of the latter cannot somehow be associated with the elimination of the projected complement position, since that position remains in the equally problematic (223), albeit with a new head.

3.1.2.2 *Postverbal Clauses*

In addition to forming near minimal pairs with prepositional structures such as in (223), sentences like (230) involving initial clauses also display a local ambiguity virtually identical to that of now familiar non-garden path examples like (235) below. As in the first two cases, an object must be reinterpreted as a subject, but, in the latter instance alone, that reanalysis is essentially cost free. Consider:

(235)   Susan knew her mother hated her.

a. **Susan knew:** Once the verb *know* has been identified and its <EXPERIENCER, THEME> theta grid recovered, the parser will construct *[IP[NP Susan][VP knew]]* via theta attachment in the expected manner.

b. **her:** *Her* is next identified as an NP and attached as the THEME: *[IP[NP Susan][VP[V knew][NP her]]]*.

c. **mother:** This is identified as a nominal and, in accord with theta attachment, is incorporated as the head of an NP, *her mother*, within the THEME position in the now familiar fashion, as the parse continues without difficulty: *[IP[NP Susan][VP[V knew][NP[Det her][N'[N mother]]]]]*.

d. **hate:** *Hate* and its theta grid, <EXPERIENCER, THEME>, are recovered. At this point the theta criterion may be maximally satisfied by reinterpreting *her mother* as the subject of *hate* and the entire clause which dominates the verb as the complement of *know*. Failure to reanalyze at this point would both prevent *hate* from locally assigning its obligatory external role and the clause from being theta marked. This reanalysis is quite similar to that required in (223) or (230), necessitating the wholesale reinterpretation of a misattached NP object as a subject, but in this instance is clearly unproblematic.

The cost free status of such sentences is of course completely predicted. While in the problematic cases the restructuring must interpret a complement as a higher subject, here the object is reanalyzed as an embedded subject. Specifically, *her mother* ceases to be the THEME of *know* but becomes the subject of the new THEME, the entire clause which now occupies the structural position previously filled by the reanalyzed NP. Notice of course that the fact that *her mother* itself comes to receive a new role from a new theta role assigner (*hate*) is not in itself predicted to cause difficulty. Both syntactic reanalyses and resulting theta role reassignments are unproblematic as long as the particulars of the TRC are not violated.

(235′)

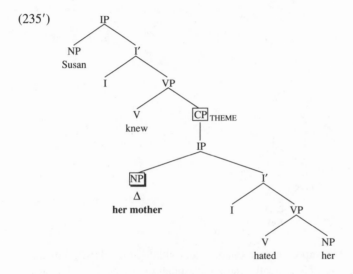

Exactly this same analysis obtains regardless of whether the objects are structurally simpler or more complex

(236) a. Ron suspected John disliked him.
　　　b. Ron believed the ugly little linguistics professor he had met the week before in Prague disliked him.

which also clearly demonstrates that length effects are nonexistent.[81] Furthermore, the tensed, infinitival, or small clause status of the embedded clause is similarly irrelevant:

(237) a. Ron believes Rex is a threat.
　　　b. Ron believes Rex to be a threat.
　　　c. Ron believes Rex a threat.

(237b′)

(237c′)

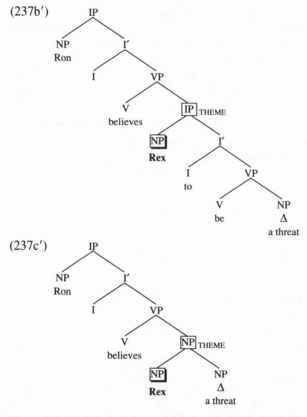

Nevertheless, it is important to recognize that although the TRC holds these analyses to be unproblematically and automatically performed by the parser, theta attachment does indeed predict the initial misattachment as object since subject attachment would locally strand the post-verbal NP without a role. This accounts for a range of experimental evidence to this effect, including the fact that locally ambiguous sentences lacking overt complementizers are processed more slowly than those in which the complementizer is phonologically realized and also that such sentences may involve regressive eye movement to the locus of the ambiguity (cf. Hakes 1972; Kimball 1973; Frazier and Rayner 1982). All such results are directly predicted by the theta attachment model as a general theory of human natural language processing.

3.1.2.3 NP Internal Ambiguities

While they do not involve object-subject ambiguities per se, NPs containing multiple nominals may require very similar internal restructuring. These include sentences involving compounding:

(238)   We admire their intelligence agency policy decisions.

(238′)

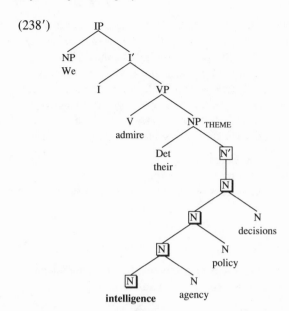

as well as recursive specifiers:

(239)   I hate her professors students papers quality.

(239′)

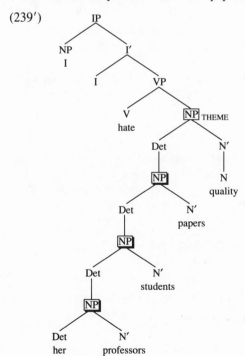

As the diagrams reveal, the complete acceptability of these structures is accounted for quite straightforwardly in precisely the same fashion as are examples such as (235). (No particular theoretical significance should be attached to the NP internal structure shown for the compound.) All relevant elements remain within their original theta domains upon each reanalysis. The analogy between the reanalysis from verbal object to subject (IP specifier) and verbal object to determiner (nominal specifier) is particularly clear. Other specifier-argument ambiguities periodically noted in the literature are handled similarly:

(240)   The grocery store always orders one.
(241)   The grocery store always orders one hundred.
(242)   The grocery store always orders one hundred bags of sugar.

or:

(243)   I know that.
(244)   I know that man.

Notice that such constructions are also predicted to be unproblematic when in subject position, though in a slightly different fashion:

(245)   a.   Their intelligence agency policy decisions scare us.
         b.   Her professors students papers quality appalled me.

Because an ambiguity exists and the parser consequently has an option, the largest NP possible will be constructed preverbally at each point during the parse in order to decrease the local strain on the theta criterion by constructing a single unmarkable NP rather than an entire series of unattachable nominals. When the verb is encountered, that roleless NP may be unproblematically incorporated into the newly licensed theta domain. A discussion of more complex NP internal ambiguity involving complicating lexical ambiguities is delayed until §4.1.

3.1.2.4 Multiple Complement Constructions

The verbs considered to this point, like prepositions, license a single internal argument. The data become even more revealing when such structures are contrasted with near minimal pairs involving verbs that assign multiple internal argument roles (excluding for the time being double NP and dative constructions which warrant a separate section—see §4.0):

(246)   ¿Susan warned the boys mother hated her.
(247)   ¿Susan convinced her friends were unreliable.

Consider first the latter example:

a. **Susan convinced:** Parsing to this point yields: $[_{IP}[_{NP}\ Susan][_{VP}\ convinced]]$, with *convince* associated with a maximal theta grid <AGENT, GOAL, PROPOSITION>.

b. **her:** *Her* is identified as an NP and attached into a position where it may receive the GOAL role.[82]

c. **friends:** This is identified as an NP and rather than being stranded without a theta role in local violation of the theta-criterion, it is reanalyzed via theta attachment as the head of the NP: *[IP[NP Susan][VP[V convinced][NP her friends]]]* in the expected fashion.[83]

d. **hate:** *Hate*'s <EXPERIENCER, THEME> theta grid is recovered. Relevant grammatical principles may be maximally satisfied at this point by reinterpreting *friends* as the subject of a clause to which the PROPOSITION role may be assigned. Failure to reanalyze would leave the clausal argument roleless and the role undischarged. However, this is an impossible reanalysis as it requires the reinterpretation of *friends* as outside of the GOAL domain of *convince* (and within the PROPOSITION domain) in violation of the theta reanalysis constraint.

(247')

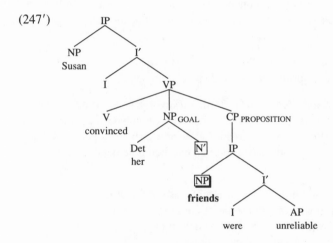

Consequently, the situation involving a verb such as *convince* which assigns two thematic roles within VP contrasts crucially with that of verbs like *know* which assign a single internal role. In the former case, when an object is reinterpreted as a clausal subject, that clause comes to be attached into the structural position originally occupied by the reanalyzed object. In crucial contrast, when object-to-subject restructuring occurs in a double complement construction, the clause does not come to occupy the original object position and consequently the reanalyzed subject is removed from its theta domain. It is the number and configuration of arguments which is crucial. These examples also reveal that the processing difficulty of (223) and (230) need not be attributed to any peculiarities concerning fronted clauses per se, as is expected given that such constructions are fully acceptable when unambiguous.

Of course, sentences such as the following are parsed without difficulty:

(248)   a.   Susan warned him friends were unreliable.
         b.   Joseph persuaded the man the boy was a fool.

In each case, when the second NP is initially processed, it must be left roleless as it can neither be incorporated into a grammatical constituent: *$[_{NP}$ *him friends]*, *$[_{NP}$ *the man the boy]* (even as the onset of a relative NP as discussed) nor directly assigned the PROPOSITION role. Consequently, it must be left unattached until the appearance of the verb when it may be unproblematically incorporated as subject.

Though the structure in (247) has been offered as a minimal pair with (235), there is one complicating factor. In the reanalysis of the post-verbal NP in the former case, the NP must be split with *her* remaining the GOAL and the former head entering a new theta domain. In (235), on the other hand, the entire NP remains a constituent under reanalysis. As was the case with fronted PPs, however, there is clear evidence that this cannot be the defining source of the difficulty:

(249)   ¿Rex·warned the ugly little man feared him.
(250)   ¿The teacher promised the students could leave.

These sentences duplicate the GP pattern, yet involve no splitting, unequivocally demonstrating that such a factor in itself cannot be the cause of the unprocessability. Recall that verbs in (249) and (250) form perfectly grammatical sentences both in the absence of an overt complementizer, a GOAL argument, or both: [84]

(251)   a.   I warned him Professor Hecht was out for blood.
         b.   I promised that the students could leave soon.
         c.   Lou warned there would be hell to pay.
         d.   Barbara promised they could leave.

Consider then (249) in some detail.

a. **Rex warned the ugly little man:** Parsing to this point proceeds as expected with *warn* yielding a theta grid, <AGENT, GOAL, PROPOSITION>, and the structure: $[_{IP}[_{NP}$ *Rex]*$[_{VP}[_V$ *warned]*$[_{NP}$ *the ugly little man]]]* projected in accord with theta attachment.

b. **fear:** This is identified along with its theta grid, <EXPERIENCER, THEME>. The theta criterion would be maximally satisfied at this point by reinterpreting the NP as outside of its GOAL domain as the subject of *fear* in the clausal PROPOSITION, but this violates the limits on possible reanalysis as characterized by the TRC and hence cannot be performed, accounting for the GP effect when a grammatical parse consequently fails to result.

It is a crucial aspect of the Government and Binding framework adopted here that thematic roles are conceived of as purely configurational phenomena at the level of syntax. As a result, the structural position of the PROPOSITION role remains distinct from that of the GOAL even in those instances where the GOAL is not overtly realized:[85]

(249′)

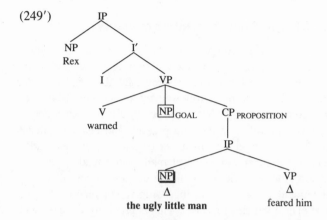

If this were not the case and, for example, were the PROPOSITION attached as the first sister of V in the absence of a GOAL (as would presumably be the case in the more surface-oriented analyses of LFG or GPSG) the TRC would fail to predict the occurring unprocessability. Instead the situation would parallel that involving verbs licensing a single internal argument, and consequently the garden path status of such structures in its own turn provides support for just such a configurational approach to thematic roles:

(249″)

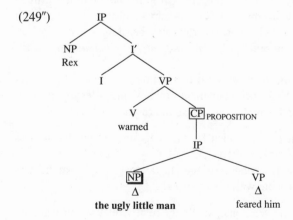

To this point, the fundamental operation of the theta attachment model has been established through an examination of a range of contrastive object-subject ambiguities.[86] The next section of this chapter begins to demonstrate that the analysis motivated above is by no means construction specific.

3.2 Complement Clause–Relative Clause Ambiguity

It is perhaps in the realm of complement clause–relative clause ambiguity that the crucial role played by the theta-assigning properties of the verb with respect to attachment is most clearly revealed. Descriptively, the ambiguity concerns whether a nominal followed by an S′ should be interpreted as forming a complex relative NP or as object NP plus an independent complement clause. Recall from the data presented in chapter 2 that it is only the relative clause readings which (under certain conditions) lead to unacceptable sentences—in other words complement clause readings are primary. This will be accounted for within the theory developed only if it is the case that theta attachment initially favors the complement reading and reanalysis as a relative clause violates the TRC. This is precisely the case with no further assumptions required. Consider a repeatedly seen example in detail:

(252)   ¿The patient persuaded the doctor that he was having trouble with to
          leave.

     a. **the patient persuaded:** By this point *persuade* will have been identified as a V, its theta grid <AGENT, GOAL, PROPOSITION> recovered, and *the patient* theta attached as subject.
     b. **the doctor:** Once identified, this NP will in the now familiar fashion be immediately attached as the first internal object of *persuade* in order to occupy a position to which the GOAL role may be assigned in local satisfaction of the theta criterion: $[_{IP}[_{NP}$ *the patient*$][_{VP}[_V$ *persuaded*$][_{NP}$ *the doctor*$]]]$.
     c. **that he was having trouble with:** It is at this point that the parse becomes interesting since the proper attachment of this string is locally ambiguous between a relative and complement clause interpretation:[87]

(253)   a.   The patient $[_{VP}$ persuaded $[_{NP}$ the $[_{N'}[_{N'}$ doctor$]$ $[_{CP}$ that he was
                 having trouble with$]]]_{GOAL}]$.
         b.   The patient $[_{VP}$ persuaded $[_{NP}$ the doctor$]_{GOAL}$ $[_{CP}$ that he was
                 having trouble with his finances$]_{PROPOSITION}]$.

Theta attachment forces the latter analysis. In the relative clause construction, a single one of *persuade*'s internal thematic roles may be locally discharged, and the CP is left roleless. In contrast, in the complement clause structure, both the GOAL and the PROPOSITION role may be discharged and the NP and CP may each receive a role. Though both locally and globally grammatical, the relative clause analysis not only strands a role but also leaves a potentially theta markable constituent unmarked, less strongly satisfying the theta criterion.[88] Consequently, the local structure built by theta attachment is as in (253b) with *the patient* receiving the GOAL role as the first argument and *that he was having trouble with* the PROPOSITION role as the second.

    d. **to leave:** Reanalysis as a relative construction must occur when the true PROPOSITIONAL complement, *to leave,* appears, but the requisite restructuring is correctly predicted to be impossible by the TRC. Remapping the complement structure into a relative clause would require the theta marked PROPOSITION, *that he was having trouble with,* to be removed from its PROPOSITION theta domain (and reinterpreted within the GOAL theta domain). According to the TRC this is an analysis which cannot be performed automatically by the parser and may only be accomplished by conscious effort. Theta attachment correctly predicts the initial complement clause attachment, while the TRC properly characterizes the difficulty of reanalysis:

(252′)

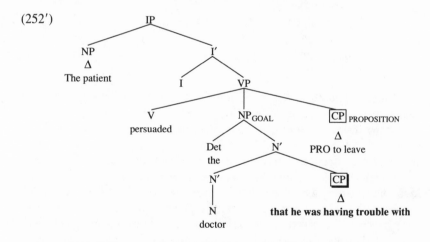

As fully expected, the identity of the constituent which forces the reanalysis is irrelevant if the TRC is otherwise violated. For instance, it is unimportant whether the actual complement clause is infinitival as above or tensed:

(254)   ¿The patient convinced the doctor that he was hated that he should leave.

or even forced by the simple termination of input, although such examples are perfectly grammatical with only a GOAL complement:

(255)   a.   ¿The patient convinced the doctor that he was having trouble with.
             (cf. The patient convinced the doctor.)
        b.   ¿The patient persuaded the doctor that he hated.
             (cf. The patient persuaded the doctor.)

In all cases, reanalysis yields the GP effect as expected.

Needless to say, in the event that the complement clause analysis proves correct, no reinterpretation is necessary and no processing difficulty occurs:

(256)   The patient told the doctor that he was having trouble with his feet.

Trivially, when *his feet* appears, it may be attached into a position so as to receive the internal theta role from *with* which is consistent with the previous complement clause attachment, further verifying the fact that it is indeed favored.

Of course, no difficulty is predicted given disambiguating information:

(257)   a.   The patient expected [$_{IP}$ the doctor that he was having trouble with to leave].
        b.   The patient forced [$_{NP}$ the doctor that he was having trouble with]$_i$ PRO$_i$ to leave.
        c.   The patient persuaded [$_{NP}$ the doctor that was having trouble with him]$_i$ PRO$_i$ to leave.

For example, lexical knowledge disambiguates the first two examples—only a single theta role is available from *expect* in the ECM example (257a), circumventing the possibility of a complement clause reading, while *force* requires its clausal complement to be infinitival rather than tensed in the Control case (257b). Syntactically, the lack of an overt subject in the substring *that was* (*having trouble with him*) bleeds the complement clause interpretation in (257c), leaving only the subject relative reading.[89] Consequently in each case, only the relative clause reading is locally available.[90] Notice that the first two examples remain completely mysterious under an "item-independent" approach (cf. Frazier 1989, alluded to in note 80) where the complement clause interpretation would be favored (by means of Minimal Attachment or a related strategy) in accord with phrase structure rules—even in those instances where ungrammatical given the actual words involved.

The above discussion clearly demonstrates that even a class of garden path sentences entirely distinct structurally from those previously considered is subject to an identical account. This strongly suggests that a unified and predictive theory of parsing and breakdown is fully possible once grammatical factors are seriously taken into account.

3.3 Matrix Clause–Relative NP Ambiguity

3.3.1 Canonical Garden Path Effects

With the concepts so-far developed in mind, a straightforward account of canonical garden path structures may be provided. In such sentences the ambiguity descriptively centers on whether an initial NP V sequence should be interpreted as the subject and verb of a matrix clause or alternatively as the onset of an NP modified by a reduced relative clause (which, by definition, lacks both a form *be* and an overt *wh*-moved passive subject). In numerous cases, the global necessity of resolving this ambiguity in favor of the latter results in severe processing breakdown, and a satisfactory theory must account for both the initial pursuit of the matrix analysis as well as the potential difficulty of reanalysis as a relative NP.

Consider then in some detail what is perhaps the most renowned exemplar of a garden path sentence:

(258) ¿The horse raced past the barn fell.

a. **the horse:** This is identified as an NP but no further action can be taken in the absence of a theta assigner.

b. **race:** This is recovered as a V along with its maximal theta grid, <AGENT, THEME>.[91] Because *raced* is ambiguous between a past tense verb form and a passive participle,[92] two independent structures associated with two distinct sets of theta-role assignments could grammatically be posited at this point. In the matrix clause analysis, *the horse* would be attached as subject in order to receive the external (here, AGENT) role from *race* in a simplex clause, leaving the THEME role locally undischarged:

(259)

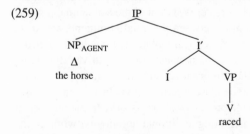

Alternatively, the THEME role could be discharged on an empty category co-indexed with a (null) operator, in a relative clause construction:

(260)

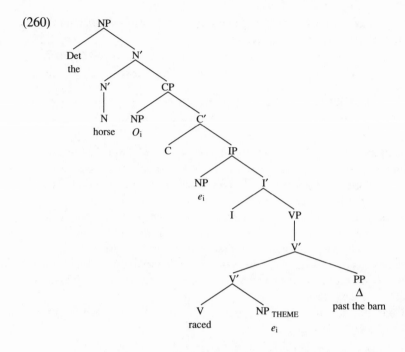

In each case only one of the available theta roles is discharged: AGENT in the case of the main clause and THEME in the case of the reduced relative. It is important to recognize that despite its apparently greater structural complexity such a configuration is clearly not inherently excessively difficult given the perfect acceptability of morphologically unambiguous examples.

Why is the former analysis pursued? Quite simply, theta attachment forces the matrix clause interpretation because, although a single thematic role is discharged in each configuration, the relative clause analysis additionally constructs a higher NP, the relativized NP itself (here headed by *horse*), for which no role is locally available, as indicated in the diagram above. This obviously constitutes a greater violation of theta attachment's goal of maintaining a one-to-one mapping between potential arguments and theta roles, therefore resulting in a more severe local violation of the theta criterion.

Notice that the processor favors a main clause over a relative NP reading in canonical garden paths for rather different reasons than it favors a complement clause analysis over a relative clause interpretation. In the matrix case, available theta roles are few and the processor attempts to keep the number of targets to a minimum by not constructing additional arguments, while in the complement clause case roles are plentiful and the parser attempts to admit targets to receive them. Since the parser will consequently build the structure in (259) rather than (260) the way is paved for an explanation of the difficulty of reanalysis as a relativized NP.

c. **past the barn:** The PP is processed and adjoined (see also §5.1).

d. **fall:** This verb's theta grid, <THEME>, is recovered and grammatical principles may be maximally satisfied both locally and globally by reanalyzing *the horse raced past the barn,* as an NP, thus permitting *fall* to discharge its obligatory external theta role. This requires *horse,* which originally headed the NP assigned an external theta role by the *race,* to be reanalyzed as the (head of the) subject of *fall* receiving its THEME role. However, since the latter structural position lies outside of the external theta domain of *race,* the TRC correctly predicts this to be an impossible reanalysis, which cannot be performed automatically by the parser:

(258′)

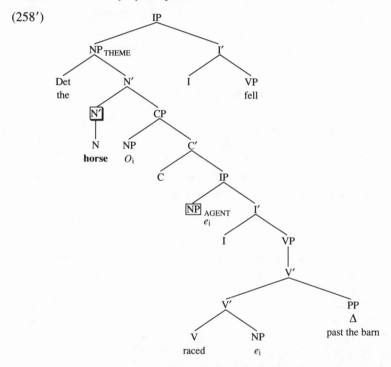

Consequently, not only is the initial analysis as a simplex clause rather than as a relativized NP predicted by theta attachment, the impossibility of reanalysis is directly accounted for by the theta reanalysis constraint. The processing failure associated with such paradigmatic garden path sentences thus proves to be subject to precisely the same account as a range of syntactically distinct local ambiguities and the structure actually possesses no special theoretical status.

It is of course obvious that in the case of a structurally parallel sentence such as

(261)   The horse ridden past the barn fell.

the requisite ambiguity never arises given the cues provided by the verbal morphology. Since *the horse* is never analyzed as the subject of *ride*, there is no subsequent reanalysis and hence no possibility of a TRC violation. Inherently, the structure itself is not significantly difficult.

3.3.1.1 Reduced Relatives as Adjectivals

There is an alternative grammatical analysis of reduced relative clauses which has certain ramifications for the theta attachment theory and is therefore worth considering. Rather than adopting the traditional view that reduced relatives are clauses which lack both a form of *be* and an overt *wh*-extracted passive subject, both Abney (1987) and McCawley (1988) treat such constructions as pure adjectivals which make no internal thematic assignments. If such a theory were adopted, theta attachment would then favor the verbal over the adjectival interpretation not only because the latter would strand an NP roleless but also because an additional theta role would be discharged, as none are within AP. Reanalysis as an adjectivally modified NP will violate the TRC in precisely the same fashion as previously discussed by forcing the impossible reinterpretation of the misanalyzed subject of *race* as a higher subject. Thus, identical predictions are made with respect to the canonical matrix garden path structures just considered.

In contrast however, the theory has slightly different implications in those instances where the ambiguity is embedded under a higher verb: [94]

(262)   ¿John believes the horse raced past the barn fell.

(263)   ¿Rex knows the boy hurried out the door slipped.

Such structures are clear garden paths, [95] but this is not straightforwardly predicted if a standard reduced relative clause analysis is adopted. Because a theta role for the complex NP is available from the higher verb, the complement clause reading would not obviously be favored over the relative NP interpretation. Though the TRC continues to clearly predict the reanalysis to be costly if required, the problem is that theta attachment does not necessarily assure the simplex clause construction when embedded.

On the other hand, if the adjectival analysis is adopted, the clausal structure will be initially favored in order to allow the ambiguous head to discharge its internal theta role as a verb, with reanalysis straightforwardly violating the TRC. It therefore appears on the basis of the processing data that an AP analysis of such structures is to be preferred. This is an interesting example of an instance where a well-articulated parsing theory may actually shed light on alternative grammatical analyses, and some additional cases are briefly considered in §4.0.4.3. Nevertheless, as the reduced relative clause analysis is generally more familiar, I will continue to adopt it when discussing the ambiguity in matrix contexts.

3.3.2 Canonical Garden Paths Avoided

Quite interestingly, there are sentences which display the canonical garden path ambiguity but which nevertheless fail to yield garden path effects (recall the discussion in §2.2.1):

(264)   The spaceship destroyed in the battle disintegrated.

Descriptively, it appears that only in those structures where the morphologically ambiguous verb is obligatorily transitive does the expected conscious processing difficulty fail to occur. More precisely, the verb must be unambiguously accusative, requiring at least two obligatory arguments (overt or implicit) at d-structure and s-structure:

(265)   a.   The bird bought in the store flew away.
      b.   The thug murdered on Thursday was pushing up daisies.
      c.   The children found in the woods were frozen.

Compare:

(266)   a.   *The bird bought in the store.
      b.   *The thug murdered on Thursday.
      c.   *The children found in the woods.

On the other hand, if the verb may select only a single argument at d- and s-structure, that is if it may be either unaccusative or unergative,

(267)   a.   The boat floated down the river.
      b.   The horse raced past the barn.
      c.   The girl pushed through the crowd.

the GP effect will occur in reduced relative constructions, other ambiguities being equal.

3.3.2.1 *The No-Misanalysis Hypothesis*

Given the theory as developed, there are two logical possibilities for accounting for this lack of processing breakdown—both of which depend crucially on properties of the ambiguous verb. The parser might ascribe a special status to an obligatory internal argument and consequently attempt to satisfy that lexical requirement before all others, thus effectively circumventing the main clause analysis. As a result, examples such as (264) would pattern with morphologically nonambiguous sentences such as (261) in requiring no reanalysis. Alternatively, it is possible that the main clause misanalysis is first made in the previously predicted manner, but that the transitivity cues available, in some manner to be discovered, prevent the theta reanalysis constraint from being violated. Although the former hypothesis might initially seem somewhat more appealing, there appears to be some evidence that an account along the lines of the latter is correct. Both hypotheses are similar in their recognition of the fact that the argument structure of the morphologically ambiguous verb is absolutely crucial, but each makes slightly different use of this information in the time course of the parse and hence yields different predictions.

Consider first how the former No-Misanalysis approach might be worked out:

(268)   The spaceship destroyed in the battle disintegrated.

a. **the spaceship destroyed:** *Destroy* has a theta grid <AGENT, **PA-TIENT**>, where boldface now indicates an obligatory internal argument. Suppose that the processor, which, employing grammatical knowledge directly, plausibly has access to such information, elects to discharge obligatory before optional arguments wherever possible in its attempt to maximally license the local structure. The parser would consequently not initially pursue the simplex clause analysis since an obligatory argument would fail to be discharged and there exists an alternative relative NP analysis which would allow this. As a result, the relative clause structure would be built in accord with some slightly augmented version of theta attachment which recognizes the special status of obligatory arguments. As a result, no reanalysis would be necessary when the higher verb is encountered, *the spaceship destroyed in the battle* having already been constructed as a (roleless) NP which is available to serve as subject.

Notice that although reanalysis would be required whenever global resolution proved to require a simplex clause interpretation, GP effects are not falsely predicted in simple transitive sentences such as:

(269)   The spaceship destroyed the planet.

When the relative clause analysis is initially pursued, the complex NP cannot be attached as a subject and will hence have no theta domain. As a result, reanalysis of *the spaceship* as a main clause subject will not violate the TRC and the acceptability of (269) is therefore compatible with the No-Misanalysis hypothesis.[96]

Despite the initial appeal of such a hypothesis and the rather natural extension of theta attachment it suggests, three objections come immediately to mind, two theoretical and one empirical. First, there does not appear to be any compelling theory-internal reason that the parser should prefer early discharge of an obligatory role when such an analysis itself creates a constituent (the relative NP) for which a role must eventually be found. Since it is equally true that a target for the obligatory role might appear at some later point in the input string, arguing for the primacy of role discharge over role receipt would appear rather stipulative and even unnatural. Second, the subject role itself is also obligatory and the primacy of an obligatory internal role over an obli-

gatory external role would remain a mystery (though this argument is complicated by the fact that it is not entirely clear how an implicit subject role is
structurally realized). Furthermore, it is at least intuitively somewhat unnatural that simplex subject+verb readings are always predicted to be secondary. Each of the above points reveals conceptual difficulties with the approach.
More convincing however are the empirical data.

3.3.2.2 Detachment and Reattachment: The TRC Revised

Insight into the proper account of these potentially costly but in practice
unproblematic transitive garden path environments can be gained from an
examination of very similar clausal–relative NP ambiguities which arise in
Japanese:

(270)   Roozin ga   kodomo o   yonda zyosee to   hanasi o   sita.
        old man NOM child   ACC called woman with talk   ACC did
        'The old man talked with the woman who called the child.'

A suggestive range of cross-linguistic data are examined in detail in §5.2, but
of concern here is the fact that the initial NP NP V sequence (*roozin ga
kodomo o yonda*) may be interpreted directly as a simplex clause (*The old man
called the child*) in accord with theta attachment. Of course, this analysis does
not prove globally correct in (270) where the need for the relative reading is
revealed by the occurrence of the nominal *zyosee* (*kodomo o yonda zyosee* =
the woman who called the child):

(270')

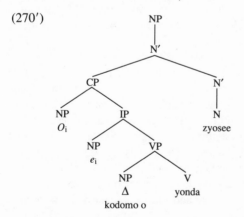

This necessitates the removal of *roozin* from the AGENT theta domain of
yonda, predicting a severe garden path effect. However, as discussed in
Mazuka et al. (1989), despite their initial clausal interpretations, such sentences involve no conscious difficulty even given the significant restructuring
involved.

The situation directly resembles the English case in two respects. First, in neither instance does the otherwise anticipated GP effect occur. In the Japanese example, however, the No-Misanalysis hypothesis is not available as an escape hatch since the string *roozin ga kodomo o yonda* straightforwardly corresponds to a completely acceptable simplex clause with global grammatical principles fully satisfied by definition. There is no way to avoid that initial analysis—nor would it be at all desirable to do so. This directly contrasts with the situation in English wherein the NP V PP substring (e.g., *The umpire murdered behind home plate*) fails to form a globally grammatical sentence and alternative local interpretations are consequently plausible as discussed above. As a result, the only apparent explanation of the unproblematic status of the Japanese structure is that the reanalysis simply does not violate the TRC despite appearances—an option which also remains open with respect to the English examples. (A demonstration of a true GP effect in Japanese is provided in §5.2.4.)

The second parallel between the two cases is one which at first glance might not appear relevant: in neither instance is the reanalysis forced by a constituent which is itself a theta assigner. In the English example, the necessity of restructuring is revealed as soon as the prepositional phrase is encountered (attributable to the local application of the Case Filter as discussed in §5.0.1.1.) since a nominal complement must occur right adjacent to its verb, unseparated from it by other arguments or adjuncts:

(271)   *The spaceship destroyed in the battle the planet.

In the Japanese example, reanalysis is prompted by a post-verbal nominal which serves as the head of a relative construction (licensing the clause via predication).

What is striking is that in each case a primary effect of the non-theta-assigning status of the cue to reanalysis is that the element removed from its theta domain in putative violation of the TRC cannot itself be immediately re-theta-attached. For example, in the English sentence, the matrix verb *disintegrated* which theta marks *spaceship* has yet to appear, while in the Japanese case the higher verb *sita* has not occurred to license *roozin* as subject. As a result, each of these elements is once again temporarily stranded roleless, just as when initially encountered. A unified account of the acceptable status of both constructions can therefore be provided if reattachment is also hypothesized to be relevant to processing failure and the TRC revised along the following lines:

(272)   **Theta Reanalysis Constraint:** Syntactic reanalysis which reinterprets a theta marked constituent as outside of a current theta domain and as within a distinct theta domain is impossible for the automatic Human Sentence Processor. [*Version 3*]

Upon this conception, it is the *combination* of detachment and reattachment rather than detachment alone which is problematic.[97] It may be easily verified that all of the locally ambiguous structures accounted for in the previous sections of this chapter are fully compatible with (272). While this version of the constraint might initially seem more complicated, it will be shown shortly below that it leads to extremely desirable theoretical and empirical simplification.

Notice that although the approach just outlined forces the immediate positing of an obligatory internal argument right-adjacent to the verb when one does not occur in its d-structure position in the input string, this may prove incorrect in certain instances, specifically in Heavy-NP Shift contexts, such as:

(273)   The spaceship destroyed e_i in the battle [the giant Kzinti cruiser which had been pursuing it for weeks]$_i$.

According to the account above, the string *the spaceship destroyed in the battle* will first be interpreted as a simplex clause and subsequently reparsed as a relativized NP. As a result, when the actual internal argument appears, re-restructuring will be required. Given the acceptability of such constructions it is important to note that this does not violate the revised TRC. *Spaceship,* as head of the relative NP, will have no theta domain and will therefore be free for construal as a simple clausal subject just as is any unattached element.

Of course, this revised version of the TRC continues to account for canonical garden path sentences like (258) since in such cases the simplex clause analysis may be maintained through the post-verbal adjunct in contrast to examples like (264) and (265):

(274)   a.   √The horse raced past the barn.
         b.   *The umpire murdered behind home plate.

It is not until the higher verb occurs that restructuring is triggered in such cases, violating the TRC since the reanalyzed element is immediately reattached within a distinct theta domain.

In this section, a comparison of paradigmatic garden paths with very similar but unproblematic structures suggested the need for a revision of the theory as developed. A change in theta attachment itself was rejected on both theoretical and empirical grounds in favor of a slight adjustment to the theta reanalysis constraint which recognizes the relevance of both an element's initial attachment site as well as the position in the parse tree it comes to occupy upon reanalysis. This revision will be further explored in chapter 4 where it proves key to a crucial simplification of the theory.

3.3.2.3 Degrees of Difficulty

A single and unified account has now been provided for several distinct garden path structures, and the homogeneous nature of the analysis itself raises an important question: Can the theta reanalysis constraint account for the fact that garden path structures themselves vary significantly in processing difficulty? The parser as it is conceived of here is a mental module in the sense of Fodor (1983), a module which knows only how to analyze syntactic structure (as argued here, by employing principles of the competence grammar directly). However, its abilities are not unconstrained and it is the TRC which characterizes its limitations. When its capabilities are exceeded, rational, nonmodular faculties may be invoked—that is, the sentence must be consciously analyzed with the native speaker essentially assuming the role of a (naïve) linguist. Consequently, although all such reanalyses are nonautomatic and hence difficult by definition, there is no reason whatsoever to expect the degree of their complexity to be uniform. Intuitively, the simpler the target structure the more easily interpretable the garden path, but such concerns will only be relevant at the conscious level once the autonomous parser has essentially given up on a particular construction. Thus, simple notions like Steal-NP (see §2.0.4) may actually be relevant at some level, not as actual recovery strategies but simply as rough descriptions of the rational abilities of native speakers to analyze linguistic structure. This supposition is consistent with the fact that hearers appear to differ radically in their ability to recover from garden paths as well as the fact that GP recovery can improve greatly with practice, though some degree of conscious awareness by definition remains. Varying levels of difficulty upon this conception are not directly relevant to the discovery of the nature of the autonomous parser, being, in a sense only measures of a hearer's conscious ability to analyze linguistic structure. From this perspective it is actually inappropriate for the parsing theory itself to make finer predictions beyond the fact that conscious reprocessing is required.[98]

At this point, it may be useful to summarize the fundamental parsing algorithm, which may be informally but accurately characterized as follows:

a. Input a word.
b. Recover lexical information, including category and theta-grid, and project the appropriate XP(s).
c. Maximally satisfy the theta criterion via theta attachment as constrained by the theta reanalysis constraint.
d. If input 'ceases' affirm that the resulting structure satisfies all relevant grammatical principles (success); and if not (failure) invoke *conscious* reanalysis, by definition yielding the GP effect; otherwise continue to the next word.

This chapter has demonstrated how a wide range of human processing phenomena may be accounted for with a model of parsing which operates by locally satisfying a global grammatical principle, the theta criterion, and whose capabilities for reanalysis are further constrained in terms of grammar-derived notions. The next chapter examines a major simplification of the model which may be achieved by further reducing the TRC to grammar and explores the theoretical and empirical benefits which result from such a move.

CHAPTER FOUR

The On-Line Locality Constraint

4.0 Ditransitive Ambiguities

The discussion to follow focuses primarily on a class of ambiguities which arise in ditransitive constructions wherein a predicate is directly able to assign a thematic role to a secondary NP argument at s-structure.[99] An investigation of the unique local ambiguities that arise given this property, coupled with the revision to the TRC just formulated in §3.3.2, suggests an important (and final) reinterpretation of the theta reanalysis constraint which significantly increases its conceptual link to grammatical theory and enhances its empirical coverage.

It is important to recognize that although the actual content of the theta role assignments in ditransitive constructions is often ambiguous, this is not problematic:

(275)　a.　Louis gave the dog to Barbara.
　　　　b.　Louis gave the dog a treat.
(276)　a.　Joe loaded the truck with bananas
　　　　b.　Joe loaded the truck onto the boat.
(277)　a.　Zeny rented the apartment to Theresa.
　　　　b.　Zeny rented the apartment from Theresa.

The first NP in an example like (275) or (276) may globally come to be assigned either a THEME or GOAL role, while in (277) the subject may ultimately prove to be either SOURCE or GOAL. Despite the uncontroversial assumption that sentences are interpreted incrementally, none of these ambiguities is costly and it consequently does not appear that the indeterminate content of the semantic roles involved is a source of difficulty. In fact, there is evidence that such gross thematic role labels have no true semantic status. Consider:

(278)　a.　John loaded bananas onto the truck.
　　　　b.　John loaded the truck with bananas.

Though in each example *the truck* would standardly be analyzed as receiving the GOAL role and *bananas* the THEME, the semantics of the sentences nevertheless differ (cf. Fillmore 1977). In (278b) but not (278a) *the truck* is full as a result of the act of loading, as revealed by the anomalous status of (279b) but not (279a):

(279)   a.   John loaded bananas onto the truck, and then he filled it up with coconuts.

        b.   #John loaded the truck with bananas, and then he filled it up with coconuts.

Sentence (279b) is bizarre unless it is assumed that John first unloads the bananas and then refills the truck with coconuts. In contrast to its content, the configurational s-structure position of the immediately post-verbal NP is not in doubt in either instance. In both cases, regardless of its theta role, it possesses canonical object properties (with respect to movement, binding, etc.):

(280)   a.   Bananas$_i$ were loaded [e_i] onto the truck.
        b.   *Bananas$_i$ were loaded the truck with [e_i].
        c.   The truck$_i$ was loaded [e_i] with bananas.
        d.   *The truck$_i$ was loaded bananas onto [e_i].

As repeatedly stressed, within the theta attachment model as in the syntactic theory from which it is derived, thematic role labels represent only a convenient shorthand for discussing argument structure positions required by virtue of the theta criterion. Though the fact that a particular structural position is assigned a semantic role is indeed crucial, what the content of that particular role is is not.

4.0.1 A False Prediction

The syntactic irrelevance of semantic role content thus established, consider how theta attachment operates in a simple double object construction:

(281)   a.   John sold Rex the car.
        b.   John sold Rex to the witches.

a. **John sold Rex:** First, *John* is attached as subject in the usual fashion. What is crucial is that *sell* assigns two internal thematic roles and that consequently *Rex* will be immediately attached as the first internal object because this position is structurally accessible to theta role assignment—something which will not change regardless of the role ultimately associated with that position: $[_{IP}[_{NP} John][_{I'}[_{VP}[_V sold][_{NP} Rex]]]]$.

b. **the car–to the witches:** When either *the car* or *to the witches* is processed, it may be attached as the second complement of the appropriate category, leaving *Rex* in its original configurational position. No structural reanalysis is involved and such sentences are expectedly unproblematic.

Far more revealing, however, are those double object constructions wherein theta attachment along with the TRC does predict conscious processing difficulty:

(282)   a.   They gave her gifts on Halloween.
        b.   They gave her gifts to Doug.

(283)   Ron sent the boys dogs to Rex.
(284)   Ron sent the boys dogs some bones.

Consider the first example, (282a).

a. **They gave her:** As in the previous example, the NP immediately following the verb will be interpreted as the first internal argument of the double object verb: $[_{IP}[_{NP}$ *They]*$[_{VP}[_V$ *gave]*$[_{NP}$ *her]]]*.

b. **gifts:** The ultimate position of this nominal is locally indeterminate. It might be attached as the head of an NP with a determiner, *her,* or as a second independent NP in the double object construction. The ambiguity is parallel to that encountered in a familiar sentence such as

(285)   They suspected her friends.

but with one crucial difference. A double object verb by definition has an additional theta role which may be assigned directly to such a nominal. While in examples like (285) a larger NP, *her friends,* is locally constructed in order to avoid stranding *friends* without a theta role, there is no such pressure here since an extra role (which may grammatically be discharged on an NP) is available from the verb. Hence, in this instance, the theta criterion may be maximally satisfied locally by discharging both roles onto two independent arguments, yielding: $[_{IP}[_{NP}$ *They]*$[_{VP}[_V$ *gave]*$[_{NP}$ *her]* $[_{NP}$ *gifts]]]* rather than $[_{IP}[_{NP}$ *They]*$[_{VP}[_V$ *gave]*$[_{NP}$ *her gifts]]]*. This predicts the interpretation unproblematically associated with (282a) or the simple string, *They gave her gifts.*

Now, however, consider sentence (282b). The analysis proceeds as above until the occurrence of the true GOAL PP *to Doug,* which forces restructuring. *Her* is reinterpreted as POSSESSOR, remaining in its original theta domain (construed of course in terms of structural position not role label). In contrast, *gifts* itself must be reinterpreted as the head of the first rather than the second internal argument in clear violation of the TRC

(282′)

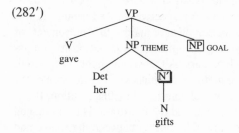

as can be seen in (282′). Unfortunately, since such sentences do not cause conscious processing difficulty, the theory has clearly made an incorrect prediction.[100] Sentence (283) makes precisely the same point, the only differences being that the ambiguous possessor, *boys,* is a lexical NP rather than a pronoun. Sentence (284) is also falsely predicted to be costly and further demonstrates that the ultimate resolution of the ambiguity in favor of an NP NP or

NP PP analysis is irrelevant. The crucial question of course is why such constructions are not problematic as predicted by the theta reanalysis constraint.

4.0.2 From the TRC to the On-Line Locality Constraint

The solution to the problem of ditransitive constructions is to be found in a somewhat altered perspective on the fundamental nature of the reanalysis constraint. Recall that in its first incarnation the TRC was formulated as a condition on the reinterpretation of a single previously attached constituent which required that the element not be removed from a current theta domain. Although this provided generally excellent descriptive coverage, one disturbing aspect of the original formulation was its reliance on the very notion theta domain, a novel theoretical construct. Although naturally formulated in terms of the primitive grammatical notions of dominance and theta role, the relation nevertheless had no source within the underlying syntactic theory. Worse, empirical difficulties surrounding the unproblematic status of certain canonical garden path structures subsequently revealed that conscious processing difficulty arose only in those cases where the reanalyzed element not only departed but also entered a new theta domain, giving increased importance to the notion. Now, the problematic empirical facts concerning double object constructions have revealed certain difficulties with any formulation of the theta reanalysis constraint in terms of theta domains. Though its descriptive coverage is impressive, the notion nevertheless proves somewhat theoretically and empirically troublesome when certain very fine predictions are considered.

Fortunately, it turns out that when viewed from a slightly different angle the revised theta reanalysis constraint given in (272) provides an unexpected key to both the empirical and theoretical problems associated with the concept theta domain. The current version of the TRC tacitly characterizes reanalysis in terms of the relationship between the structural position into which an element is originally attached and the position it assumes upon reanalysis (henceforth the *source* and *target* positions respectively). As formulated, this requirement is still mediated via the notion theta domain—the 'movement' of a constituent from the source position it occupies to the target position it assumes cannot cross a theta domain boundary. A theta domain therefore essentially serves to divide the sentence into distinct chunks via an extension of the notion thematic position to include material dominated by that position. If this approach is taken to its logical conclusion and the constraint is reformulated as an *explicit* condition on the structural relationship between the source and target positions rather than on the movement of a constituent from one to the other, not only are the empirical problems resolved but the notion theta domain may be dispensed with altogether.

This change in perspective yields the following final revision of the TRC formulated in terms of the purely configurational syntactic concepts, *government* and *dominance*:

(286)   **On-Line Locality Constraint (OLLC):** The target position (if any) assumed by a constituent must be *governed*[101] or *dominated*[102] by its source position (if any), otherwise attachment is impossible for the automatic Human Sentence Processor.

Note that this statement is general enough to encompass initial attachment as well as reanalysis. The definition is largely self explanatory, with only a few comments required before it can be examined in operation. Where the existence of intermediate nonbranching projections might have empirical consequence, the source and target positions will be construed as the highest projection dominating the constituent to be reanalyzed.[103] The occurrences of the parenthetical *if any* allow for those unproblematic situations wherein a constituent either is unattached when licensed (cf. §1.5) or is not immediately reattached (cf. §3.3.2). The constraint is of course simply irrelevant to any subconstituents of a reanalyzed category which are themselves not directly re-licensed or internally restructured. Making crucial use of the syntactic relations government and dominance, the OLLC reveals even more clearly than the TRC that abstract grammatical configuration rather than its surface word patterns determine processability. Descriptively, one of its primary predictions is that reanalysis of an argument as a lower or co-argument may be acceptable whereas reanalysis as a higher argument or an adjunct is illicit.

Though it remains conceptually similar to the TRC, the revised reanalysis constraint is rechristened here to reflect the theoretical importance of the elimination of the theta domain concept and to emphasize its imposition of a strict grammar-derived locality condition between an element's source and target structural positions. A formulation in terms of government and dominance (more will be said about the apparent disjunction below) is both natural and desirable as each is a near primitive structural notion of fundamental importance within the source grammatical framework, employed to characterize or enforce locality conditions on anaphora, case assignment, long distance dependencies, and thematic role assignment, etc.[104] Although clearly theoretically desirable, the first and most crucial question facing the OLLC is whether it is indeed capable of handling the empirically troublesome ditransitive data which partially motivated it.

4.0.2.1 Some Immediate Implications of the OLLC

   In light of this revised reanalysis constraint it is now possible to reconsider the previously troublesome ditransitive structures

(287)   a.   They gave her books to Ron.
        b.   Susan gave the boys dogs some bones.

and contrast them with minimally differing true garden path examples:[105]

(288)   a.   ¿I put the candy in the jar into my mouth.
             (I put the candy which was in the jar into my mouth.)
             (cf. I put the candy from the jar into my mouth.)

b.   ¿I sent the letters to Ron to Rex.
(I sent the letters which were to Ron to Rex.)
(cf. I sent the letters from Ron to Rex.)

c.   ¿I gave the package to Rex to John.
(I gave the package which was to Rex to John.)
(cf. I gave the package for Rex to John.)

d.   ¿I loaded the bananas on the truck into the boat.
(I loaded the bananas which were on the truck into the boat.)
(cf. I loaded the bananas beside the truck into the boat.)

Unlike the TRC, the OLLC correctly predicts reanalysis in (287a′) and
(287b′) to be cost free. Quite simply, in the final structure, the second argument position, originally occupied by *books* or *dogs,* governs the target head
position, N, since it governs N's maximal NP projection:

(287a′)

(287b′)

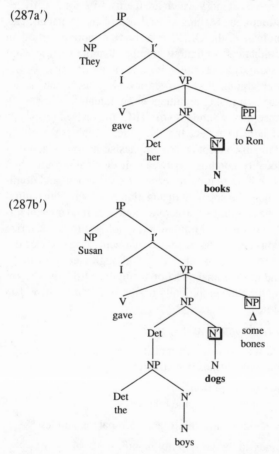

The OLLC consequently succeeds where the TRC failed.

In striking contrast to these examples, the sentences in (288) do require conscious processing. In (288a), by theta-attachment *the candy* will first be interpreted as the direct object of *put* and *in the jar* as its prepositionally headed locative complement: $[_{IP}[_{NP} I][_{VP} [_V put][_{NP} the candy][_{PP} in the jar]]]$. When this analysis is obviated upon the appearance of the actual complement PP, *into my mouth,* reanalysis must occur. Although the requisite restructuring is on the surface quite similar to that encountered in the unproblematic (287), the garden path effect nevertheless results as predicted since the government requirement is not satisfied:

(288a′)

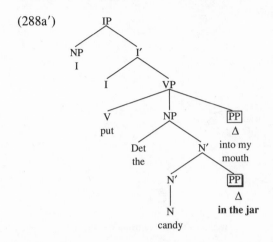

The source position of the argument PP does not govern the PP adjunct modifying *candy* given the intervening maximal NP projection.[106] This minimally contrasts with the former situation where the reanalyzed element became the governed *head* of the governed NP. An identical account pertains to the remaining examples in (288). The extreme surface similarity of these contrasting sets of examples constitutes rather striking confirmation of the grammar-derived approach to parsing and demonstrates the crucial effect of subtle structural differences with respect to processing. All of these factors sharply set the theta attachment theory apart from alternatives.

4.0.3 (Re)Establishing the OLLC

Before investigating a wider variety of double object ambiguities, it is first necessary to briefly reestablish that the processing data previously accounted for are still explained given this revised conception of the TRC. Notice also of course that theta attachment itself has not been altered and continues to operate as expected. The question is whether the new OLLC is capable of predicting the concomitant processing failure.

4.0.3.1 Complement-Relative Ambiguity

Consider first problematic double complement constructions which, in contrast to ditransitive constructions, involve clausal arguments:

(289)   ¿The doctor persuaded the patient he was having trouble with to leave.

In (289) the second internal argument position originally occupied by the *that*-clause m-commands but does not govern its target position since an NP maximal projection intervenes and the reanalyzed constituent is not the nominal's head, but rather an adjunct:

(289′)

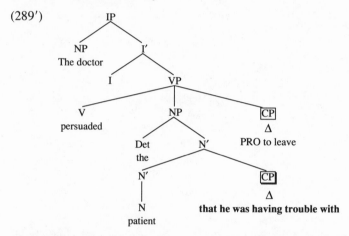

Like the original TRC, the OLLC directly predicts the unacceptability of such problematic constructions. Notice that this construction is subject to an account that is virtually identical to that of an example like (288). In each, a constituent which was an argument becomes an adjunct modifying a separate argument. This minimally contrasts with acceptable examples like (287) where an argument comes to head an independent argument.

4.0.3.2 Costly Object-Subject Ambiguity

Recall also several representative examples of costly object-subject ambiguity:

(290)   a.   ¿Susan convinced her mother was mad.
        b.   ¿Ron warned the ugly little man hated him.
(291)   ¿Without her donations to the charity could not be obtained.
(292)   ¿After Susan drank the water evaporated.

The costly status of each is predicted straightforwardly by the OLLC in the following ways. In (290a), the head N′ position originally occupied by *mother* fails to govern its target NP position as at least a CP and an IP intervene:

(290a′)

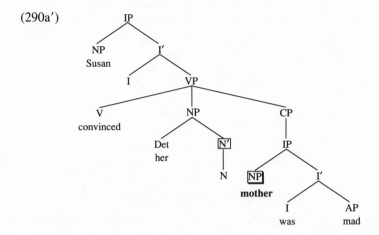

yielding the expected failure. Nearly the same is true in (290b) where the first internal argument position m-commands but does not govern the IP subject given the intervening CP and IP:

(290b′)

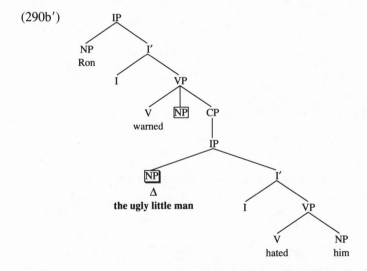

This example also emphasizes the obvious but important point that the OLLC holds for potentially abstract phrase-markers since the source position need not necessarily be filled within the final parse tree, as in the current example. It is fundamental tree geometry which is relevant, and it is perfectly coherent to pose the general question of whether the first internal argument of a particular predicate governs the specifier of the second.

In an example involving an initial PP, the source N′ position within the PP fails to m-command and hence to govern its target N′ (or NP) position:[107]

(291′)

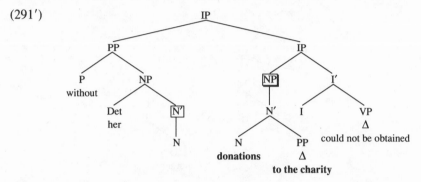

Similarly, the reanalyzed NP's source position as the complement of *drink* does not govern the target position of the matrix subject, again failing even to m-command the latter:

(292′)

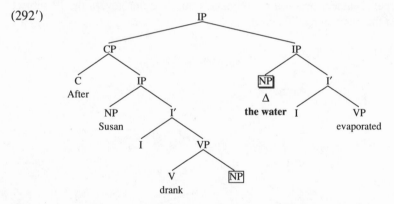

The OLLC continues to make precisely the right predictions.

4.0.3.3 Canonical Matrix GPs

Finally, reconsider the paradigmatic garden path structure:

(293)   ¿The boat floated down the river sank.

This is easily accounted for since the source position of *the boat* as the subject of *float* fails to m-command and hence govern the NP subject of *sink* in the final structure:[108]

(293')

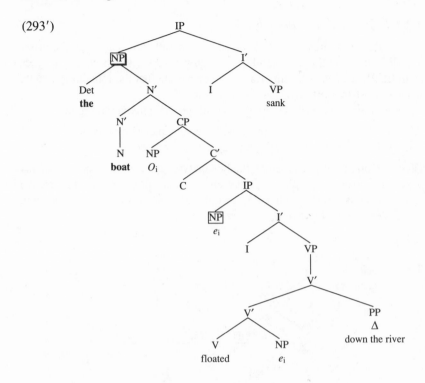

Notice that the dominance clause of the OLLC is not satisfied as the target position here dominates the source, not vice versa as required.

It is important to recognize that since this parser is lexically driven, there is no sense in which the reanalysis of *the boat* constitutes a nonreanalysis of matrix subject (of *float*) as matrix subject (of *sink*). What is relevant is the reinterpretation of a nominal from its position as external argument of *float* to a position as the external argument of *sink* in the final structure. The processor is simply not able to perform a reanalysis which requires it to reach outside of the domain governed (or dominated) by the original attachment site of the to-be-reanalyzed element. As a result, since *the boat* will have been initially attached as subject of a particular predicate, *float,* reanalyses will be (maximally) restricted to the subject position's governed domain.

The OLLC thus directly accounts for the range of garden path effects so far considered. What is striking about local ambiguity as exemplified by each of the constructions examined above is that the problematic reanalyses involve elements which remain linearly adjacent. The undeniable relevance of their increased structural distance constitutes rather overwhelming confirmation of the entire grammatical approach.

4.0.3.4 Unproblematic Reanalyses

While it has already been demonstrated that the OLLC (unlike the original TRC) predicts the acceptability of unproblematic ditransitive ambiguities as in (282), it is equally important to demonstrate that the remaining crucial range of cost-free reanalysis is also accounted for.

Consider first sentences involving multiple NP internal ambiguities:

(294)   a.   Susan hates her professors students papers quality.
         b.   Joe studies intelligence agency policy decisions.

Focusing on the representative final reanalysis of *her professors students papers* from verbal complement to specifier of that complement in (294a), the restructuring is clearly predicted to be unproblematic since its source position dominates its target position:

(294a′)

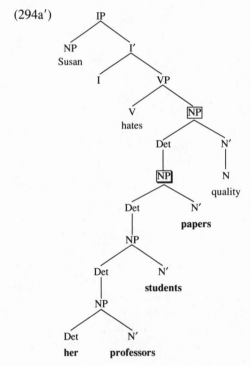

The same holds true of every prior reanalysis of VP complement to SPEC-NP (*her* → *her professors*[109] → *her professors students* → *her professors students papers*). The multiple compounding example in (294b) is subject to a parallel explanation (and this remains true upon alternative imaginable NP-internal structures).

A similar account holds as well for other familiar unproblematic examples which also satisfy dominance directly:

(295) Ned expected the professor of linguistics to bully him.

(295′)

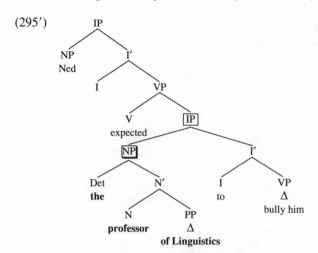

Here, *the professor of linguistics* is first attached as the IP complement of *expect* and later reanalyzed as its specifier, a constituent dominated by the complement position. Nearly the same is true when the complement clause is tensed as in (296), though the NP becomes not the specifier of the complement CP but of its IP daughter, again satisfying the dominance clause of the OLLC:

(296) Ned knew the professor would cheat him.

(296′)

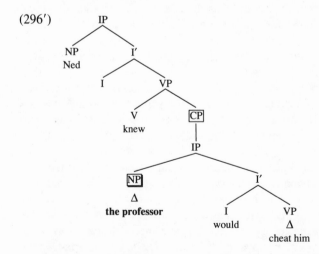

Although the acceptable examples just considered all happen to rely on the dominance clause of the OLLC, recall that the unproblematic double object constructions discussed above rely on government as do a number of additional cost-free ambiguities to be considered below.

This brief review demonstrates that the on-line locality constraint appears not only to account for all of the same data as the theta reanalysis constraint but also to provide an explanation for the previously troublesome unproblematic status of certain ditransitive sentences, and it is the OLLC which will consequently henceforth be assumed.

4.0.3.5 Disjunctive Government and Dominance

The theta attachment model holds that the parser employs the grammatical concepts of dominance and government directly to enforce a locality constraint between reanalyzed elements in parsing similar to those enforced by the grammar. By hypothesis, this may be attributed to the supposition that the parser, being derivative, has access only to grammatical constructs. That this relationship may be satisfied by either government or dominance, however, raises the question of whether this disjunction is acceptable.

Disjunctions are odious only to the degree that they obscure a generalization. Within grammatical theory, government and dominance are complementary concepts. Dominance is a notion used almost solely to characterize categorial identity and constituency (e.g., head, daughter, ancestor) whereas government enters into the definition of various relationships which hold only between nodes which are not constituents of each other (e.g., case marking, theta marking, binding). What the two concepts have in common of course is that both characterize certain structural node-to-node relationships, but in practice they are relationships whose functions do not overlap.

Government is typically defined (via the command relation) with an explicit proviso that in order for α to govern β, α must not dominate β. Were this stipulation removed, examples (294) and (295) could be explained directly since immediate dominance would, upon reasonable assumptions, also constitute government. Example (296) could also be accounted for, despite the intermediate IP projection, given the common hypothesis that whatever governs a tensed clause also governs its specifier, perhaps as a result of SPEC-head agreement (cf. the discussion in Chomsky 1986a). Under such assumptions, the dominating complement position would govern both its daughter IP and its specifier. An alternative approach to (296) might appeal to a relativized definition of government in terms of barriers, taking advantage of the fact that IP cannot be an inherent barrier in the system of Chomsky (1986a). Since, the grammatical relationships which government and dominance enter into are largely complementary, these changes would not necessarily have the dire repercussions for syntactic theory that one might expect. Nevertheless, as a thorough investigation into this possibility with respect to the grammar would be a substantial undertaking, it will be left unexplored here and the disjunctive definition allowed to stand.[110] It does not appear to affect any significant generalizations.

4.0.4 Ditransitives Redux

Returning, finally, to double object ambiguities, there is a range of sentences which are structurally more complex than those originally motivating the revision to the TRC but which are handled straightforwardly by the OLLC.

4.0.4.1 Object Relative Clauses

Consider first some examples involving object relative clauses:

(297)   ¿I handed the boy the dog bit the bandage.

a. **I handed the boy the dog:** In accord with theta attachment, this substring is parsed as a simple double object construction. It bears restating that since the parser does not match patterns of phrase structure rules there exists no relative NP ambiguity at this point for as far as theta attachment is concerned, no element is present which could license the projection of a clause (for example, an operator in SPEC-CP, a complementizer, or inflectional material) or the attachment of its subject.

b. **bit:** The appearance of the verb *bite* (<AGENT, PATIENT>) does reveal the availability of the relative clause analysis, which is also the only possibility since *hand* does not license an S′ complement. However, such a reanalysis would constitute an OLLC violation as the second NP daughter of VP clearly does not govern the subject position of *bite* in the relative clause:

(297′)

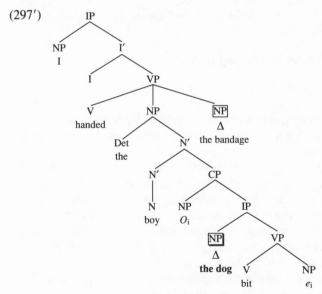

As commonly misinterpreted, the final NP in such sentences (*the bandage*) is construed as the object of the embedded verb (*bite*), something which would be grammatically impossible in the relative clause construction since an object bound by the null operator already exists. This is completely consistent with what has been suggested above about violations of the reanalysis constraint—that they simply exceed the capabilities of the processor. Hence the relative clause interpretation cannot be automatically obtained and the parser simply continues to employ its fundamental strategies (e.g., theta attachment), attaching incoming material as best it can even in the light of apparently ungrammatical input. It is quite clear that this fact is not significant with respect to the actual source of the garden path phenomenon but is merely a side effect. A structurally parallel example involving a verb which is not obligatorily ditransitive reveals this quite directly:

(298)   ¿Joe threw the vase the ball broke.

    a. **Joe threw the vase the ball:** This sequence is interpreted as a double object construction.

    b. **break:** Precisely as in the previous example, the verb forces reanalysis as a relative clause in violation of the OLLC. The requisite reinterpretation is impossible and since no further input is forthcoming the source of the difficulty can be isolated at this point, as predicted. Since *throw* does not require a second object, no subsequent NP need appear to yield a grammatical sentence and the potentially obscuring effect of final NP in the previous example is eliminated.

Of course, it is unsurprising that verbs which are not ditransitive do not produce parallel GP effects:

(299)   Joe punched the ball the dog chewed.

    a. **Joe punched the ball:** In accord with theta attachment, this is interpreted as a simplex clause.

    b. **the dog:** No theta role is available when this NP is first processed (and the relative reading is not yet visible) so a temporary local violation of the theta criterion results.

    c. **chew:** *Chew* ($<$AGENT, PATIENT$>$) is identified and further attachment may take place. Since *punch* does not select an S' complement, the string *the ball the dog chewed* may only be interpreted as a relative clause. Because *the dog* was previously unattached, the OLLC is not violated and the sentence is correctly predicted not to yield any conscious processing difficulty. (*The ball,* of course, continues to occupy its original locus of attachment and hence to satisfy the OLLC.)

A similar analysis obtains in the unproblematic (300) where in contrast to (298) it is the second object rather than the first that is relativized:

(300)   Joe threw Katrina the ball the cat chewed.

    a. **Joe threw Katrina the ball:** This is parsed as a double object construction.

    b. **the cat:** This NP cannot be attached to the local structure.

    c. **chew:** The verb forces a relative clause interpretation. The previously unattached *cat* is construed as the subject of a relative clause and the relativized NP *the ball* continues to occupy its original attachment site, satisfying the OLLC.

The above examples all involve double object constructions wherein one of the verbal objects is modified by an object relative clause and are accounted for directly by the principles developed. The interaction of double object verbs and subject relative constructions, although somewhat more intricate, is also fully predicted.

4.0.4.2 Subject Relative Clauses

While in the object relative examples, GPs result when available arguments are prematurely attached into the parse tree in accord with theta attachment, in the case of subject relatives, the number of theta roles requiring discharge from distinct theta assigners may locally exceed the number of available targets, creating ambiguity of a rather different sort:

(301)   ¿Katrina gave the man who was eating the fudge.

    a. **Katrina gave the man who was eating:** This string is interpreted via theta attachment as a simplex SVO sequence modified by an unambiguous subject relative clause. *Eat* has a theta grid, <AGENT, PATIENT>.

    b. **the fudge:** The identification of *the fudge* results in an interesting situation. A single target NP is available as are two thematic roles, THEME from *give* and PATIENT from *eat*. The principle of theta attachment apparently makes no prediction in this instance concerning which role will first be discharged, since either assignment will provide the NP *the fudge* with a theta role, releasing a single role from one grid and stranding another, and thus equally satisfies the principle.

One interesting fact immediately becomes apparent, however. Though the THEME role of *give* is obligatory, and the PATIENT role of *eat* is not, the garden path status of this sentence clearly demonstrates that the choice of which theta role to assign is not made based on this criterion. Assume that the NP *the fudge* is initially assigned the PATIENT role by *eat*, the subsequent reanalysis, motivated by the global absence of a THEME for *give*, will violate the OLLC since the complement of *eat* does not govern or dominate the complement of *give:*

(301′)

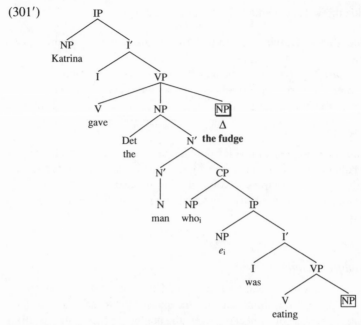

In contrast, the initial assignment of *give*'s THEME role to *the fudge* would result in the grammatical structure without the need for reanalysis. Local ambiguity in this case thus has two resolutions consistent with theta attachment: one which is predicted to be unproblematic and another which is predicted to necessitate conscious reprocessing. Interestingly, the empirical data bear this out. Though there is no clear discussion of such structures in the literature, hearers appear to judge this sentence either as unprocessable or unproblematic. In other words, some individuals are led down the garden path, some aren't.[111] This is consistent with the hypothesis that the ambiguity is resolved essentially randomly in such instances. Choosing to assign the PATIENT role of *eat* results in an unprocessable sentence, while discharging *give*'s THEME role circumvents reanalysis altogether and immediately results in the grammatical interpretation. This situation may obtain whenever the number of theta assigners locally exceeds the number of targets.

By far the most striking aspect of these results is the fact that the global obligatoriness of one of the roles appears locally irrelevant.[112] Similar conclusions concerning the relevance of obligatory transitivity in steering theta attachment were reached in §3.3.2 with respect to rather different data concerning cost-free variations on paradigmatic garden path patterns. There it was concluded that although such factors could signal the need for early reanalysis and consequently allow GP effects to be circumvented, theta attachment itself was not guided by sublexical features such as role obligatoriness. These double object findings are perfectly consistent with the previous results. Notice also, that as the following examples reveal, prematurely postulating an argument based on transitivity factors may itself very well lead to garden path effects. In general it thus appears that given the local nature of processing, transitivity information may force early reanalysis in unambiguous cases (when no overt argument occurs in its expected DS position) but does not effect the initial structure built via theta attachment, whose decisions are entirely local.

Now consider the converse case wherein the NP immediately following the embedded verb must globally be interpreted as its complement but is locally misconstrued as a matrix object:

(302)   ¿Katrina gave the man who was eating the fudge the wine.

a. **Katrina gave the man who was eating the fudge:** Assume that theta attachment has been resolved so as to incorrectly attach *the fudge* as the complement of *give* rather than *eat*, yielding: *[IP[NP Katrina][VP[V gave][NP the man who was eating][NP the fudge]]]*.

b. **the wine:** For this NP to be interpreted as the complement of *give*, reanalysis is required in which *the fudge* is attached as the object of *eat* in violation of the on-line locality constraint. The second complement of *give* (the position originally occupied by *the fudge* and globally by *the wine*) does not govern or dominate its target position inside the relative clause as complement to *eat* since several maximal projections intervene:

(302')

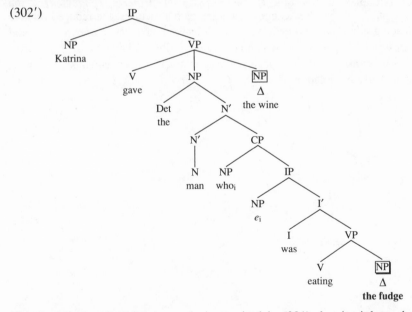

This is the opposite of the reanalysis required in (301), but it violates the OLLC as well. Alternatively of course, had *the fudge* been initially attached as the complement of *eat*, *the wine* could have been unproblematically incorporated as the complement of *give*. Like the previous example, this sentence appears to be a sporadic garden path with individuals apparently either experiencing severe processing failure on this sentence or finding it unproblematic, and, further, being inconsistent across tokens. The resolution of the equally weighted theta assignment ambiguities again appears essentially random.[113] In those simplex double object constructions exemplified by examples such as (282), the source position governs the target satisfying the on-line locality constraint. In contrast, the introduction of additional structure in the form of a relative clause disrupts the government relationship and blocks reanalysis.

It should by now be obvious that parallel sentences involving embedded intransitive verbs will display no garden path effects since the predicate will license no internal argument and thus no structural change will ever be required:

(303)   Sue gave the boy who was arriving the book.

But again, this fact is not transparently accounted for in a non-lexically driven model as the V NP sequence will match a PS rule such as VP → V NP regardless of the verb's subcategorization requirements.

Finally, consider the related case of paradigmatic garden path sentences involving a double object verb:

(304)   ¿The dealer handed the forgery complained.

a. **The dealer handed the forgery:** This is interpreted as the onset of a simplex (double object) clause: *[IP[NP the dealer][VP[V handed][NP the forgery]]]*. As in other canonical garden path structures, the reduced relative reading is not pursued as it would both leave the NP *the dealer* roleless and construct a larger NP for which no role is locally available.

b. **complained:** The occurrence of this verb forces reanalysis as a relative clause in violation of the OLLC:

(304′)

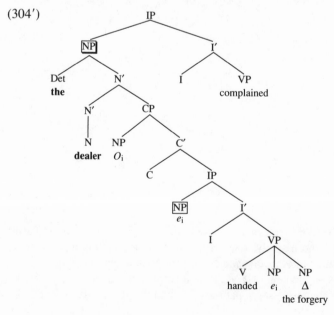

Such constructions are accounted for in precisely the same fashion as those with monotransitive predicates, the only difference being that the simplex reading is pursued through the appearance of a complement rather than an adjunct.

4.0.4.3 Small Clauses

There is one additional class of multiple NP ambiguity which warrants attention here. These involve predicates which license object controlled small clause complements:

(305)   We voted [$_{NP}$ the boys]$_i$ [$_{NP}$ PRO$_i$ congressmen].

In order to maximally satisfy the theta criterion and discharge the secondary internal theta role, theta attachment will immediately yield a structure such as the following:[114]

(305′)

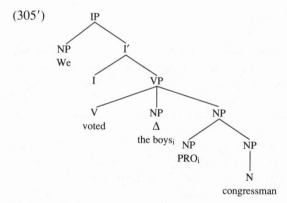

which is of course perfectly acceptable.

However, contrast (305) with the following ambiguous example in which input continues:

(306)   ¿We voted the boys congressmen senators.

The structure in (305′) proves untenable when *senators* appears, necessitating the following structure:

(307)   We voted [$_{NP}$ the boys' congressmen]$_i$ [$_{NP}$ PRO$_i$ senators].

Analyses of both the categorial identity and constituency of the small clause vary (cf. Williams 1980, 1983; Chomsky 1981; Stowell 1981), but all that is crucial for purposes here is the shared assumption that the second NP is a constituent of some secondary maximal projection, as reflected above. Consequently, the revision from (305) to (307) violates the OLLC since *congressmen* must be reanalyzed as the head of the initial NP complement rather than of the predicate. The latter NP does not govern the former N (or its maximal projection), failing to m-command it:

(307′)

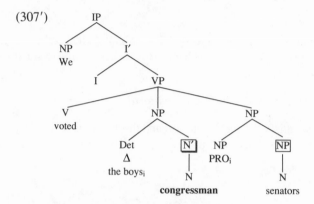

Notice that this argues strongly against a naïve surface analysis of the construction as a flat double object structure wherein *congressmen* directly occupies the secondary complement position. In such a configuration, the reanalysis would be identical to that involved in an unproblematic example such as *We handed her presents to Ron,* where the second NP position does indeed govern the first as discussed. Hence, in this instance, not only does the grammar-derived nature of the parser predict occurring GP effects, the behavior of the parser itself is able to shed light on competing linguistic analyses. This use of parsing effects to test grammatical structure is an exciting potential consequence of a strongly grammar-derived theory and deserves further exploration, though it will unfortunately not be possible to pursue the issue much further here.

　　Notice finally that the status of the small clause above as a secondary complement is crucial. In contrast, as noted in §3.1.2.2, multiple NP sequences which constitute a single small clause in an ECM construction, such as (308a), are fully acceptable:

(308)　　a.　　We considered the boys enemies.
　　　　　b.　　We considered the boys enemies friends.

Just as in the case where the object clause is infinitival or tensed, *the boys* is first interpreted directly as the verbal object then subsequently as the subject of the small clause complement, satisfying the dominance requirement of the OLLC:

(308a′)

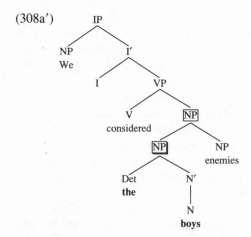

In contrast to (307), the sequence of three NPs in example (308b) is fully acceptable. Again, this is fully predicted. When *enemies* appears it causes *the boys* to be restructured as a specifier within the subject, transparently fulfilling dominance. More interestingly, it further requires the reinterpretation of *enemies* from small clause predicate to head of its subject, as shown in (308b′). Since the subject and consequently its head are governed by the predicate, this is not costly:

(308b′)

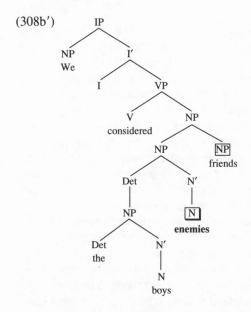

Such reanalyses may continue to be unproblematically iterated in rather striking fashion, as in *We considered the boys enemies friends fools*. What this discussion of small clauses begins to reveal rather clearly is that the OLLC is capable of making very precise distinctions between acceptable and unacceptable structures. Processability is extremely sensitive to abstract grammatical configuration.

The following section (§4-1) continues to demonstrate the wide empirical scope of the OLLC through an examination of what is often considered to constitute an independent processing phenomenon, lexical ambiguity. Crucially and perhaps unexpectedly, only the structural consequences of such ambiguity appears relevant to the associated processing effects, and an account proves to be fully consonant with the theta attachment theory as developed to this point. It is important to bear in mind throughout the following discussion that an explanation of the range of examples to be discussed crucially depends upon the revisions to the theory introduced in the OLLC. As should become self-evident, there is no obvious sense in which the theta reanalysis constraint could even be applied to many radical lexical reanalyses (cf. N-V ambiguity). It is only recognition of the fact that the relationship between a constituent's source and target positions constrains restructuring which permits a unified account of lexical and structural ambiguity.

4.1 Lexical Ambiguity

It is traditional to classify linguistic ambiguity (whether global or local) as either lexical or structural, but it is not a priori clear that this descriptive distinction is in itself empirically relevant with respect to human language processing. It was repeatedly demonstrated throughout the previous chapter that a wide range of environments which induce processing failure may be handled perspicuously in purely structural terms even when an ambiguity that is arguably in some sense lexical is also present (e.g., *her* as an NP versus *her* as an inherent Det or *raced* as a past active verb versus *raced* as a passive participle). In this, theta attachment was consistent with several models reviewed in chapter 2 which also held these ambiguities to be fundamentally structural. The discussion of the contrary view advocated by Ford, Bresnan, and Kaplan (1982) further demonstrated that the presence of lexical ambiguity per se was not only an unnecessary but also an insufficient condition on processing breakdown (cf. §2.2.1). Given these findings, the simplest hypothesis is that lexical ambiguity will adversely affect human parsing performance only in those cases where theta attachment leads to the wrong initial parse, and the resultant structural ambiguity is of a sort predicted to be problematic by the relevant constraints on structural reanalysis, e.g., the on-line locality constraint.

4.1.1 Intracategorial Ambiguity

From this perspective, there are numerous situations involving lexical ambiguity which are not predicted to be problematic. The simplest such cases arise when the ambiguity is intracategorial:

(309)   a.   Rex forgot about the *ball* which he had lost in the weeds.
       b.   Rex forgot about the *ball* which he had been eager to attend.
(310)   a.   The old man's *glasses* were filled with beer.
       b.   The bartender's *glasses* were filled with tears.
       c.   The astronomer kissed the *star*.
(311)   a.   John *set* the alarm clock to noon.
       b.   John *set* the alarm clock on the table.
(312)   a.   The construction workers *raised* the building with a crane.
       b.   The construction workers *razed* the building with dynamite.

Though the italicized words are indeed ambiguous and lead to distinct interpretations, there is no cost in obtaining the intended readings of the sentences. This is directly accounted for, given the structural approach to reanalysis in terms of the OLLC, because no syntactic reconfiguration is required in such cases, although the lexical content of the ambiguous item may have to be reevaluated. For example, in both (309a) and (309b), *ball* heads an NP prepositional complement which is modified by a relative clause, while in (311a) and (311b), *set* serves as the matrix verb selecting *the alarm clock* as its first internal argument. Reanalysis of lexical content may be necessary, but no structural change need occur. Notice that theta attachment makes no predictions concerning intracategorial sense preferences and priming,[115] so the mild surprise effect which might be associated with certain of the above sentences (for example those in 310) is perfectly consistent with the approach developed; what is crucial is that obtaining the correct reading is automatic even though it may require reaccessing the lexicon. Of course, it is predicted that examples of intracategorial ambiguity which do necessitate structural reanalyses will be subject to the OLLC, but the existence of such cases is not readily apparent.

4.1.2 Structural Ramifications of Lexical Ambiguity

In actuality, what is commonly intended by the term "lexical ambiguity" is the more narrow phenomenon of intercategorial (or cross-categorial) ambiguity. As lexical indeterminacy of this sort does frequently have direct structural ramifications, it is unsurprising given a configurational theory of reanalysis that associated processing breakdown may occur depending on the nature of the resultant restructuring.

4.1.2.1 NP-Subject+Verb Ambiguity

Consider the following examples of such intercategorial and prototypically lexical ambiguity:

(313) a. ¿The *prime number* few.
           (There are few prime.)
           (cf. The prime horrify all students.)
       b. The *prime number* seven is well-known.
(314) a. ¿The *old train* the young.
           (Those who are old train the young.)
           (cf. The old teach the young.)
       b. The *old train* chugged along the track.

Contrast the above with sentences such as the following, none of which leads to parsing failure:

(315) a. The *church pardons* set the demons free.
       b. The *church pardons* several demons each year.
       c. The *bakery stands* on the corner of Mass. Ave.
       d. The *bakery stands* sell hot crossed buns.
       e. The *warehouse fires* numerous employees each year.
       f. The *warehouse fires* kill numerous employees each year.

In (313) and (314) the ambiguous sequence is apparently interpreted as an NP to the exclusion of the NP V reading, whereas in contrast both interpretations are somehow available for the sentences in (315). The fact that such examples appear so similar yet pattern so differently might seem to confirm the widespread belief that the resolution of intercategorial lexical ambiguities is subject to complex independent principles beyond the usual processing heuristics (cf. Frazier and Rayner 1987 and references); the sentences appear to be structurally similar yet yield strikingly different performance effects.[116]

The first thing to notice in accounting for this contrast is that the sentences in (313) and (314) actually involve not merely a single lexical ambiguity but rather multiple and interdependent ambiguities (*old* and *train; prime* and *number*). Second, and of even greater importance, there actually is a clear structural difference between the two cases—the NP in an example like (314b) has the internal structure, $[_{NP} AP N]$, while in (315a) it is structurally a compound, $[_{NP} N N]$. This raises the possibility that the differing performance effects associated with these two sentences may indeed be accounted for in purely configurational terms. Notice that it must simply be a fact that in an example like (314a) the parser initially chooses to construct $[_{NP}$ the $[_{AP}$ old] $[_N$ train]] for otherwise the strong garden path effect will not be predicted. Simply assuming this to be the case for the moment, what must then be asked is whether reanalysis from that structure to the required $[_{IP}[_{NP}$ the old] $[_{VP}$ train . . .]] constitutes a violation of the OLLC. This is indeed quite clearly the case:

(314a')

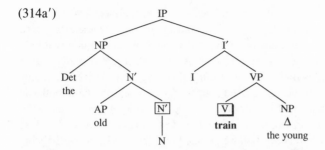

There are two reanalyses involved here. On one hand the AP *old* must be re-interpreted as the head N of the subject NP, but this does not violate the OLLC since the AP governs the head N (and hence this is not indicated in the diagram). The second analysis involves restructuring *train* as the V head of VP. In this case, the OLLC is violated since its original attachment site as the N head of the subject does not govern the matrix V target position. Recall that government is standardly construed so that *if α governs β, α governs the head of β*, not *if α governs β then the head of α governs β*. Consequently, N does not govern V in this configuration. This failure of government (and obviously dominance) straightforwardly predicts the associated processing difficulty.

Given that the OLLC reveals the reanalysis to be problematic, what remains to be determined is why it is the A N rather than the N V interpretation which is initially pursued. Indeed, it might appear that theta attachment would mistakenly predict the latter to be favored in order to maximally satisfy the theta criterion in *[$_{IP}$[$_{NP}$ the old][$_{VP}$ train]]*, rather than creating a roleless noun phrase, *[$_{NP}$ the old train]*. Fortunately there is a straightforward explanation for this apparent exception to theta attachment. The fact of fundamental relevance is that *old* is a zero-derived nominal and consequently does not display the full range of properties associated with either nonderived Ns or morphologically identified derived nominals (cf. Chomsky 1970). For example, zero-derived nouns must be interpreted as generics and cannot appear as plurals, with adjectives, with PPs, with quantifiers, or with determiners other than *the*:[117]

(316) a.   *Olds like children.
       b.   *The ugly old visited Spain.
       c.   *The old from Spain visited France.
       d.   *An old hit me today.
       e.   *That old is my best friend.
       f.   *Every old likes to wake up early.
       g.   *This old dislikes sushi.

Furthermore, such de-adjectival zero-derivation constitutes a productive process in English, and it would consequently be neither theoretically necessary not desirable to maintain that every such form (e.g., *the tautological, the prime, the lunar, the arcane,* etc.) possessed an independent lexical entry. Granting its undeniably restricted nominal status then, *old* in some clear sense is not a noun and not ambiguous within the lexicon at all; consequently it may only be initially recovered as an adjective. As a result, there is really only a single local analysis available for *old train.* Of course, zero-derived nominals will ultimately have to be recognized, but it is a very reasonable hypothesis that unidentified syntactically restricted derived forms are not accessed when the simplex lexical entry is compatible with the existing analysis. Given this, the unambiguous A N reading will be pursued until reanalysis is forced, correctly predicting breakdown when the N is reinterpreted as a V as discussed.

It is important to recognize that there are two independent issues of relevance here. First, does the theta attachment theory force the initial A N interpretation? Second, does the OLLC predict the resultant processing breakdown in the reanalysis from $[_{NP}$ *AP N]* to $[_{IP}$ *NP $[_{VP}$ V]]?* The answer to the first question is affirmative given reasonable assumptions concerning the non-ambiguous status of restricted zero-derived nominals, and the answer to the second is an unequivocal "yes." Note again that it is the reanalysis from N to V not A to N which is problematic, and a sentence such as, *The old teach very well,* may be unproblematically reanalyzed.[118]

Given this analysis of (314), consider the unproblematic (315a) and (315b). The fundamental difference is that the first element of the sequence, *church,* is an unambiguous N (unlike *old*). When *pardons* appears two possibilities arise. It could be interpreted as an N also and incorporated with *church* into a nominal compound or it could be recovered as a V, allowing *church* to be construed as an NP subject. The former option would yield a local theta criterion violation by constructing a roleless NP, *church pardons,* while the latter is capable of discharging a role from *pardons* onto *church* in accord with theta attachment. Since there is a true ambiguity in this instance in contrast to the case just discussed, theta attachment applies as expected and the latter option is selected. This analysis may of course continue uninterrupted through a sentence along the lines of (315b)

(317)   The church pardons many demons.

correctly predicting the lack of processing difficulty. On the other hand, if additional material indicates that *pardons* should actually have been recovered as a noun, reanalysis will be required, and *pardons* necessarily incorporated into the subject NP:

(315a′)

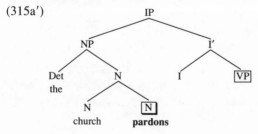

But the position originally occupied by the VP *pardons* in this instance does govern its target position for it governs its maximal projection. Notice that the source position here is VP (not V) since *pardons* constituted not only the head V but the entire phrase. This contrasts with the previous example where it was only the head N, *train,* not the entire branching NP with its additional lexical material which was reanalyzed. This is in full accord with all previous analyses in the text, as the source position has been consistently identified as the highest projection dominating all of the relevant lexical material. Notice that were the compound reading initially preferred (contra theta attachment), the OLLC would predict resultant processing difficulty since the head of a branching nominal compound would fail to govern the head of VP just as in the case of the adjectival modification in the previous example. Consequently, it is the interaction of theta attachment and the OLLC which is crucially responsible for making precisely the right predictions.

This account of nominal compounds itself provides some additional evidence for the previous derived-nominal approach to apparent A-N ambiguity. It turns out that strings containing a truly ambiguous A-N alternation in which the items are not synchronically related by zero-derivation do not yield the same GP effect as examples like (314). Consider (318):

(318)   a.   The Japanese push their merchandise abroad.
         b.   The Japanese push held off the allies.

Since, unlike *old, Japanese* has full status as an N (e.g., *a famous Japanese, every Japanese, Seven Japanese from Tokyo,* etc.) as well as an A ($[_{NP}$ *Japanese N]* structures receive phrasal (final) not compound (initial) stress, e.g., *Japanese antiques*), theta attachment predicts a preferred N V interpretation just as in the situation involving compounds. In (318a) this of course proves correct, but examples such as (318b) are also unproblematic. This sentence involves a reanalysis of *push* from V to N precisely parallel to that encountered with respect to acceptable compound ambiguity in examples such as (315).[119] Consequently, the restricted status of zero-derived nominals is crucial, but only in terms of its structural consequences rather than some inherent property of A-N ambiguity per se.

4.1.2.2 Interactions with Relativization

Before leaving the topic of NP versus N V ambiguities, notice that the possibility of relativization introduces additional complication:

(319)   a.   ¿The building blocks the sun faded toppled.
         b.   ¿The church pardons many sinners obtained burned.
         c.   The old train the children rode crashed.

Restricting attention to (319a) and (319b) for the moment, in the simplex case, as in (315), neither an initial N V reading:

(320)   a.   The *building blocks* the sun.
        b.   The *church pardons* many sinners.

nor an initial NP reading:

(321)   a.   The *building blocks* broke.
        b.   The *church pardons* burned.

directly results in processing breakdown. This is predicted given that the N V
interpretation is pursued in accord with theta attachment but cost-free reanalysis as an NP occurs just as in the analysis sketched above. However, if
the N V analysis is subsequently obviated along the lines of (319), a garden
path does indeed occur in a variation on the canonical GP pattern. Specifically, in the latter instance the original N V reading will be pursued through
the attachment of the post-verbal NP, *the sun* or *many sinners,* as a verbal
complement. Upon reanalysis this constituent comes to be reanalyzed as the
subject of a relative clause modifying *building blocks* or *church pardons,*
a position that the VP complement certainly does not govern, for example:

(319a′)

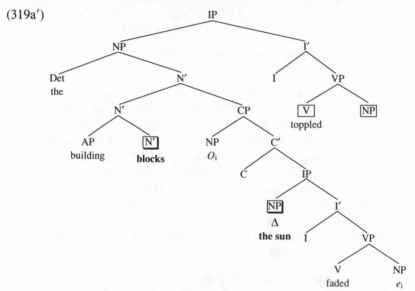

In this structure, the reanalysis of *blocks* or *pardons* from V (not the branching VP which contains additional lexical material after the attachment of *the
sun*) to N also violates the OLLC.

Notice in contrast that neither of these reanalyses is required in an unproblematic example containing an overt relative pronoun:

(322)   a.   The building blocks which the sun faded toppled.
        b.   The church pardons which many sinners obtained burned.

The overt relative operator of course prevents the attachment of *the sun* or *many sinners* as a verbal complement, and at the point of reanalysis, *blocks* or *pardons* will constitute the entire VP, which does govern the head N of the subject NP, just as in a simpler structure such as (322'):

(322')

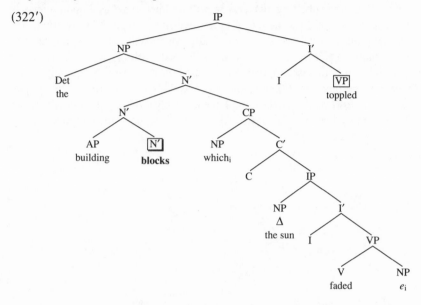

Note finally that (319c) in contrast to (319a) and (319b) is not costly to process. This is directly attributable to the fact that *the old train* is parsed as an unambiguous NP, as discussed, and reanalysis as a subject-verb is simply beyond the capabilities of the processor. Consequently, the string *the old train the children rode* constitutes an unambiguous relative NP with no reanalysis required. All of these examples demonstrate rather clearly that it is not lexical ambiguity per se but its structural consequences which are relevant to an account of human processing performance.

4.1.2.3 Demonstrative-Complementizer Ambiguity

As repeatedly demonstrated, common NP-determiner ambiguity (e.g., *her, that,* possessives in *-s*) is directly predicted to be unproblematic. In the case of *that,* however, in addition to its readings as a demonstrative determiner and NP, there is an alternative interpretation as a complementizer available. Furthermore, in instances where the specifier reading is prior, reanalysis as a complemetizer is problematic (cf. Fodor and Frazier 1980):

(323)   a.   ¿I saw that white moose are ugly.
        b.   ¿That white moose are ugly surprised me.

In the complement case (323a), *that* will first be directly interpreted as an NP object and then unproblematically reanalyzed as a determiner. In the subject example (323b), it is unimportant whether the parser first identifies *that* as a complementizer, determiner, or NP as it will be unable to perform any attachment. Next, the substring *that moose* will be interpreted as a noun phrase in order to avoid the construction of either two independent NPs, *[NP that]* and *[NP white moose]*, or an embedded clause which will both need a role itself and contain an element (*moose*) which will need a role, *[CP[C that][IP[NP white moose]]]*. In both cases, agreement features on the verb subsequently reveal *moose* to be plural and hence that *that* may only be construed as a complementizer. However, since the complementizer position is neither governed nor dominated by the specifier of its embedded IP's subject, the GP effect consequently results:

(323′)

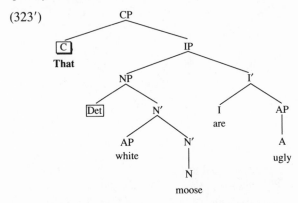

Of course, in those cases where there is no commitment to the determiner reading of *that*, perhaps for morphological reasons (e.g., *I saw that newts were a necessary ingredient*, or, *That warlocks can cast spells is self-evident*), there is no consequent reanalysis and hence no difficulty. Again, this reveals quite clearly that it is not the indeterminancy of lexical ambiguity in itself which may be a source of difficulty, but rather the structural ramifications which result.

4.1.3 Structural Constancy and Multi-Element Chains

Since the OLLC predicts only structural change to be potentially problematic, it is instructive to investigate the processability of sentences which are configurationally identical at a certain level of abstraction but otherwise lexically (and semantically) distinct. Interestingly, there are more subtle examples than those cases of intracategorial ambiguity in (309)–(312).

4.1.3.1 Verb-Auxiliary Ambiguity

In each of the following sentences, *have* is ambiguous between an auxiliary and a lexical verb but neither sentence is a garden path despite the fact that the structure is not disambiguated until the late appearance of *by the tigers* or *their dinners*:

(324)   a.   Have the boys devoured their dinners?
       b.   Have the boys devoured by the tigers!

As previously noted, Marcus (1980) invokes data of this sort as one argument for a look-ahead capability in the human sentence processor since the distance between the ambiguity and its resolution may be unboundedly increased by relativizing the pre-verbal NP. However, these data may be accounted for by theta attachment and the OLLC directly without an appeal to look-ahead.

     It appears that theta attachment should initially favor the auxiliary reading of *have* since an AUX, possessing no associated theta role, places no local strain on the theta criterion. Kurtzman (1985) provides experimental evidence that this is indeed the human preference, and this assumption will be adopted here. Consider, then, the partial local interrogative structure which will be built prior to the appearance of the disambiguating information:

(324a′)   *Question*

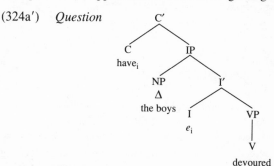

If the sequence continues *their dinners,* no reanalysis is required of course since an NP complement is simply introduced via theta attachment.

     On the other hand, if the continuation is *by the tigers,* (324a′) must be remapped into (324b′) (unnecessary details suppressed):

(324b′)   *Imperative*[120]

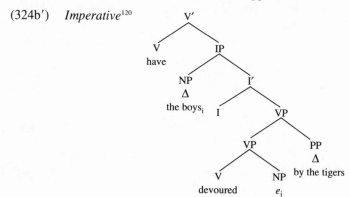

This obviously requires the introduction into the tree of the *by*-phrase itself as well as an empty NP complement coindexed with *the boys*. Theta attachment of course predicts such initial chain formation to be subject to the local application of the relevant global grammatical principles, for example, that the head c-command the tail. This condition (among others) is clearly satisfied here and chain formation is licit. Beyond these changes, the two structures differ only in the category labels associated with certain nodes, the head C is changed to V and this feature percolates through the projection. If, as is commonly assumed (somewhat tacitly within GB theory, explicitly within G/HPSG), category specifications per se are simply features associated with nodes-as-complex-objects, then it is predicted by a purely configurational theory of reanalysis that such features may be freely altered without significant processing cost if the relevant structural constraints are not violated as a result.[121] Consequently, the OLLC predicts no processing difficulty in the mapping from (324a′) to (324b′) as there is actually no reanalysis of phrase structure involved—only on-line chain formation and node relabelling.[122]

The examples in (324) contrast interestingly with the following, also pointed out by Marcus (1980):

(325)   a.   Have the boys given gifts to their friends?
        b.   ¿Have the boys given gifts by their friends!

Like (324a), (325a) is fully processable, but in contrast to (324b) the imperative in (325b) presents difficulty (providing additional evidence that the auxiliary reading is indeed primary). Notice that the two examples differ in one respect of potential importance—in the latter instance, the auxiliary reading may continue through the occurrence of a post-verbal NP, here *gifts*. This is construed as a complement via theta attachment, prohibiting, as a side effect, the immediate association of *the boys* with that position:

(325a′)

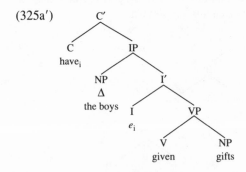

If *to their friends* next appears, there is of course no difficulty since this conforms to the anticipated interrogative structure. However, if the agentive phrase occurs, (325a′) must be remapped into:

(325b′)

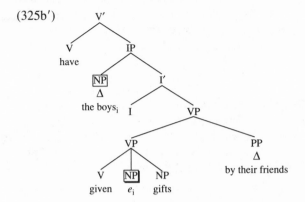

Now, the reanalysis of *gifts* from first to second object of *give* satisfies the government clause of the OLLC and is therefore predicted to be unproblematic. However, another reanalysis also takes place. As initially constructed, both the head and tail of *the boys'* chain occupy the subject position of *give*. Upon reanalysis, however, the tail must be reinterpreted as the inner object of *give*, a position which it obviously neither governs nor dominates. This clearly violates the OLLC, predicting the encountered difficulty. It is crucial to recognize that in contrast to the previous example this is indeed a case of reanalysis rather than on-line chain formation. The inner object position had been previously introduced into the tree and occupied by *gifts*. Although the reanalysis of *gifts* presents no difficulty, the corollary reanalysis of the tail of the chain headed by *the boys* does, and it is this to which the processing failure may be attributed.

The generalization of the OLLC to chains is an extremely desirable result. It should be the null hypothesis in a grammar-derived theory of processing that global principles, locally applied, hold of the same theoretical substantives. Initial chain construction is subject to theta attachment while the OLLC constrains their reanalysis. Indeed, throughout all previous discussion the theta attachment theory has been applied to chains, albeit typically of length zero. The discussion here simply generalizes the relevant conditions to chains of greater length, and this natural extension of the theta attachment model to multi-element chains is fully compatible with the data as analyzed throughout the previous chapters. Although numerous questions are of course immediately raised (e.g., the status of head-movement chains), the full implications of the hypothesis appears ripe for further investigation. An additional example is discussed in §4.1.3.3 below.

4.1.3.2 Node Feature Respecification

One important aspect of the previous analysis is the hypothesis that categorial identity per se may be freely altered. There is further evidence that simply altering a feature specification associated with a node is unproblematic if the structural configuration remains unchanged. Consider:

(326)   I saw her duck . . .

This sentence is globally ambiguous between an NP and small clause VP. Initially, *her* will be attached in the familiar fashion as the complement to *see*. Regardless of whether *duck* is recovered as an N or V, *her* will be reanalyzed as a specifier (of NP or VP respectively) with neither of these analyses predicted to be problematic. Furthermore, no matter how the sentence continues, no GP effects result:

(327)   a.   I saw her duck into an alleyway.
         b.   I saw her duck fly away.

This may be directly attributed to the fact that the structure of *her duck* is arguably configurationally identical in the two instances (cf. Kuroda 1987):[123]

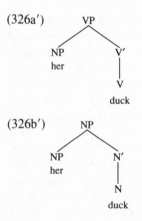

(326a′)

(326b′)

Since it is a fact that simply altering the category feature specification of a node does not change structure, the relevant question is whether reinterpretation of the entire subtree itself constitutes a violation of the OLLC in either instance. If the NP interpretation (326b′) is first pursued and reinterpreted as a small clause VP as in (327a), then all that is required is node relabeling. The entire construction remains a complement of *see*, its structural position is not altered, and reanalysis is predicted to be unproblematic. If the VP analysis is first preferred, but the NP structure required as in (327b), then, after relabeling, the complement need merely be reinterpreted as the embedded subject, satisfying the dominance clause of the OLLC in the familiar fashion. The internal phrase structure of the constituent is not itself altered:

(327b')

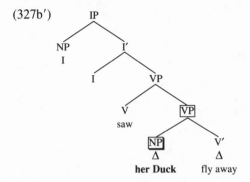

Consequently both reanalyses are perfectly acceptable and the ease of switching between two very different interpretations for a lexically distinct string is directly predicted.

Notice, more simply, that a similar account holds of the processing of an item which is arguably ambiguous between a preposition and a complementizer, e.g., *after* as discussed with respect to example (230). A string such as *after John* will initially be interpreted as a PP in accord with the theta criterion but may be acceptably reanalyzed as a C in *after John left* precisely because there is no resultant structural change involving the head or its projection. This and similar analyses provide rather appealing processing evidence for the generalized X′ schema (Chomsky 1970, 1986b; Jackendoff 1977).

4.1.3.3 Adjectival Predicate-Causative Ambiguity.

Finally consider the following contrasting pair:

(328)   a.   The boy got fat.
        b.   ¿The boy got fat melted.

Unlike (328b), other causative alternations are completely unproblematic:

(329)   a.   The boy $\begin{Bmatrix} got \\ had \end{Bmatrix}$ (a) cake.

        b.   The boy $\begin{Bmatrix} got \\ had \end{Bmatrix}$ (a) cake baked.

The reanalysis from (329a) to (329b), is familiar and does not violate the OLLC:

(329b′)

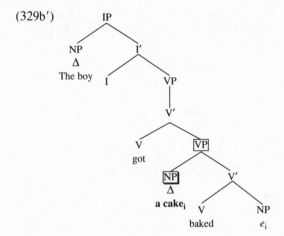

The boy remains the IP subject and *cake* remains dominated by the complement position of *get*; the initial coindexation of the VP subject and complement positions is a simple instance of on-line chain formation.

There is a crucial contrast between these examples and (328b), however. The adjectival interpretation is pursued in the latter case in order for *the boy* to receive a theta role through predication with *fat* and due to *fat*'s status as a derived nominal.[124] The situation in (328a) may be captured in various ways (for example, see Bowers 1991 and references) but a defensible structure involves raising:

(328a′)

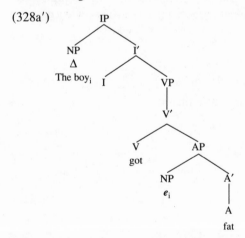

where *the boy* is the DS subject of *fat* and forms a chain with that position at SS. The results of subsequent reanalysis are shown in (328b′):

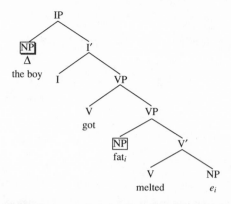

Although *the boy* remains the IP subject, the reanalysis of the empty category terminating the chain through which *the boy* received its thematic role violates the OLLC. That is, the tail of *the boy*'s chain is initially construed as SPEC-AP (structurally corresponding to the relabeled VP's specifier subsequently occupied by *fat*) but must be reinterpreted as IP subject, a position identical to its head but one which the reanalyzed tail itself does not govern. Thus the situation is very similar to (325b) above. The lexical ambiguity of *fat* is indeed relevant, but only insofar as it affects the initial structural attachment decisions. The processing breakdown itself is independent of the need to recategorize the adjective but rather is attributable to the resultant structural changes in *the boy*'s chain which must take place in violation of the OLLC. Such examples strongly support the null hypothesis that the OLLC itself applies to chains.

What this section has revealed is that the distinction between lexical and structural ambiguity is useful only as a descriptive device to characterize the source of a processing indeterminacy. Both the initial resolution of that ambiguity and the effects of reanalysis are accounted for in purely structural terms via a combination of theta attachment and the OLLC, just as is true of more obviously configurational cases. Whether its origin is lexical or structural, ambiguity is only problematic when theta attachment forces a local choice whose later reanalysis violates the on-line locality constraint. Recategorization is never a significant cost; restructuring may be.

Contrary to the widely held performance-oriented views of human language processing, it appears clear from the discussion in the last two chapters that a cognitively plausible model must be formulated explicitly in terms of grammatical principles operating on precisely articulated grammatical structure rather than on vague, albeit putatively more general, human cognitive constraints. The next chapter expands the model to encompass principles beyond the theta criterion, a move which both simplifies the principle and extends its scope.

CHAPTER FIVE

Generalized Theta Attachment

This chapter explores various empirical and theoretical extensions to the theta attachment theory. Of greatest importance, a generalization is made which introduces the local application of principles of grammar beyond the theta criterion. This proves to be not only theoretically desirable but also allows for a simplified analysis of some previous empirical data as well as an account of certain additional processing phenomena, both in English and cross-linguistically.

5.0 Beyond the Theta Criterion

Theta attachment constitutes not only a strong empirical thesis concerning human parsing performance but also a theoretical hypothesis with respect to the Grammar-Parser relationship. As it is derived from a grammatical principle rather than a (language specific) rule of syntax, theta attachment potentially possesses significant universality, and it is fully natural to expect that other global principles apply locally in a similar fashion. It has been suggested numerous times throughout the preceding chapters that this is indeed the case, and the following sections demonstrate that an extension of theta attachment which encompasses additional grammatical principles leads to desirable simplification of the theory as a whole as well as increased empirical coverage.

5.0.1 Eliminating Role Content

As discussed briefly in chapter 1 and tacit throughout the subsequent chapters, in certain instances the parser has apparently been steered in its initial decisions by the content of the thematic roles it assigns. For example, recall the earliest discussion of the following contrast:

(330)   I believe her professors hated me.
(331)   ¿I informed her professors hated me.

In (330) *professors* was first attached as the THEME complement of *believe* and then reanalyzed as the subject of the complement PROPOSITION. This was not predicted to be problematic since both roles were realized on the same argument position. On the other hand, *professors* in (331) was first attached as a GOAL and then reanalyzed as the subject of a structurally distinct secondary PROPOSITION. The crucial fact that *professors* was not originally attached directly as the second argument was accounted for by an appeal to role content—quite simply that *professors* could not be a PROPOSITION in an initial structure *[$_{VP}$[$_V$ *informed*] [$_{NP}$ *her*][$_{NP}$ *professors*]], therefore its attachment into that position would not locally satisfy the theta criterion.

This is disturbing on several grounds, however. Theoretically, since the syntax in general and the theta criterion in particular make no reference to the semantic content of thematic roles, it is undesirable that the derived processor employ such information. As discussed in §4.0 with respect to the so called *spray-load* alternation, there is also evidence that gross role labels do not actually have any true lexical-semantic status. The use of such nonlinguistic knowledge on-line would thus run contrary to the widespread assumption that the human sentence processor is necessarily informationally encapsulated (cf. J. A. Fodor 1983 for a discussion of the influential modularity hypothesis). Further, there is the simple empirical fact that, aside from the issue under consideration, the model of human parsing performance developed is otherwise formulable solely in terms of structural principles. Finally, it turns out that it is not even truly the case that propositional arguments must be clausal, and consequently an account of the distributional facts in terms of thematic roles fails in any event:

(332)   I informed Bob of the comic book's value.
(333)   I warned her about the vampires.

For all of these reasons, it is highly desirable to eliminate all reference to role content from the parsing theory. Clearly, with respect to the grammar, and, by extension, the parser, the crucial contrast between verbs like *inform, tell, persuade, warn, convince* on the one hand and examples like *know, believe, see, suspect, discover* on the other, is that the latter may only assign a role to a single internal complement, while the former may assign roles to two distinct positions.[125] How their content is described should be irrelevant.

5.0.1.1 Case Theory

Given the hypothesis that theta attachment, like the theta criterion, has access only to information concerning argument structure configurationality and not actual semantics, the obvious question that arises is how the contrast between (330) and (331) is actually to be accounted for. The monotransitive sentence (330) remains unproblematic as *professors* will first be attached into the sole internal argument position and then reanalyzed as the subject of the actual clausal complement, satisfying the on-line locality constraint as before. What is at issue is how, in an example like (331), theta attachment is to be prevented from prematurely construing *professors* as the second internal argument, more fully satisfying the theta criterion but incorrectly circumventing costly reanalysis.

There is an appealing solution to this problem in the form of the fact, alluded to above, that NPs may occur as secondary propositional arguments only if they appear in a particular structural configuration. As standardly analyzed within the Government and Binding framework, the following examples are held to be ungrammatical not because a certain role cannot be assigned to the second NP argument but because it lacks Case: [126]

(334)   *I informed Bob the comic book's value.
(335)   *I warned her the vampires.

Only if a case marker, specifically a preposition, is present will the representation be licit, as exemplified previously in (332) and (333).[127] Consequently, a local appeal to the Case Filter will prevent the initial attachment of *professors* into a Caseless position in (331), with no reference to role content required.

The hypothesis that the parser attempts to satisfy locally Case theory as well as Theta theory may be subsumed into a (final) revision to theta attachment along the following lines:

(336)   **Generalized Theta Attachment:** Every principle of the Syntax attempts to be maximally satisfied at every point during processing. [*Final Version*]

Syntactic principles are increasingly satisfied to the degree that each element in the local representation is licensed, and, beyond this, the greater the number of licensing features (e.g., Cases, theta roles) discharged. It is absolutely crucial to recognize that this is not equivalent to the claim that the processor attempts to construe each local string as globally grammatical, though at times it may have the same effect.[128] This interpretation of theta attachment, emphasizing the local representation, was of course unavailable when formulated in terms of only a single principle. Although the discussion which follows will largely restrict itself to Case and Theta theory, there is also evidence that other principles, such as those of Binding theory, Control theory, and Bounding theory, apply on-line (cf. Nicol and Swinney 1989; MacDonald 1989; Kurtzman 1985) and it seems desirable to state the heuristic in the strongest terms possible in the absence of counterevidence. The term theta attachment should henceforth be understood in this broader sense.

In most monotransitive and ditransitive constructions, Case and theta role assignment arguably coincide, and, as a result, both the original and generalized versions of theta attachment make the same predictions in essentially the same fashion. However, generalized theta attachment does handle some previous double complement constructions in a somewhat novel fashion as well as provide an account of certain new data. Each of these cases is worth examining in more detail.

5.0.1.2 *Some Previous Data Reconsidered*

One obvious benefit of generalized theta attachment is that it provides a simple explanation for the unproblematic status of obligatorily transitive variants on the canonical garden path pattern:

(337)   The warlock cast into the pit vanished.

Early reanalysis may now be directly attributed to the local application of Case theory. The adjacency requirement on Case assignment reveals an obligatory argument to be missing as soon as the PP appears. The motivation for the immediate restructuring is now far more transparent than when discussed in §3.3.2.

Now consider in somewhat more detail the solution to the problem of PROPOSITIONAL complements sketched above:

(338)   a.   ¿I warned the werewolf was after Ron.
        b.   ¿I convinced her witches would fly by.

Upon standard assumptions, thematic roles are associated with configurational positions, for example the (first) sister of V, and, in the case of double complement verbs, the second sister (or perhaps the sister of V'). The first internal theta role is associated with a position which is structurally Case marked, while the second is associated with a position which is not. As a result, in (338a) the NP, *the werewolf,* is initially attached into the first internal argument position in order to receive both a theta role and Case, rather than into the second thematic but Caseless position. In (338b), *her* is attached as the first internal argument for the same reason. *Witches* could then be structured either as the head of this argument or assigned the second internal role directly, given that thematic content is irrelevant. Although the latter choice would increase satisfaction of the theta criterion, it would violate the equally important Case Filter. In contrast, in the alternative configuration *witches* and *her* may both be fully licensed, locally receiving a theta role and Case, and hence this is the analysis pursued in accord with generalized theta attachment. In both examples, subsequent reanalysis of *the werewolf* or *witches* violates the OLLC as expected.

It must be emphasized that the non–garden path status of sentences such as

(339)   a.   I warned he was after me.
        b.   I convinced her Bob stole the comic book.

continues to be predicted. In (339a) the nominative form *he* is incompatible with first internal argument position since it is obligatorily associated with accusative case. Instead, *he* is attached as the second internal argument, which is not a Case position and therefore does not disallow the nominative. This permits *he* to obtain at least a theta role and satisfy grammatical principles to the greatest degree possible. (Note again the distinction between maximal licensing and grammaticality.) Observe that this does not conflict with the previous analysis since *witches* failed to attach as the second argument only because the parser had an alternative that more fully satisfied the grammar by assigning it both a theta role and Case. Similarly in (339b), *Bob,* as a full noun phrase, cannot be incorporated as the head noun of the previous theta and Case marked NP, so it may be directly attached as the second argument (and subsequently reanalyzed as its subject). In both instances, any Case assignment is impossible but the theta criterion may be locally fulfilled.[129]

In other double complement constructions, the generalized theta attachment account differs from the original approach only in being more specific as to the point when the second internal role is assigned. Consider familiar relative-complement clause ambiguities:

(340)   a.   The monk convinced the priest he was having trouble with his
             manuscripts.
        b.   ¿The monk convinced the priest he was having trouble with to
             convert.

Since there is no way to incorporate *he* into a theta and Case position within the first NP, the pronoun may be immediately attached as the second internal argument in order to avoid a local theta criterion as well as Case Filter violation, just as in (339) since no NP, $[_{NP}$ *the priest he]*, can be formed. Subsequent reanalysis as a complement subject is of course unproblematic in both cases, but later restructuring as a relative in (340b) violates the OLLC as before. Similarly, if an overt complementizer (*that*) were present, attachment could also occur immediately at that point in order to allow the second internal role to discharge.[130] Notice that in such cases both the complement and relative representations would be equally licensed at that point, but the complement is preferred under generalized theta attachment just as under the original interpretation as it releases an additional theta role, all other things being locally equal.

As mentioned, the remaining monotransitive and ditransitive data considered throughout the previous chapters require no further comment since Case and theta role assignment coincide, and, as a result, both versions of theta attachment operate in essentially identical fashions. However, the revisions just outlined do also yield an explanation of certain otherwise problematic double complement sentences whose costly status was not previously so clearly predicted.

5.0.1.3 Additional Complex Data Explained

Each of the garden path sentences to be considered in this section would have presented a problem for the processing theory as outlined in chapters 3 and 4. The difficulty does not stem from theta attachment making a wrong prediction (nor from a failure of the OLLC), but rather from the principle's inability to select between two alternative constructions. This problem is completely resolved under generalized theta attachment, which, as seen, is able to disregard role content by taking a broader range of syntactic principles into account.

Consider for example the following:

(341)   ¿I informed the boy the dog bit Sue would help him.

Under prior assumptions, *inform* would assign AGENT, GOAL, and PROPOSITION roles. While *the boy* would be immediately assigned the GOAL role, *the dog* could not be directly attached as a PROPOSITION. Consequently, when *bite* was encountered, two possibilities arose. On one hand, a PROPOSITION theta role might be assigned to *the dog bit* (its clausal status clear) and an AGENT role assigned to *the dog,* leaving the PATIENT role of *bite* undischarged. Alternatively, the surface string *the boy the dog bit* could be analyzed as a relative NP receiving the matrix GOAL role with the PATIENT role discharged on the VP internal gap, stranding only the higher PROPOSITION. The θ-criterion alone does select between these two alternatives as each strands a single role. Obviously, however, the latter correct analysis cannot represent the preferred interpretation since the sentence is an unequivocal GP. Fortunately, this is predicted by the revised approach since *the dog* will be immediately attached as the second internal argument once role content is disregarded; there is no alternative position where it may be more fully licensed by receiving Case also. Subsequent reevaluation as a relative violates the OLLC since the NP position neither dominates nor governs the clausal subject. Structurally this ambiguity is very similar to one exhibited by true ditransitives, discussed in §4.0.4.1, which were amenable to earlier explanation given their ability to directly theta license a second NP. The account of the two parallel constructions is now identical.

(341′)

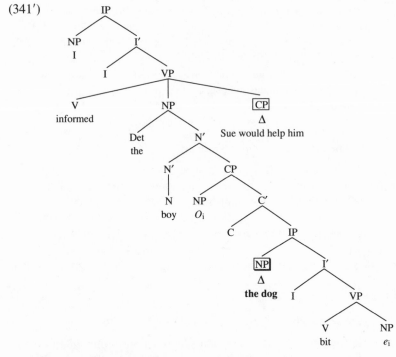

These revisions also yield an account of certain more complex matrix clause–relative NP ambiguities:

(342)   a.   ¿The Russian men killed fled the country.
         b.   ¿The cotton fields produce makes warm clothing.

Consider the string, *the Russian men killed* in (342a). The original version of theta attachment fails to select between the two possible structures. What sets such examples apart from paradigmatic reduced (subject) relative garden path structures is the additional NP-internal ambiguity. This admits a possible object relative reading wherein the external as well as the internal role may be discharged, rendering the matrix and object relative constructions equivalent as far as the theta criterion alone is concerned. The former analysis would strand one of *kill*'s roles, while the latter would leave only the roleless relative NP. However, once generalized theta attachment is adopted, the simplex clause reading is clearly favored since all elements are fully licensed (though the structure is not globally grammatical) while the alternative leaves the NP headed by *Russian* both roleless and Caseless. When restructuring is forced at *fled*, the reanalysis of *Russian* from (a constituent of) the subject of *kill* to the head of the relative clause subject of *flee* violates the OLLC. The revised approach clearly predicts the initial misanalysis and hence the resultant GP effect.

(342a′)

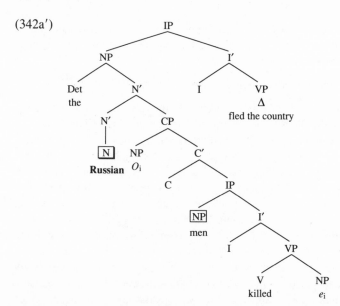

The account of sentence (342b) is ultimately identical, though there exists one additional ambiguity whereby *cotton fields* is initially structured as a Subject + Verb, then unproblematically reanalyzed as a compound subject of *produce*, as discussed in §4.1.2.1 (e.g., the unproblematic *The cotton fields produce large crops*), before being reanalyzed once again as independent nominals in a relative construction in violation of the OLLC, just as in the previous example.

The fact that generalized theta attachment is able to disregard role content by encompassing Case as well as Theta theory (and by hypothesis additional principles) can thus clearly be seen to provide not only a natural theoretical generalization and simplification but also to result in improved empirical coverage. The following section continues to investigate topics beyond the purview of the theta criterion alone, turning to adjuncts, elements which by nature are not Case or theta marked by a head.

5.1 Adjunct Attachment

Quite naturally, the grammar-derived parsing model motivated up to this point has concerned itself primarily with the attachment of arguments— selected elements which, by definition appear in positions structurally accessible to theta role and Case assignment. Recall from chapter 2, discussion of the influential perceptual processing model originally motivated in Frazier (1978), which is founded on the notion that the parser locally performs Minimal Attachments as determined by matching explicit phrase structure rules. One claim which is frequently made in favor of this approach is that it is capable of providing a unified account of both argument and adjunct attachment effects. The crucial data concern the preferred readings of globally ambiguous sentences such as the following:

(343)   Rex slapped the man with the board.

It is held that in (343) the PP is preferentially interpreted as an instrumental adverbial modifying the verb phrase rather than as a nominal adjunct. According to proponents of the model, this is directly attributable to Minimal Attachment since the VP construal is the simplest, introducing the fewest new nodes into the tree. (Recall that this notion of simplicity is functionally rooted in purported (vague) cognitive constraints rather than any aspect of grammar.) That the preference for verbal over nominal adjunction may apparently be accounted for by an appeal to the same heuristic which predicts various argument attachment preferences may thus be taken as evidence in favor of the MA model. (Of course, this assumes that an MA-based theory provides an adequate account of argument attachment effects, a claim which is strongly disputed in chapter 2, but which will be granted here for the sake of discussion.) Given such data, it appears that the question consequently arises of whether the theta attachment model is also capable of capturing these putatively parallel processing effects in a natural fashion.

5.1.1 The Failure of Minimal Attachment

The burden of proof actually lies with the theta attachment theory only if the Minimal Attachment account of adjunct effects is truly sound. Contrary to popular belief, it turns out that the preference for verbal over nominal adjuncts is simply not predicted by MA. Consider the standard X′ theoretic structures of such sentences, common to a number of syntactic frameworks including the very one Frazier herself adopts in current work:

(343′)

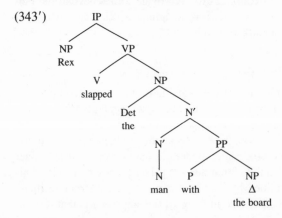

(343″)

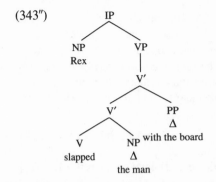

PP attachment into each tree is equally simple in terms of MA, introducing (in addition to the PP itself) a single additional X′ projection (either V′ or N′) into the local structure. There is simply no way for MA alone to select between the two alternative trees. Typically in other such indeterminate situations (as discussed in chapter 2 in reference to argument attachments, e.g., *Since John jogs a mile seems like a short distance*) an appeal is made to the supplementary principle of Late Closure (a.k.a. Right Association) which simply stipulates that new material is to be attached to the lowest open node. Although this stipulation produces the correct result in the case of arguments, it unfortunately predicts the lower N′ attachment of (343′) to be preferred, precisely what is held not to be the case in human parsing.

It turns out that the structures which must actually be assumed in order for MA to function as desired are as follows:

(343‴)

(343⁗)

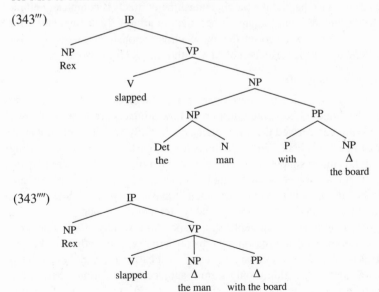

The sister attachment of the PP in (343'''') would indeed be more minimal than the adjunction in (343''') which introduces an additional NP node, but these are structures that few if any linguists would postulate. First of all, these phrase markers simply fail to capture the proper constituency of the relevant substrings with respect to a range of elementary syntactic tests which clearly reveal *man with a board* in the nominal construal and *slapped the man* in the verbal to form independent constituents:

(344) a. Max saw a [$_{N'}$ man with a board] and [$_{N'}$ boy with a brick].
           (*Coördination*)
       b. Max likes that [$_{N'}$ man with a board]$_i$ but Guy likes this [$_{N'}$ one$_i$].
           (*Anaphora*)
       c. Max likes this [$_{N'}$] and Guy likes that [$_{N'}$ man with a board].
           (*Right Node Raising*)

(345) a. Max [[$_{V'}$ slapped the man] with a board], but Guy did with a stick. (*Deletion*)
       b. Max [[$_{V'}$ slapped the man]$_i$ with a board], but Guy did so$_i$ with a stick. (*Anaphora*)
       c. [$_{V'}$ Slap that man] Max very well may with that heavy board.
           (*Preposing*)

Furthermore, to adopt the structures necessary for MA to function as desired is simply to abandon the claim that both involve adjunction. VP adjuncts behave like arguments in these constructions precisely because, as structural sisters of V, they are indeed arguments by definition. Hence, any appeal to MA as a common cause behind the parallel attachment effects is completely eliminated as "argument" and "adjunct" become but arbitrarily distinct labels for the same structures. As a result the approach is viciously circular. (See also Abney 1989 for further criticism of MA within the X' framework.)

5.1.2 Quasi-Arguments

Having shown that a rule-based parser founded on MA itself provides no account of adjunct effects, the question of how adjuncts are locally licensed within a grammar-derived theory, remains open. Only an initial attempt at an answer can be made here, but the findings are suggestive. The crucial starting observation is that a simple argument-adjunct asymmetry, while extremely insightful, is not sufficient. As has long been recognized, certain classes of adverbials behave as what might be termed "quasi-arguments." Specifically, locative, instrumental, and, more variably, temporal adjuncts pattern with clearly subcategorized constituents with respect to a variety of syntactic processes, while manner and reason adverbs are prototypically adjunct-like (cf. Rizzi 1990). To take an arbitrary example, a locative PP may be extracted from a *wh*-question, yielding only a mild subjacency violation whereas extraction of a manner PP produces a far stronger Empty Category Principle (ECP) effect:

(346)   ?[In what shop]$_i$ do you wonder what we bought e_i.

(347)   *[In what way]$_i$ do you wonder what we fixed e_i.

The locative trace behaves as if head-governed by the lower verb while that of the manner adjunct does not. Additionally, unlike manner and reason adverbials, instrumentals and locatives cross-linguistically often pattern with selected arguments with respect to various processes which alter grammatical relations. Again, to take an example at random, consider the following applicative alternation facts (see Baker 1988, pp. 69–70 for this example as well as a variety of additional evidence):

(348)   *Chichewa*

    a.   Msangalatsi a-ku-yend-a   **ndi** ndodo.
          entertainer SP-PRES-walk-ASP with stick
          'The entertainer is walking with a stick.'

    b.   Msangalatsi a-ku-yend-**er**-a   ndodo.
          entertainer SP-PRES-walk-**APPL**-ASP stick
          'The entertainer is walking with a stick.'

    c.   Mkango u-ku-yend-a   **ndi** anyani.
          lion   SP-PRES-walk-ASP with baboons
          'The lion is walking with the baboons.'

    d.   *Mkango u-ku-yend-**er**-a   anyani.
          lion   SP-PRES-walk-APPL-ASP baboons.
          'The lion is walking with the baboons.'

Despite the fact that the same preposition (*ndi*) is involved in each case, only the instrumental may undergo incorporation, patterning with subcategorized arguments such as GOALS in dative constructions. Thus there is a variety of syntactic evidence which supports the notion of certain "adjuncts" as quasi-arguments.

What does this imply with respect to the theta attachment model? Quite simply, if predicates in some fashion do actually select certain adjuncts, then their immediate verbal construal is predicted via theta attachment in the standard fashion. What needs to be investigated is whether the behavior of pure verbal adjuncts (manner and reason) truly contrasts with quasi-arguments (locatives, instrumentals, temporals) as the theta attachment theory as developed so far would predict. Unfortunately, the distinction has not been widely made within psycholinguistics and the relevant data are largely lacking. Nevertheless, there is certain intuitional evidence, consider:

(349)   Frank visited the man with a suitcase.

As it stands, the theta attachment model predicts no preference between true V' and N' adjuncts since neither is selected, and it does appear to be the case that the nominal construal is more readily accessible in (349) than (343).

On the other hand, if quasi-argument adjuncts are in some fashion selected, theta attachment and the OLLC will predict processing breakdown in the relevant environments. Although for independent grammatical reasons most such constructions are somewhat marginal in English, examples such as the following are suggestive:

(350)   a.   ¿While the hunter waited in the field appeared a tiger.
        b.   ¿While Joe was sitting there appeared a ghost.
        c.   ?Before John arrived in the car sat a unicorn.

Sentence (350a) contains a PP which is ambiguous between a local locative attachment and the initial PP in an inversion construction. *In the field* will first be construed as a locative quasi-argument of *wait* via generalized theta attachment but subsequently require reinterpretation as the inverted matrix PP, a site clearly not governed by the embedded source position. Sentences of this sort do display clear GP effects and thus bear out the prediction. A similar point can be made in *there*-Insertion contexts as exemplified by (350b). On the other hand, as predicted, examples involving unselected manner adjuncts like (350c) seem somewhat more acceptable. Unfortunately, constructing sentences wherein the PP is naturally ambiguous between a manner and locative reading is quite difficult and the grammatical marginality of the data interferes with clear judgements. Nevertheless, there does seem to be a contrast and the predictions of the theta attachment theory appear confirmed.

In a sense then, Frazier's Minimal Attachment model achieves some accidental success by tacitly treating adjuncts as structural arguments precisely because the data typically marshalled in support of the analysis involve truly argument-like elements. Even given this, however, the precise structures that must be adopted in order for MA to make the desired predictions remain wholly unjustified, and the fact that quasi-arguments do also display adjunct-like behavior is unaccounted for. (For instance, they are rarely obligatory and do not uniformly pattern with arguments with respect to relation-changing processes; see Higginbotham 1985 for one possible syntactic approach.) In contrast, the theta attachment model explicitly acknowledges the fact that certain verbal adjuncts are selected and attributes their behavior to their argument-like status. However, as there is no fully satisfactory grammatical account of the range of adjunct behavior, a full explanation of the associated processing effects and the contrasts among subclasses of adverbials waits upon increased syntactic understanding.

The previous two sections of this chapter have explored some theoretical and empirical extensions to the theta attachment model, investigating both a generalization of theta attachment itself to encompass principles of grammar beyond the theta criterion, and taking an initial look at the far muddier facts surrounding adjunct attachment effects. The following section continues to expand the descriptive envelope with an initial exploration of one of the most exciting aspects of the theory, the potential universality which results from its emphasis on grammatical principles over specific grammatical rules.

5.2 Cross-Linguistic Predictions

Human parsing performance has not been well studied cross-linguistically, and relevant data are in general unavailable. Nevertheless, the theta attachment theory as formulated succeeds widely in providing an account of the known garden path effects as well as in predicting configurations in which processing breakdown is expected to occur in languages where such data is otherwise unavailable. No ad hoc language specific assumptions are required, as expected of a strongly grammar-derived theory which should be as universal as the principles upon which it is founded. Such a model in principle offers a natural account of both parsing similarities (the same principles are employed) and differences (their on-line application varies as the parameterized syntax varies) across languages. Consider then a range of garden path phenomena from a variety of typologically and genetically diverse languages.

5.2.1 Mandarin

Gorrell (1991) provides the following sentence as an exemplar of the GP effect in Mandarin Chinese, apparently like English a surface SVO language:

(351) ¿Zhangsan yi   du   shu jiu diao le.
       Zhangsan as-soon-as read book then fall PERF.
       'As soon as Zhangsan read, the book fell.'

As should be obvious, the explanation for its garden path status precisely parallels that of its English translation. *Shu* is first interpreted as the complement of *du* via generalized theta attachment but must subsequently be reanalyzed as the subject of *diao* in violation of the OLLC. In contrast, although sentence (352a) demonstrates that the verb *wang* may select a simple NP object, there is nevertheless no processing difficulty associated with an example such as (352b) since reanalysis satisfies the dominance clause of the OLLC:

(352) a. Wo wang le   Zhangsan.
           I forget PERF Zhangsan
           'I forgot Zhangsan.'
       b. Wo wang le   Zhangsan yao qu.
           I forget PERF Zhangsan will go
           'I forgot Zhangsan would go.'

Note that nothing special need be said about Mandarin language processing.

5.2.2 Hebrew

An essentially identical ambiguity can also be found in Hebrew, a surface SVO language:[131]

(353) ¿Axrey she-shatiti   maim hitgalu   be-b'er.
       after COMP-drank-1s water were-found in the well
       'After I drank water was found in the well.'

Again, the example precisely parallels the familiar case found in English and Mandarin. Such cases are easily constructed in numerous other head initial languages where the possibility of sentence initial adverbial clauses creates the potential environment for problematic misconstrual of an object as a subject.

5.2.3 German

Slightly more involved and interesting examples arise in certain verb-final constructions found in German. Consider the following embedded clause, cited by Crocker (1990, p. 12) as an example of a conscious garden path:

(354)   ¿daß der Entdecker von Amerika erst im
         that the discoverer of   America first in
             18. Jahrhundert erfahren   hat
             18th century   learned-of has
         'that the discoverer originally learned of America in the 18th century'

Again, theta attachment directly predicts the initial misanalysis which occurs in such sentences. *Entdecker* possesses an internal theta role which allows it to immediately license *von Amerika*. This local misanalysis as a complement necessitates global reinterpretation as an argument of the obligatorily transitive *erfahren*. Since the NP-internal attachment site does not govern the verbal complement position e_i or the site the PP ultimately occupies, the OLLC predicts the associated processing failure.

(354')

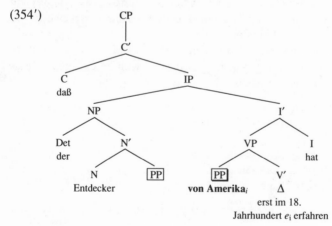

Quite interestingly, the following example, also from Crocker, in contrast is not a garden path according to native informants:

(355)   daß der Nachbar mit dem grossen Hund verzweifelt gerungen hat.
         that the neighbor with the big   dog desperately struggled has
         'that the neighbor desperately struggled with the big dog'

The distinction between the two sentences is of course attributable to the fact that *mit dem grossen Hund* will not initially be attached as an adjunct since it is not directly licensed by any feature of the nominal *Nachbar*. Consequently, it remains free for later incorporation as the complement of *ringen*. This constitutes additional evidence for a core argument-adjunct distinction in parsing as well as grammar and, given the distinct ambiguities afforded by German syntax, provides a clearer exemplar than the more marginal English example (350c).

5.2.4 Japanese

The German ambiguities just considered arise in embedded verb-final constructions due to the possibly delayed appearance of a constituent's true licensing head. Even more complex examples occur in strictly head-final languages, such as Japanese.[132]

Based on experimental data of various sorts, Mazuka et al. (1989) suggest that, ". . . Japanese speakers do not seem to encounter particular constructions that cause *consistent* and *severe* processing difficulties comparable to English garden path sentences . . . ," (emphasis the authors'). This is surprising given that, from the traditional perspective of top-down rule-driven phrase structure parsing, Japanese sentences are highly locally ambiguous even taking into account the existence of overt case particles (which may typically be dropped in any case). Consider just one representative example. An *NP-ni NP-ga* sequence is locally ambiguous between a dative-nominative and a double subject analysis (for independent grammatical reasons, these examples are most natural when embedded):

(356)   a.   *Dative -ni*

        Rex ni   John ga   hanasita.
        Rex DAT John NOM spoke
        'John spoke to Rex.'

    b.   *Subject -ni*

        John ni   nihongo ga   wakaru.
        John DAT Japanese NOM understand
        'John understands Japanese.'

There is overwhelming syntactic evidence that the *NP-ni* in (356) is the (sole) subject (cf. Kuno 1973; Shibatani 1977), displaying fundamentally different behavior from the dative:

(357)   *Dative -ni*

        *John_i ni   Rex ga   zibun_i no   tomodati ni tuite hanasita.
        John   DAT Rex NOM self   GEN friend   about   spoke.
        'Rex spoke to John about John's friend.'

(358)   *Subject -ni*

No !
John-ni   nihongo ga   zibun no tomodati
John DAT Japanese NOM self   GEN friend
yori yoku wakaru
more better understands.
'John understands Japanese better than John's friend.'

In addition to its ability to antecede reflexives, the *NP-ni* in (358) is also capable of triggering subject honorification and controlling certain temporal clauses, all of which are strictly properties of subjects in Japanese. Nevertheless, neither this nor a host of other local particle ambiguities which can be found throughout Japanese yield conscious processing difficulty, as reported by Mazuka et al. (see Whitman 1991 for syntactic analysis of many of the relevant constructions).

   This fact is of course fully accounted for within the grammar-derived processing model which has been developed, given the head-final syntax of Japanese. As far as the theta attachment theory is concerned, there is essentially no ambiguity since attachments cannot be made until licensed by the verb, and it is the verb itself that disambiguates the structures. Nevertheless, despite the conservatism theta attachment displays in head-final languages, a knowledge of the theory leads directly to the discovery of truly problematic configurations and reveals Mazuka and her associates' empiricist conclusions to be too strong. For example, consider, the following biclausal sentence:

(359)   [$_{IP}$[$_{CP}$ Frank ni   Tom ga   Guy o   syookai suru to]$_i$
              Frank DAT Tom NOM Guy ACC introduce   COMP
         John wa   *e*$_i$ omotte-iru].
         John TOP   think-ing
         'John thinks that Tom will introduce Guy to Frank.'

In general, it is possible in Japanese to scramble an entire complement clause to pre-subject position. As (359) is processed, the first three constituents will initially be left unattached until the appearance of the first verb. *Syookai* selects three arguments and theta attachment will yield the following grammatical simplex clause structure (roughly), with *Frank ni* also scrambled out of VP to clause initial position:[133]

(360)   [$_{IP}$[$_{NP}$ Frank ni]$_j$ [$_{IP}$[$_{NP}$ Tom ga] [$_{VP}$[$_{NP}$ Guy o] *e*$_j$]
            [$_V$ syookai suru]]]] (to)
         '(that) Tom introduced Guy to Frank'

Notice that before the occurrence of *to*, there is no commitment to the status of the clause as matrix or embedded. Subsequently, an additional NP followed by the matrix verb *omotte-iru* is encountered, which licenses its own external and internal argument. The previously constructed clause may be attached as the complement with its internal constituent structure undisturbed, and *John wa* may be attached as the subject (more precisely its topicalized binder) un-problematically resulting in a grammatical structure as in (361). The embedded clause has been scrambled out of the matrix VP to presubject position and *Frank ni* has been scrambled within the embedded clause to a position before the embedded subject (unnecessary details omitted):

(361) $[_{IP}[_{CP}[_{NP}$ Frank ni$]_j$ $[_{IP}$Tom ga Guy o e_j syookai suru$]$ to$]_i$ $[_{NP}$ John wa$]$ $[_{VP}$ e_i $[_V$ omotte-iru$]]]$.

Such sentences are both fully grammatical and acceptable and yield no conscious processing difficulty whatsoever.

   Now, contrast the following example, which is quite similar on the surface:

(362)   ¿Frank   ni   Tom ga   Guy o   syookai suru to
         Frank   DAT Tom NOM Guy ACC introduce   COMP
         John wa   iwaseta.
         John TOP said-CAUSE
         'John made Frank say Tom introduced Guy.'

Once again, when *syookai suru* is identified, the structure initially built is as in the simplex clause (360), *Tom introduced Guy to Frank*. In this instance, however, when the lower verb is encountered, it is found to be a causative which selects *three* arguments, including an obligatory *-ni* marked CAUSEE. As a result, *Frank ni* must be reinterpreted as an argument of *iwaseta* in a structure like the following:

(363) $[_{IP}[_{NP}$ Frank ni$]_j$ $[_{CP}$ Tom ga Guy o syookai suru to$]_i$ $[_{NP}$ John wa$]$ $[_{VP}$ e_i e_j $[_V$ iwaseta$]]]$

As in the previous example, the embedded clause has been grammatically scrambled to a pre-subject site and *Frank ni* to sentence-initial position. Obviously, the source position of *Frank ni* as a complement of *syookai suru* does not govern (or dominate) the target matrix complement position. The OLLC is violated and a severe garden path effect results as predicted. It is important to note that the perfect acceptability of the following sentence reveals that long distance multiple scrambling is itself not a source of significant difficulty:

(364) $[_{IP}[_{NP}$Frank   ni$]_j$ $[_{CP}$Tom ga   Guy o   korosu-daroo   to$]_i$
         Frank   DAT Tom   NOM Guy ACC kill-SUSPECTIVE COMP
         John wa $[_{VP}e_i$ e_j iwaseta$]]$.
         John TOP   said-CAUSE
         'John made Frank say Tom would probably kill Guy.'

The difference is of course due to the fact that *korosu* does not select the dative NP which is consequently free for attachment as the CAUSEE when *iwaseta* is encountered. While garden paths are rare in Japanese given its head final structure, examples can can be constructed as predicted by the theta attachment theory.[134] This predictiveness in itself constitutes rather striking confirmation of the entire grammar-derived theta attachment approach.

5.2.5 Korean

Although the historical relationship between Japanese and Korean is unclear, the languages are indisputably similar typologically, and as in Japanese, case marking is by no means an unambiguous indicator of surface grammatical relations in Korean. Also as in Japanese, case particles may be omitted entirely under certain syntactic conditions, and it is not uncommon for a sentence to consist of a (potentially scrambled) sequence of bare NPs followed by the predicate. Such unmarked NPs of course provide no information of use to the parser in performing local attachments, and consequently Korean too provides rather direct evidence of the crucial role played by licensing heads with respect to processing as well as grammar. In contrast, from the perspective of a top-down theory which performs (minimal) attachments throughout the time course of the parse, such typical head-final languages appear malignantly ambiguous.

Given the structural similarity of Korean and Japanese, it is perhaps not surprising that the construction exemplified in (362) above is equally problematic in Korean:

(365)   ¿Kelley-eykey   Charles-ka   tola   o-ass-ta-ko
        Kelley-DAT   Charles-NOM return come-PST-IND-COMP
        Richie-ka   malha-key hay-ss-ta.
        Richie-NOM say-COMP do-PST-IND
        'Richie made Kelley say Charles returned.'

The substring, *Kelley-eykey Charles-ka tola o-ass-ta-ko,* will first be structured as a simplex clause with *Kelley-eykey* a dative argument of the embedded verb. Subsequently, this will require restructuring wherein the NP is construed as the matrix CAUSEE. As in the Japanese example, the OLLC is violated and processing failure results as expected.

The preceding section has clearly revealed that, although parsing differences exist, this warrants no fundamental change within the general theory of human natural language processing. Given generalized theta attachment, it is the linear and structural position of licensing heads which will be expected to constitute the primary locus of the cross-linguistic variation. Innumerable issues remain to be explored across languages, but the predictions of the theory are quite clear, and, given the facts available, quite strikingly successful.

5.3 Conclusions

Two questions were posed in the first chapter:
  i. How is it that humans are able to (rapidly and automatically) assign
     grammatically licit structure to incoming strings of words?

ii. What is the relationship between the parser and the grammar which makes this possible?

A single hypothesis was put forth in response:

iii. The core of syntactic parsing consists of the local application of global grammatical principles.

Chapter 2 established the primary data through an exploration of the range of empirical difficulties faced by numerous performance-based models of parsing which found their functional motivations in perception, computation, word knowledge, or semantics rather than grammar.

Drawing data primarily from facts concerning processing breakdown in English, chapter 3 provided an initial formalization of (iii) and outlined a relatively theory-neutral grammar-derived model of processing which relied heavily on one fundamental principle of grammar, the theta criterion, both to steer initial attachments and constrain reanalysis.

Chapters 4 and 5 simplified the model by increasing its theoretical linkage to Government and Binding theory, in turn strengthening its empirical coverage. Specifically, chapter 4 further reduced the theta reanalysis constraint to grammar, recasting it solely in terms of government and dominance, while chapter 5 generalized theta attachment to encompass grammatical principles beyond the theta criterion.

Ultimately, the following two principles of attachment and re-attachment were motivated:

(366)   **Generalized Theta Attachment:** Every principle of the Syntax attempts to be maximally satisfied at every point during processing.

(367)   **On-Line Locality Constraint:** The target position (if any) assumed by a constituent must be *governed* or *dominated* by its source position (if any), otherwise attachment is impossible for the automatic Human Sentence Processor.

Together, these two principles characterize both the initial resolution of local ambiguity as well as the constraints on possible reanalysis, both structural and lexical and both in English as well as cross-linguistically.

More generally, what this work has attempted to demonstrate is that approaches to parsing not formulated directly in terms of grammatical principles are cognitively insufficient. The result is a purely configurational theory of attachment and reanalysis effects. Though much investigation remains to be done, the success of the theory in covering a wide body of compelling data strongly suggests that models not functionally motivated in terms of grammatical theory are also unnecessary. In its strongest form, this suggests that human natural language processing may be characterizable wholly in terms of a Grammar, where the Grammar is viewed not as a system of rules, but as a set of conditions on representation, and where the parser applies the principles of grammar locally at every point during the processing of the input string.

More broadly, both processability and grammaticality are accounted for

by the same principles, though in somewhat different fashions. Ungrammaticality results from the *global* violation of some grammatical constraint.
Unprocessability, on the other hand, is attributable to certain *local* violations
of grammatical principles. Success in accounting for an extremely wide range
of processing phenomena in a simple and unified fashion both in English and
across typologically distinct languages has provided strong evidence that the
core of Parsing theory is derived from the theory of Grammar.

NOTES

1. This was first proposed in the literature in Pritchett 1987.

2. Certain investigators within computational linguistics have of course been extremely concerned with the parsing efficiency of particular grammatical formalisms, an independent question which itself presupposes particular notions of parsers and grammars and their interrelationship; Bresnan (1978); Gazdar et al. (1985); Barton, Berwick, and Ristad (1987).

3. These comments are intended to hold for syntactic models of processing—even, for example, those as radically functionalist as Hawkins (1990). Given the overwhelming evidence amassed within grammatical theory that syntactic structure is necessary for interpretation, radically nonsyntactic models, e.g., Schank and Birnbaum (1984), or the associationist models of the connectionists, e.g., McClelland and Kawamoto (1986), will be touched upon only very briefly in subsequent discussion. This is further justified by the simple fact that, as far as I can see, such models are simply too underdeveloped at the current time to make any predictions whatsoever with respect to the sorts of data we will be considering.

4. Throughout this work every attempt is made to remain as "subtheory-neutral" as possible. I endeavor to formulate analyses in terms of the essential notions of Government and Binding and not to appeal ad hoc to peripheral or controversial analyses of specific constructions. For example, with respect to the theory-internal notion *government*, I have attempted to remain true to its core definition in terms of shared maximal projections and to avoid more recent and less established relativized approaches with respect to parsing phenomena. Though it is of course impossible to predict theoretical shifts given that research within grammatical theory itself continues, overall I believe this goal is achieved and that nothing crucial in these analyses is attributed to seemingly transient assumptions of the theory.

5. Hence the human language processor appears to be a paradigmatic example of a modular input system in the sense of J. A. Fodor (1983).

6. I employ the symbol "¿" to indicate garden path sentences (as defined in the text). Through chapter 2, GPs will generally be glossed with interpretable paraphrases followed by structurally equivalent but unambiguous examples where possible.

7. Though uncontroversial, this condition is not self-evidently necessary given the difficulty imposed by arguably nonambiguous structures such as multiple center embeddings:

(1)   The rat the cat the man chased caught squeaked.

I will adopt the standard position that that processing difficulty which is the result of ambiguity is not only empirically but also theoretically distinct from that which is not (cf. Kimball 1973) and will focus on processing ambiguity. However, in an interesting analysis, Gibson (1991) (adopting certain aspects of Pritchett 1987 discussed below) attempts to integrate the two notions, attributing the difficulty to the presence of stacked NPs. However, Gibson's framework fails to account for the simple fact that such sequences of multiple NPs are the norm in head final languages, ←

157

contrary to his claim. (Gibson's example, from Japanese, involves a predicate, *suki,* with ambiguous surface case-marking properties which may have contributed to the confusion.) See Pritchett (1991a) and §5.2 below for further discussion of left-branching languages.

8. In general, in representing structure, I will follow the notation of Chomsky (1986b) where I abbreviates INFL (inflection) and is the head of IP ($=$S) and C abbreviates complementizer and is the head of CP ($=$S'). In the textual discussion, I will interchangeably speak of IP or S and CP or S'. Also note that O represents an empty operator and e an A or A' trace. Certain aspects of structure may be omitted in labeled bracketings and tree diagrams where irrelevant to the discussion.

9. In order to more directly investigate the nature of syntactic processing strategies, I adopt the widespread technique of omitting cues that would be provided in writing by punctuation and in speech by intonation. Judgements of acceptability given in the text should be interpreted as holding for sentences in either modality in the absence of such information. For example, a layman's explanation of the processing difficulty associated with:

(1)   After Mary drank the water had evaporated.

is that it "needs a comma," a naïve way of suggesting that it lacks the appropriate intonational contours. Quite obviously, however, preposed adverbial clauses are certainly not ungrammatical in the absence of such information, for they are perfectly acceptable when there is no ambiguity:

(2)   After Mary drank she fell off the stool.

But even if the function of a comma or intonational information in such instances is to circumvent the ambiguity, this merely raises the question of why such a cue is not required in similarly ambiguous examples like (3):

(3)   Mary discovered the water had evaporated.

It appears that prosodic cues may aid one in avoiding garden paths but apparently cannot themselves force them. For example, strong relative clause intonation (whatever it may be precisely) may aid in disambiguating an example like (4):

(4)   ¿The mortician told the mourners he was having trouble with to get out.

but that same intonation, misapplied to (5):

(5)   The mortician told the mourners he was having trouble with the graves.

evidently does not cause a garden path effect. Crucially, no intonational cues are needed to interpret (5), which is easily processed even in neutral speech (again, whatever that may be), while intonational or semantic cues are required to prevent GP effects in sentence (4). Thus to claim that a sentence is unacceptable because it lacks certain orthographic or intonational cues is merely to rephrase the question—but it in no sense provides an answer to that question.

Similar points are made with respect to contextual information in §2.3. As Janet Pierre-Humbert (personal communication) has pointed out, the parsing model proposed here could easily incorporate intonational information on-line by treating it as an additional type of grammatical principle whose "licensing conditions" are respected locally. Nevertheless, a detailed investigation of intonation and ambiguity resolution, however interesting, is orthogonal to the primary concerns of this work.

Finally, note that it is sometimes proposed that examples such as (1) are actually ungrammatical in the absence of some intonational feature associated with the fronting of the clause. However, this cannot be maintained in light of the simple fact that such sentences are unacceptable only given ambiguity:

(6)   √After Mary arrived she sat down.

10. Though the discussion here is couched in terms of a serial processing model, this is not crucial at this point. Any model, whether backtracking, parallel, or deterministic, must in some way be able to distinguish between problematic and unproblematic ambiguity. For expository ease, I will continue to speak of backtracking and reanalysis.

11. Both of these definitions of garden path are narrower than that adopted by some researchers for whom condition (a) alone is sufficient (cf. Frazier 1978) and who reserve the phrase "severe garden path" or "conscious garden path" for use when (b) is also intended. This is merely a terminological difference, however, and any complete theory of human NLP must also provide an account of what others have called weak garden path effects and I will call unproblematic reanalyses.

12. Except where noted, judgements of processing difficulty associated with particular structures were confirmed in a survey of 50 students conducted at Harvard University in 1987. Certain informal follow up surveys were also conducted at Northwestern University during 1988–89. Since the results of both are consistent with the general results reported in the literature to be reviewed below and are also subject to introspective verification, I do not formally present them.

13. There is a traditional distinction between structural and lexical ambiguity, which, although descriptively useful, is not sufficiently precise. Lexical ambiguity very frequently results in structural ambiguity, and in chapter 4 it will be argued that no special theoretical distinction need be made between the two within the parsing theory.

14. Some objections which have been raised to this claim will be considered when semantic approaches to processing are discussed in §2.3.

15. In this work I will be concerned solely with issues of ambiguity and not with theoretically independent questions of computational space-time complexity. Additionally, since the psycholinguistic predictions made by the parser's grammar-derived operative principles are essentially independent of implementational details, I will have little to say here about such issues. Nevertheless, the theory is fully intended to be implementable, and Pritchett and Reitano (1990) sketch a strongly type-transparent object-oriented approach in which the parser operates in a strictly head-driven fashion, projecting phrasal structure as determined by lexical properties and licensing local attachments which maximally satisfy on-line principles of Universal Grammar at every point. Other less transparent implementations are imaginable, though I believe far less likely to explain the psycholinguistic effects which will be seen to motivate the approach in the first place. See Berwick, Abney, and Tenny (1991) for various approaches to what has come to be known as principle-based parsing.

16. The term theta grid is adopted from Stowell (1981) and is here intended in its most general sense simply as a specification of what roles a given head assigns to what structural positions.

17. Although the analysis is cast in the argot of Government and Binding theory, it should be obvious that the concepts employed are common in some form to all major current syntactic theories. Although this will remain the case through chapter 3, the theory as discussed in the final two chapters relies increasingly upon notions specific to that particular grammatical framework.

18. See Chomsky (1986b) for a discussion of genitive case and theta marking. I will not consider the more controversial hypothesis of Abney (1987) that what are traditionally thought of as NPs are actually determiner phrases (DPs); the processing analyses proposed are largely unaffected by this alternative.

19. But see Gibson (1991) for an approach which posits a mild but cumulative cost in such situations.

20. Although its essence will remain as expressed in (30), the TRC will be refined several times as new empirical and theoretical issues are considered.

21. It will become apparent below that the "splitting" of the NP constituent *her contributions* cannot in itself be the source of the difficulty.

22. An external role is one assigned by a head to a structural position outside of its maximal projection (roughly, the subject), whereas an internal role is assigned within that projection

(roughly, to complements), the latter representing the more usual case. For our purposes it is not crucial whether verbs theta mark their subjects directly, indirectly, or compositionally through VP (cf. Chomsky 1981, 1986b; Marantz 1984; Williams 1984).

23. What I am calling computational approaches to human NLP should not be confused with computational linguistics which is (partially) concerned with the complexity of grammar formalisms and parsing efficiency but not, in general, with specific psycholinguistic issues (though there are, of course, areas of overlap).

24. In practice, these attachment strategies have typically been uncovered more through an investigation of the preferred interpretations of globally ambiguous sentences than through the study of processing breakdown. Arguably, this lack of attention to parsing failure has imposed unnecessary hardship on the investigation of language processing and created something of a poverty-of-stimulus situation for the investigators. In some ways it is as if one had attempted to construct a grammar while largely ignoring ungrammatical data.

25. Bever's strategies in general, though necessarily applied to the surface, were geared toward the ultimate recovery of deep structures (then the sole input to semantic interpretation). Though its functional motivation may not be self-evident, the CSS was a clear progenitor of later more obviously perceptual approaches.

26. As such, it also raises an important theoretical question: how are such rule-based strategies to be learned? Heuristics such as (67) and the CSS presuppose knowledge of (English) grammatical rules for their operation, but it is not at all apparent how the language learner could come to acquire such specific rules in the absence of an ability to parse. A circle exists, and it seems to be a vicious one. Quite generally, any parsing strategy which is heavily dependent on particular phrase structure rules will be subject to similar criticism.

27. In passing, Kimball also suggests incorporating a limited look-ahead capability of one or two symbols into the model. As he does not employ this systematically, it is difficult to evaluate. Models explicitly employing look-ahead (Frazier and Fodor 1978; Marcus 1980) are examined in subsequent sections.

28. Kimball's reasons for distinguishing Closure from Right Association are highly dependent upon the particular PS rules he assumed and facts about coördination. Recently there has arisen a general consensus that the processor prefers to keep phrases open (Late Closure) and that Kimball's apparent (Early) Closure effects are actually due to something more like Right Association which is therefore retained as a separate strategy. I will return to this distinction in the discussion of the so-called Sausage Machine model (Frazier and Fodor 1978) below.

29. However, see Hawkins (1990) for a more sophisticated processing-functional approach to this and related issues concerning the form of grammars.

30. Kimball must assume that a phrase is closed when all of its major constituents have been recognized, even if they have not been fully parsed (hence S is closed when NP and VP are identified rather than completed). Otherwise multiple left and right embeddings of greater than degree two would also be incorrectly predicted to be unprocessable by principle 4.

31. Potentially problematic for this account is the fact that *that* is of course not an unambiguous signaller of an S node:

(1)   a.   I know that.
      b.   I know that man.
      c.   I know that dogs are nice.

32. There is a clause in principle 6 which states, "unless the next node parsed is an immediate constituent of that phrase," but this is apparently not intended to prevent Closure in sentences like (84), since Kimball himself claims Closure occurs after *the girl* (but this further ignores the additional issue of why Closure cannot occur immediately after *know*, given that it may be intransitive).

33. Actually, the possibility that the unit is not the word is left open: "The capacity of the

PPP may be defined not in terms of words, but in terms of syllables or morphemes or conceivably in terms of time. Its proper definition is a very interesting question, but we have not attempted to disentangle all of these alternatives . . ." (Frazier and Fodor 1978, 293). Given their crucial reliance on the PPP, this is somewhat disturbing since reinterpreting the identity of the unit potentially alters every single empirical prediction of the model.

34. This is a paraphrase as there are several variant but essentially equivalent wordings of MA in Frazier's works (see references).

35. This account of VP versus NP attachment of adjunct PPs is suspect is structures consistent with the X' theory are adopted, since (100a) and (100b) will each involve X' adjunction, to V' in the former case and N' in the latter:

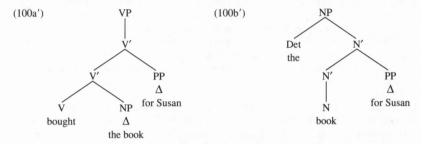

Both (100a') and (100b') are equally minimal under this conception, a severe theoretical problem which potentially undermines the entire MA approach. See §5.1 for further discussion.

36. Following Kimball (1975), the authors also attempt to derive MA effects in terms of rapid path construction from a terminal to a root node given memory considerations, drawing attention to the fact that the model is clearly perceptual with nonlinguistic roots. However, as MA is usually stated as an independent principle and the shift has no obvious empirical effect, I will continue to treat it as such.

37. Though not discussed explicitly, this was a somewhat tacit motivating hypothesis behind many of Kimball's seven principles. As originally formulated, many of Kimball's strategies are actually compatible with either of two positions with respect to the source of processing difficulty: (a) that it is the necessity of syntactic reanalysis or backtracking which is the relevant factor, or (b) that the number of nodes that must be stored on-line (i.e., open) simultaneously is the determining factor. While Kimball apparently leaned toward the former view in the 1973 paper as discussed, in a later work (Kimball 1975), he opted for the latter, which may be classified as an example of a *complexity metric*, as opposed to a *reanalysis* approach to relative processing difficulty.

This blurs certain important issues, however, since such metrics generally characterize the gross *syntactic* complexity of a string generated by a grammar based on such factors as depth of embedding (Yngve 1960), the number of transformations applied (the *Derivational Theory of Complexity;* Jenkins, Fodor, and Saporta 1965; Fodor, Bever, and Garrett 1974) and nonterminal to terminal node ratios (Miller and Chomsky 1963), among others. Such an approach predicts identical complexity for identical constructions regardless of the lexical items involved. Though well-suited to providing an account of inherent structural difficulty which is arguably not the result of ambiguity (e.g., center-embedding, object versus subject relatives) they are incapable of distinguishing garden paths from syntactically parallel unambiguous structures:

(1) ¿The dealer sold forgeries complained.
(2) The dealer given forgeries complained.

Though these may indeed be equally *syntactically* complex in some sense, they are certainly not equivalent in terms of *processing* difficulty. Where ambiguity is involved, it appears unavoidable that a reanalysis rather than an open nodes approach must be taken (at least within a serial model—but see Gibson 1991 for complexity metric approach within a parallel-processing framework).

38. In a well-known volley of articles, the criticisms levelled by Wanner (1980) eventually prompted, directly or indirectly, Fodor and Frazier (1980) to (temporarily) reintroduce a stipulated principle of Local Attachment (see also Wanner and Maratsos 1976). This ad hoc move addresses only Wanner's observation that given more than one grammatical option, RA applies in short as well as long sentences and hence cannot be derived from the architecture of their model. The modification is irrelevant to the garden path examples discussed.

Wanner himself handles RA and MA effects by rules of scheduling within an Augmented Transition Network (ATN) model. Such rules specify the order in which arcs exiting a state in an ATN are considered. He notes that Minimal Attachment can be captured by scheduling both WORD and CAT arcs before SEEK arcs. Since, roughly, within the ATN formalism, following an arc results in the attachment of the constituent admitted by that arc to the constituent whose network is being traversed, scheduling WORD and CAT arcs (which admit words and lexical categories) before SEEK arcs (whose function is to admit phrasal constituents) insures MA by forcing the attachment of words and lexical categories before the hypothesizing of new phrasal nodes. On the other hand, Right Association can be captured by scheduling JUMP arcs and SEND arcs after arcs of all other types (WORD, CAT, SEEK). JUMP arcs skip over parts of the network (hence ignoring possible attachments) while SEND arcs exit subnetworks entirely. Since the purpose of RA is to delay closure, that is, to attach as much as possible to existing material, scheduling those arcs which skip through or exit from the network as late as possible insures that legitimate local attachments will not be ignored. Because ATNs are so powerful and because Wanner in general accepts the descriptive adequacy of Right Association and Minimal Attachment (though not Frazier and Fodor's account of them), I will not consider the particular ATN model he proposes to capture the effects of the Sausage Machine. In general, it makes the same predictions as Frazier and Fodor's model modulo length effects, and it will be shown in the next section (§2.0.4) that there are a large number of arguments against models incorporating strategies similar to Minimal Attachment above and beyond these length effects. Of course an ATN account of MA and RA is also stipulative in the sense that all arcs might have been scheduled in the reverse order, as nothing in the theory or formalism would prevent this. Along similar lines, Pereira (1985) presents an interesting formal characterization of Right Association and Minimal Attachment in terms of a *shift-reduce* processor claiming that the resolution of shift-reduce conflicts in favor of *shifting* corresponds to Right Association, while resolving reduce-reduce conflicts in favor of the option that pops the most symbols from the stack yields Minimal Attachment. Like all approaches that implement MA and RA in some form, this approach is completely dependent upon the particular phrase structure rules posited and is of course subject to the general criticisms levelled against the two strategies.

39. On the basis solely of examples such as (127) one might hypothesize that breaking up the previously constructed NP is somehow more difficult than simply extracting a complement, as in (122) and (123). However, as previously alluded to, minimally contrasting sentences such as (126) and (128) reveal that this simply cannot be the correct explanation. Actually the examples do not show that splitting up an NP is not costly, but that it cannot be the sole source of the processing difficulty. Because splitting an NP will necessarily involve a violation of the Theta Reanalysis Constraint further motivated in chapter 3, it will always be "accidentally" costly for that reason—though the splitting itself will not be the source of the difficulty.

40. Recall that computational approaches to human NLP are quite distinct from mainstream computational linguistics which concerns itself primarily with the formal and/or practical aspects of grammars and parsing architectures and only very rarely addresses psycholinguistic issues.

41. Just as an attempt has been made to reduce the power of serial models by constraining the

reanalysis strategies they may employ, so-called "ranked parallel" models have been proposed, which limit the number and type of structures which may be maintained on-line. Gorrell (1987) provides experimental evidence in favor of such an approach, while Clark and Gibson (1988) and Gibson (1991) develop a processing model along such lines. Because this very interesting theory adopts certain of the notions originally proposed in Pritchett (1987, 1988) and further discussed in chapter 3 (though it employs them quite differently within a unique framework entirely distinct from that developed here) I will not discuss it explicitly. While the approach is quite radical in some respects (its basic ranked-parallel architecture) it is quite conservative in others (processing effects are explained in terms of memory load), and the reader is referred to Gibson's own work for further details.

42. Actually he originally made the claim only for English, though clearly the results would be fairly uninteresting if his claims were true only for certain natural languages.

43. The existence of global ambiguity appears to raise an immediate problem. Marcus points out, however, that the reanalysis required in such instances is quite different from that encountered in instances of strictly local ambiguity. In the case of globally ambiguous sentences, entire rather than partial structures are discarded, new legitimate parses being formed from scratch, in effect by giving the parser a whack. Marcus allows for multiple legitimate parses and reasonably claims that they do not violate the determinism hypothesis. Actually, it is not self-evident that it is necessary for each global interpretation to be begun from scratch, but it is certainly possible that they are. Exactly how and when the normal principles of processing are overridden to obtain alternative global parses remains unclear, as it does in most perceptual models.

44. Prior to Marcus, look-ahead had been fairly commonly employed in the processing of artificial languages, where a very small fixed look-ahead of perhaps only a few characters is generally sufficient to disambiguate (Aho and Ullman 1972). As noted, Kimball (1973, 1975) also suggested that the human parser might employ some look-ahead capability, but provided few details. The PPP of the Sausage Machine was a quasi-look-ahead device. None of these models were deterministic, however.

45. Unfortunately, Marcus is later driven to hypothesize that different languages and possibly even different individuals have look-ahead buffers of various sizes. He also finds it necessary to allow the routines which parse NPs to have access to five rather than three buffer cells. All of these constitute extremely undesirable weakenings of the theory, especially since the buffer's size is vaguely motivated in terms of the size of working memory. Virtually all empirical predictions are changed when buffer size is altered.

46. Since the grammatical rules employed by Marcus's parser are organized into "packets," rule ordering can also be used to force various processing effects. As this approach is both stipulative and orthogonal to Marcus's primary hypothesis concerning garden path phenomena, I will not pursue the possibility here.

47. Initially, an appeal to the fact that prepositions license arguments and hence can't be closed immediately might seem plausible, but the same is of course true of many nouns (e.g., *dislike* as in *my dislike of soup*) so this cannot distinguish the two cases.

48. See Briscoe (1983) for additional arguments that PARSIFAL is incapable of accounting for an even wider range of problematic structures, including examples like:

(1)   ¿After Todd drank the water proved to be poisoned.

(2)   ¿Todd gave the boy the dog bit a bandage.

Demonstrating this would require a deeper investigation into the internal structure of PARSIFAL than I will undertake here given subsequent changes in Marcus's theory to be discussed in the following section.

49. Marcus (personal communication) has indicated that he had actually intended only to make the weaker claim that a sentence was a garden path if, not if and only if, it was not deter-

ministically parsable by PARSIFAL. Hence, there could be other causes of processing break-down. As he acknowledges, this is obviously a far less interesting claim which leaves numerous questions unanswered. This escape also remains open within the D-theory version of determination discussed below.

50. Although the reasons for this error may not be entirely obvious given the previous discussion (they are somewhat theory internal), the basic problem for Marcus is the unproblematic bidirectional status of these now familiar object-subject ambiguities regardless of the structure and length of the ambiguous NP.

51. As Amy Weinberg has noted, as originally presented the D-theory model is so unconstrained as to make no predictions at all. Though it is obviously not what Marcus intended, all attachments could minimally be made to the matrix S with additional dominance predicates added only after all lexical input had been received, thus entirely eliminating local ambiguity. See Weinberg (1990) for a very interesting minimal commitment model, which also reinterprets certain notions proposed in Pritchett (1987, 1988).

52. Marcus stipulates two constraints on the addition of domination predicates to a syntactic description under construction:

(1)   *Rightmost Daughter Constraint*
       Only the rightmost daughter of a node can be lowered under a sibling node at any given point in the parsing process.

(2)   *No Crossover Constraint*
       No node can be lowered under a sibling which is not contiguous to it. (Marcus, Hindle, and Fleck 1983, 133)

However, though few details are given, it seems that neither of these constraints is relevant to an account of (160). *My aunt from Peoria* will initially be attached as a rightmost daughter and it is lowered under a contiguous S in both (159) and (160).

Marcus (personal communication) suggests that D-theory could be made to handle such cases if primitives for thematic roles are introduced. The source of the difficulty of (160) would then be attributable to the fact that *my aunt from Peoria* is initially construed as dominated by the role GOAL, which later proves to be false. As will become clear in chapter 3, there is something correct about such a move. However, it appears dubious that it is semantic content which is relevant, as will be discussed in §5.0.1. To anticipate slightly, it is not at all obvious under such a conception why either (3) or (4)

(3)   I loaded the truck$_{GOAL}$ with hay$_{THEME}$.
(4)   I loaded the truck$_{THEME}$ onto the ship$_{GOAL}$.

or (5) or (6):

(5)   I sent the dog$_{GOAL}$ a birthday card$_{THEME}$.
(6)   I sent the dog$_{THEME}$ to Tom$_{GOAL}$.

does not lead to garden path effects since the proper role cannot be unambiguously associated with the immediately post-verbal NP in every instance.

53. In fact, it is not clear that Marcus's D-theory parser will fail even on longer garden paths of the sort PARSIFAL was capable of handling. Though Marcus appears to retain his previous assumptions with respect to look-ahead, the incorporation of minimal commitment essentially eliminates most arguments for decision delay, as pointed out by Weinberg (1990).

54. Much work has of course been conducted concerning lexical recovery (cf. Seidenberg et al. 1982; Simpson 1984, and references) but far less on its role in processing breakdown. One exception among the approaches we have considered is Marcus (1980), who discusses examples such as:

(1)   ¿The prime number few.
        (There are few primes.)

However, his account hinges more on particulars of implementation than on the general architecture of his parser.

55. A somewhat similar though far less developed model is presented outside of any particular theoretical framework by Milne (1982) who focuses primarily on the narrow range of garden
path sentences which uncontroversially involve lexical categorial ambiguity:

(1)   The *old man* sailed down the river.
(2)   ¿The *old man* the boats.

He adopts a deterministic approach but proposes that lexical (and, he suggests, structural, but this
is made far less clear) ambiguity is not resolved in accord with any purely syntactic heuristics but
instead through semantic-pragmatic considerations (and in this regard his has more in common
with theories to be discussed in 2.3.2). Specifically he proposes:

(3)   *Semantic Checking Hypothesis (SCH)*
        When a person encounters a situation which syntactic context implies might lead to a
        garden path, instead of using lookahead they decide which alternative to pursue based on
        semantic information. They do this without regard to the following words in the sen-
        tence. If their preference for this leads to an analysis different from that demanded by the
        remainder of the sentence, they will garden path. (Milne 1982, 362)

where, "a situation which syntactic context implies might lead to a garden path" should evidently
be interpreted as "a local ambiguity." Consequently the contrasting difficulty of sentences (1) and
(2) is attributed to the fact that $[_{NP}$ *old man]* is somehow a semantically natural concept.

Quite oddly however, the Semantic Checking Hypothesis actually requires Milne to treat the
dual ambiguities associated with sequences such as *old man* (A N or N V) as if they involved
some sort of look-ahead for they must be resolved simultaneously as pairs. This not only contrasts
with the generally accepted hypothesis that the parser makes lexical and structural decisions rapidly as each new word is input, but also with his own explicit rejection of look-ahead and reanalysis. Resolution of the ambiguity of the initial lexical item will immediately eliminate one of
the structures, but it is consequently unclear how the SCH could ever actually apply. Furthermore, even if the two ambiguous elements can somehow be considered simultaneously, the SCH
makes incorrect empirical predictions. For example,

(4)   ¿The old baby the young.

should not be a garden path upon this conception since *old babies* arguably represent an unnatural
concept, but the sentence is obviously quite unacceptable. On the whole, the predictions of the
model are extremely unclear and the coverage is limited. In general, where it does make predictions it is subject both to the same criticisms which hold of Ford, Bresnan, and Kaplan's far more
sophisticated and broader lexical approach as well as those to be levelled at the more developed
semantic approaches considered in §2.3.

56. The authors actually hedge somewhat, stating that recategorization is a necessary condition but possibly not a sufficient one. Since additional factors which potentially contribute to the
GP effect are not characterized, I will continue to interpret their claim in its strongest form.

57. This is not an arbitrary distinction, though it is dependent upon LFG internal assumptions
concerning the structure of the lexicon and the nature of rules which relate lexical items.

58. Though it is not entirely clear how it is to be interpreted, Ford, Bresnan, and Kaplan's
rider that it is reanalysis, "within the functional structure of a completed constituent" which is
problematic might conceivably mediate in certain cases where the theory overpredicts processing

difficulty. In (190) adjectival *fat* will not ever be incorporated into the f-structure of *obtain* since it does not select an adjective.

However, this will not rescue the theory from the far more severe problem of underprediction. In other words, at best the approach characterizes only a small subset of occurring GP effects while at worst it also classifies many perfectly acceptable sentences as problematic.

59. Although this assumption has dominated work in psycholinguistics, it is of course by no means uncontroversial. Spurred largely by the explicitness of J. A. Fodor's (1983) modularity hypothesis, debate surrounding the subject has recently intensified. Very broadly, there are three fundamental possibilities concerning the role of contextual information in the resolution of syntactic parsing ambiguity.

What might be called the strong-syntax position maintains that parsing decisions are driven by purely syntactic strategies with no input from semantics possible at any point. The version of determinism exemplified by PARSIFAL constitutes a clear instance of such an approach.

On the other hand, from a mixed syntax-semantics point of view, both syntactic and semantic strategies are available. One version of this hypothesis posits that syntactic strategies operate initially (hence accounting for the directionality of garden paths) but that contextual information may be rapidly employed by the parser to facilitate reanalysis, possibly to the degree that it is rendered nearly unproblematic. Frazier appears variously sympathetic with this approach, as do Crain and Steedman (1985) who discuss it explicitly. Alternative mixtures can also easily be imagined (for example see Trueswell, Tanenhaus, and Garnsey 1991).

In opposition to both of these, the strong-semantics perspective holds that all ambiguity is initially resolved based on contextual factors rather than structurally based strategies. Milne, discussed in note 55, is an example, as are Altmann and Steedman (1988) and Steedman and Altman (1989). This approach is quite controversial and experimental counterevidence is presented in, for example, Ferreira and Clifton (1986) and Clifton and Ferreira (1989). In addition to the specific works cited, Garfield (1987) clearly presents the fundamental hypothesis and collects numerous additional papers covering all sides of the issue.

Unfortunately, as with much of the cognitive psychology literature, the modularity debate too often degenerates into methodological squabbling devoid of any real theoretical interest. Rather than participate explicitly, I will simply continue to assume, based on the sort of evidence reviewed here in chapters 1 and 2, that parsing strategies are basically syntactic. The success of the model outlined in chapters 3 through 5 should then be interpreted as additional evidence to this effect, but I will not explicitly cast it in such terms.

60. As reflected in these two approaches, the term "semantic" is vague and variously employed in two rather different senses to indicate both the actual interpretation of a sentence (however it is to be properly represented) and the contextual information (be it pragmatic, stochastic, real-world, etc.) used in obtaining a semantic (in the previous sense) or syntactic representation.

61. Frazier's theory of Constraint of Extraction Domain (CED; cf. Huang 1982) effects provides a device to prevent premature closure, but were this adopted here no account of garden path effects whatsoever could be derived from the interpretive island hypothesis.

62. The fact that such sense ambiguity typically does not result in GP effects is discussed in §4.1.

63. Despite appearances, the authors do not explicitly argue for a strongly semantic model and remain somewhat vague on the question of whether thematic grids are selected based solely on such grounds. They variously appear to maintain strategies such as Minimal Attachment and Late Closure although it is not clear that this is coherent within their model given their contention that thematic roles are purely conceptual rather than configurational; how such nonstructural theta roles are ever unified with the independently built syntactic structure remains a mystery.

64. Just as every judgement of grammaticality is a miniature experiment, so is every judgement concerning the interpretability of an input string. A native speaker's introspective judgement concerning the status of an utterance ($\pm$grammatical or $\pm$processable) is perfectly acceptable

data and should not be confused with naïve introspective theory construction (an entirely different matter altogether). While this distinction has always been clear within linguistics, it is less so within psychology with its empiricist roots. Nevertheless, a CRT is not prerequisite for data collection and statistics don't necessarily make science.

65. Though such ambiguities have been noted in the literature they have rarely received an explicit analysis (but see Gibson 1991). They will be treated in detail in §4.0 as they raise issues of crucial importance.

66. Recently, a variety of approaches to so-called principle-based parsing have also been explored. Although all are interesting, they actually have little in common beyond aspirations toward some degree of input-output compatibility with syntactic structures licensed by Government and Binding theory (for example, see Clark 1988; Correa 1991; Fong 1991; Johnson 1991; Wehrli 1988; Weinberg 1988). I intend both the terms "grammar-derived" and "principle-based" parsing in a more restrictive sense to indicate a psycholinguistic processing theory which employs global grammatical principles directly on-line in order to build structure.

67. See §§3.1.2.3, 4.1.2, and 5.1 for some discussion of NP-internal parsing.

68. Though I will informally continue to refer to it as such, it is important to recognize that theta attachment should ultimately not be viewed as an independent parsing heuristic, but rather simply as the local application of a single, albeit extremely important, global grammatical principle. The application of additional principles is the subject of chapter 5.

69. I will necessarily assume that the parser has access to the core syntax of the language under discussion and not simply universal principles. In order to emphasize the theoretical and psycholinguistic issues of primary concern within this work, I will remain purposefully non-committal concerning precisely how theta attachment might be computationally implemented, though a great deal should become clear throughout the discussion. Although a head-driven approach appears by far the most natural, nothing in the psycholinguistic theory developed crucially depends solely on this assumption. Unlike top-down approaches, a parser adhering to a head-driven control structure never projects a constituent until its head is encountered but, unlike a bottom-up model, may formulate hypotheses based on features of the head. There appears to be some cross-linguistic evidence that, in addition to heads, specifiers, but not complements, may trigger the projection of a higher category. This is briefly discussed in §5.2. See Pritchett and Reitano (1990) for discussion of an implementation founded on the Projection Principle; see also Pritchett (1991b).

70. I will somewhat arbitrarily refer to the role assigned by prepositions as THEME, a decision to which no theoretical import should be attached since role content will prove irrelevant to the theory being developed.

71. Precisely the same analysis obtains even if *her* is held to be inherently categorially ambiguous; see §4.1 for a discussion of this.

72. The same results should obtain under a DP analysis of NPs (cf. Abney 1987). Initially the NP *her* would be interpreted as the complement of a null D in accord with theta attachment and then reanalyzed as the head of the DP itself licensing a complement *donations*, a reanalysis permitted by the TRC as *her* would remain within its initial theta domain in DP. In general, I will adopt the more commonly assumed NP analysis, but the core theory developed should be compatible with both.

73. Notice unsurprisingly that neither the presence nor status of the PP is relevant to the GP effect:

(1) ¿Without her donations in envelopes failed to appear. (adjunct PP)
(2) ¿Without her donations failed to appear. (no PP)

74. Since the preposition *to* may not be intransitive, *the charity* is not available for reanalysis (and would violate the TRC in any case). I will ignore here the possible intransitive adverbial use

of *without* since equivalent cases are discussed in §3.1.2.1 below and violate the TRC in a completely straightforward fashion.

The reader may notice that the reanalysis of the specifier *her* as a complement in (223') should also constitute a TRC violation with respect to the its POSSESSOR domain (though not the higher THEME). However, since this prediction is not necessary for an account of the GP effect and will, in any case, be altered given the subsequent versions of the TRC motivated below, I will simply ignore this aspect of the analysis here.

75. Theta attachment cannot, of course interpret such strings as the onsets of relative NPs, as in *[NP her donations to the charity [S' Bob discovered]] proved to be fraudulent*. In the absence of a theta assigning verb there is nothing to license a local subject attachment of *Bob* and therefore no ambiguity exists. (More generally, in the absence of inflection or a complementizer, there is nothing to reveal potential clausal structure if a head-driven approach is assumed.)

76. I am grateful to John Whitman (personal communication) for bringing this issue to my attention.

77. Though not evident at this point, there is another possible explanation suggested by a revision in the TRC to be discussed in §3.3.2, where it is proposed that the reanalyzed element must not only depart its current theta domain but also enter a new theta domain for reanalysis to be problematic. Consequently, since auxiliaries assign no role to the subject, it might appear that they should not lead to TRC violations. However, this is completely untenable as the following GPs reveal:

(1)   a.   ¿Without her contributions would be impossible.
       b.   ¿Without her contributions seemed to arrive.

Both auxiliaries and raising verbs yield GP effects despite the fact that neither assigns a theta role to its subject. The garden path status of such sentences follows directly from the revised TRC given in §3.2 if coupled with a slightly refined definition of theta domain which more clearly emphasizes what we have been assuming all along, the importance of argument structure (of syntactic positions) over semantic roles per se:

(2)   **Theta Domain:** α is in the γ theta domain of β iff α occupies a position structurally accessible to the assignment of some theta role γ by β or α is dominated by a constituent structurally accessible to the assignment of that role.

However, because far more significant theoretical alterations in the conception of the TRC are introduced in chapter 4, it is not worthwhile to pursue such transient changes in too much detail here.

78. The d-structure argument-adjunct status of the initial clause is irrelevant (as is its status as base generated or moved):

(1)   ¿That the tiger ate Rex knew.
       (cf. That the tiger ate she knew (but that the cow did she forgot).)

However, due to the potentially confounding contextual effects of the acceptability of topicalization, I will generally employ fronted adjuncts in the examples.

79. To avoid introducing an irrelevant lexical ambiguity here, I will follow Emonds (1985) and assume prepositions may select both nominal and sentential complements. I will continue to refer to this construction as a fronted clause, however, in order to distinguish it from the contrasting simplex PP examples. Section 4.1.3.2 demonstrates that category relabelling is completely cost free, so a more traditional analysis of the fronted adverbial with *after* as a complementizer in C is also perfectly compatible with the parsing theory.

80. In fact, Frazier (1989) argues that item-specific (i.e., lexical) information is ignored during the parser's first stage analysis and hence predicts *the water* to be misattached as the object of

arrive on item-independent grounds, (e.g., by virtue of a general phrase structure rule such as VP→V NP). Citing Mitchell (1987), Frazier claims that there is in fact reading-time evidence that NPs are initially attached as direct object even when the preceding verb is obligatorily intransitive. Nevertheless it is clear that the garden path data do not support this claim whatsoever as there is simply no need for conscious reprocessing in examples where the lexical properties of the embedded verb prevent its licensing the following NP. This strongly suggests that Mitchell's results have been misinterpreted. A likely explanation is the fact that at least some of the predicates tested are not true intransitives at all; they may indeed theta mark a postverbal NP. For example, Frazier herself cites:

(1)   After the audience had departed the actors sat down for a well-deserved drink.

However, *depart*, in contrast with true surface intransitives like *arrive* or *belch*, can cooccur with an object:

(2)   The actors departed the stage.
(3)   a.   *The actors arrived the stage.
       b.   *The actors belched the stage.

And, furthermore, such verbs do indeed induce GP effects (contrast (233)):

(4)   ¿After the actors departed the stage collapsed.

In light of these grammatical facts as well as the garden path data, there appears to be little evidence for Frazier's claim. Notice that while *arrive* is unaccusative, *belch* is clearly unergative. This seems relevant insofar as unaccusatives, licensing a deep object, absolutely proscribe surface complements whereas unergatives may co-occur with a very restricted range of cognate objects, as in *J. B. belched a juicy belch*. Examples such as (3b) do seem better than (3a) and structures such as (4) seem slightly worse with unergatives than with unaccusatives. This is perfectly consistent with the analysis to be developed below (see §4.1.3), but I will continue to treat both unaccusatives and unergatives as if strictly intransitive at s-structure.

It may be the case that the NP licensed by a verb such as *depart* is actually theta marked by a null preposition:

(5)   The actors departed (from) the stage.

The NP behaves in a fashion consistent with a prepositional object with respect to both *wh-* and NP-movement:

(6)   Which city did the actors depart (from)?
(7)   *The stage was departed (from) by the actors.

However, this has no effect on the theta attachment analysis.
     81. Embedded clausal elements are less acceptable:

(1)   ???John knew that Ron disliked Rex disturbed Todd.

but this does not appear to be either a length or ambiguity effect. First, short clauses also yield the same results:

(2)   ???John suspected that Ron left disturbed Todd.

Second, nominalizing the subject vastly improves such examples without reducing length or eliminating the ambiguity:

(3)   a.   John knew the fact that Ron disliked Rex disturbed Todd.
       b.   John suspected that Ron's leaving disturbed Todd.

If, as argued by Koster (1978), sentential subjects are obligatorily topicalized (or perhaps, Left Dislocated), then their unacceptability in embedded contexts needs no further explanation. Given these facts it seems more likely that a grammatical rather than parsing theoretic explanation for these data should be sought.

82. For now, we may assume that the parser makes no attempt to associate the second internal role with the NP phonologically adjacent to the verb since this would effectively block the possibility of ever realizing the first role (possibly modulo certain rightward movements beyond the scope of discussion here). Such a local analysis is further constrained by Case theory as discussed in §5.0.1.1.

83. As discussed in chapter 1, I will simply assume temporarily that the role PROPOSITION cannot be assigned directly to an NP. This stipulation is satisfyingly eliminated in chapter 5 by an appeal to grammatical principles beyond the theta criterion, and should be viewed only as a transitory simplifying assumption.

84. Given this, sentences such as:

(1)   ¿Susan warned her friends would deceive her.

are actually ambiguous (with both *friends* and *her friends* possible subjects of the lower clause), but both interpretations are correctly predicted to be garden paths.

85. This might be revealed more clearly given the structure:

(1)

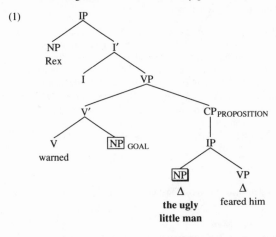

For simplicity, however, I assume a flat VP internal structure in double complement constructions of all types. Nothing crucial hinges on this decision and a binary branching analysis would serve equally well. (Somewhat more abstract analyses have been proposed (cf. Larson 1988) but will not be considered here.)

Notice that there is clear syntactic evidence that clausal elements simply may not appear as the first sister of V in such constructions. For example, "Dative Incorporation" is obligatory in precisely those cases where one of the arguments is sentential:

(2)   I told Susan-Mary the story.
(3)   I told the story to Susan-Mary.
(4)   I told Susan-Mary that she should publish the book.
(5)   *I told that she should publish the book to Susan-Mary.

86. I am aware of only a single sort of object-subject ambiguity that does not consistently appear to yield the expected processing difficulty:

(1)   (¿)I was fixing the brake and the engine started.

According to the principles outlined, *the engine* should initially be interpreted as the object of *fix* and reanalyzed as the subject of *start*, outside of its original theta domain in violation of the TRC. All such examples involve coördination, whose syntax is not well understood and speakers' judgments seem to vary on such examples. Conceivably, if an analysis in terms of parallel structures (not parallel processing) along the lines of Goodall (1987) proves correct, then it may be possible to provide a natural account of this apparently anomalous behavior.

87. It is by no means necessary to assume that the attachment does not occur until this entire string has been processed. Rather, it should occur as soon as its potential sentential status is identified, logically at either the CP or the IP head. However, for ease of discussion I will continue to speak as if no attachment occurs until the point immediately prior to the locus of disambiguation.

88. Notice that this example clearly reveals the contrast between a theory which attempts to maximally satisfy independent principles of grammar and a logically conceivable alternative which attempts to interpret each local substring as fully grammatical. In the latter case, one might expect the relative clause interpretation to be primary since a string such as *the doctor that he disliked* would constitute a grammatical relative clause, though not a grammatical NP S' sequence. This is clearly the wrong prediction.

89. The unproblematic status of the sentence does present difficulty for the strong hypothesis that attachments are immediately head triggered (a hypothesis compatible with but not crucial to the analyses elsewhere in the text) since the attachment does not appear to occur immediately given the head of CP, *that*. However, it is quite conceivable that clauses are not actually licensed until the occurrence of the true head of S, INFL, rather than the head of CP, C, and it is this assumption that I will informally adopt. At INFL (here *was*) the string is unambiguous given the absence of an overt subject. See also note 130 below.

90. Though I will say little about the issue, I assume that relative clause attachment itself is both globally and locally licensed by the predication of the relative operator with the head of the relative clause as required by Full Interpretation (cf. Chomsky 1986b). Notice that there may be evidence that this licensing requirement must also be satisfied on-line when there is no alternative thematic attachment possible:

(1) ¿Despite the scorecard that we lost remained undiscovered.
     (Despite the scorecard the fact that we lost remained undiscovered.)
     (cf. Despite John that we lost remained undiscovered.)

Rather than remaining locally uninterpreted, the string *that we lost* is evidently immediately licensed by predication with reanalysis as a sentential subject violating the TRC as expected.

91. There is a danger here that the use of thematic role labels may appear to raise a problem that does not actually exist. Arguably, in its surface transitive and unaccusative uses, the semantic content associated with the surface subject position of a verb like *race* may differ:

(1) a. The jockey$_{AGENT}$ raced the horse$_{THEME}$ past the barn.
     b. The horse$_{THEME}$ raced past the barn.

However, crucially, the syntactic position of that surface subject does not change (regardless of whether a movement or lexical analysis of unaccusatives is adopted). There is no syntactic ambiguity with respect to the subject-verb sequences in examples such as (1), and, as expected, switching from one analysis to another yields no processing difficulty (cf. also §2.3.2):

(2) a. The vase broke (the glass table).
     b. The match burned (the paper).

Recall that although the configurationality of thematic roles, item specific lexical information, is absolutely fundamental, their content is irrelevant to the syntax and by hypothesis the parser.

Of course, there is likely much of interest to be investigated with respect to the processing of unaccusatives and their subclasses which might shed light on their lexical and syntactic status, but this is somewhat beyond the scope of the discussion here (though cf. Pritchett 1991c).

92. As discussed in §2.2, in certain theories, the passive participle is considered to belong to a different (possibly adjectival) lexical category than the past tense verb form. It is worth reiterating that this ambiguity in itself cannot be the source of the difficulty. Theoretically, in both functions the ambiguous verbal occupies an identical structural position as the head of a predicate. Empirically, in addition to the general failure of lexical approaches to processing, recall that there are numerous examples which conform to the canonical garden path pattern which display the requisite categorial ambiguity but are completely unproblematic

(1)   The umpire murdered behind home plate made a lousy call.

as will be further discussed in some detail below. Finally, it will be argued in §4.1 that only the structural ramifications of lexical ambiguity are relevant to a theory of reanalysis in any event.

93. It is important to recognize that although the head of the relative NP may be predicated of the null operator in SPEC-CP which binds the passivized empty object (cf. Chomsky 1986b), it is uncontroversial that the the syntactic position occupied by *horse* is not directly assigned *race*'s internal role in the relative construction which is rather discharged on the trace.

94. Note of course that these ambiguities crucially depend on the "reduced" nature of the relative clause (its passive status and the absence of *wh-* and *be*) and are quite distinct from those cases considered in §3.1.2.4 involving double complement verbs.

95. Similarly, the relative NP reading of globally ambiguous sentences such as

(1)   Auntie knew the horse raced past the barn.
(2)   Jeane expects the boat floated down the river.

is not easily relinquished. But note of course that when no clausal reading is possible given the selectional properties of the higher predicate, the relative NP reading is perfectly acceptable:

(3)   Susan sang the song played on the radio.

96. This could conceivably even be interpreted as a reason that the parser might follow the obligatory argument strategy—it would always fail to yield GP effects, though it would produce local misanalyses. I will not pursue such a functional line of investigation here—as it ascribes to the parser far more metaknowledge than appears justified.

97. There are a couple of additional pieces of evidence in favor of the revised TRC over the no-misanalysis approach. First, the latter but not the former correctly predicts the unacceptability of

(1)   ¿The spaceship destroyed disintegrated.

Though it is unarguable that reduced relative clauses which are this light are only marginally grammatical in English, the sentence does seem more problematic than:

(2)   ?The spaceship seen disintegrated.

Second, though they clearly require no conscious processing, examples such as (268) do seem slightly more complex than morphologically unambiguous relative clauses, suggesting reanalysis, and experimental data would be quite welcome here.

98. I believe that this also explains the fact that *right* context may aid in interpreting garden path sentences, an initially puzzling fact for any on-line models of processing:

(1)   (¿)The horse raced past the barn fell over the sacks of potatoes that I had carelessly left its way.

Unlike the autonomous parser, the consciously processing hearer is free to use whatever types of information become available to interpret the sentence. Notice that this claim is quite distinct from the hypothesis that contextual information may aid the parser directly. Under the former conception, contextual information may be used only by the hearer-as-linguist in situations involving conscious reprocessing as the result of parsing failure, but may not steer the processor per se.

99. Although some of the constructions to be discussed here actually involve NP PP sequences, I will refer to them all interchangeably as "ditransitive," "double object," or "dative."

100. Pritchett (1988) follows the predictions of the theta attachment theory as developed to this point and actually holds these sentences to be mildly unacceptable, which, as pointed out by various researchers (personal communications) and reflected in the analysis here, does not appear to be the case.

101. The core definition of government in terms of shared maximal projections will suffice:

(1) **government:** α governs β iff α m-commands β and every γ dominating β dominates α, γ a maximal projection. (Adapted from Chomsky 1986a)

where m-command is simply c-command with "branching node" replaced by "maximal projection":

(2) **m-command:** α m-commands β iff α does not dominate β and every γ that dominates α dominates β, γ a maximal projection. (Adapted from Chomsky 1986a)

Additionally, it is uncontroversial that *if α governs β then α governs the head of β.* For example, as in traditional grammar, case and agreement features are assigned to a phrase under government but typically realized on its head. This is simply a natural result of the notion that heads and their projections share all features except bar level. Hence if some constituent governs an XP it will also govern its head X, but not its specifiers, complements, or adjuncts.

102. It is important to recognize that this use of dominance to characterize locality is absolutely distinct from that found in a minimal commitment model such as D-theory. In such cases it is used to enforce a constant relationship between a constituent and a hypothesized ancestor, say between an NP and a VP. In complete contrast, the OLLC requires that a relationship hold between the source and target positions assumed by an element during reanalysis, and the two approaches make numerous distinct predictions, as, for example, with respect to the contrast between (287) and (288) as well as the range of data discussed in §2.1.3. Furthermore, the OLLC requires no additional assumption of underspecification, a notion which appears extremely difficult to justify on psycholinguistic grounds concerning immediate on-line interpretation. (Though see Weinberg 1990 for a discussion of a very interesting Minimal Commitment model which essentially adopts a version of theta attachment.)

103. Alternatively, it would be possible to interpret the source position as the lowest projection dominating all relevant material by redefining m-command in terms of branching maximal projections.

104. Conceived of in more traditional parsing terms, the on-line locality constraint might be thought of as providing a formal characterization of how close two elements must be in order for "backtracking" to be successful. Crucially, this closeness is characterized directly in terms of configurational grammatical concepts, rather than simple parsing notions like adjacency or distance across the terminal string. From this perspective, the OLLC allows the parser to restrict its attention to the domain governed by the structural position of the constituent to be reanalyzed, whose own identity is of course determined by the licensing requirements of the element which forces reanalysis.

Alternatively, it is possible to conceive of theta attachment and the OLLC in terms of a parallel parsing model. All possible syntactic structures would be built, but those constructed in accord with theta attachment would be most highly valued and any representations more distant from this preferred structure than allowed by the OLLC would be immediately pruned and made unavailable.

Neither of these more traditional characterizations is crucial, and, I believe, both are actually misleading. The OLLC, like the TRC, enforces an essentially grammatical locality condition which could be implemented in numerous ways, and it is the nature of the former rather than the latter which fundamentally characterizes the limitations on human natural language processing. (But for a comprehensive parallel approach along the lines sketched above embodying a largely distinct set of assumptions and a memory-based complexity metric, see Gibson 1991.)

105. This contrast was pointed out by Gibson (1991).

106. Of course, unambiguous adjuncts do not require reprocessing:

(1)   I called the man with brown hair from Italy.

Refer also to the discussion in §5.1.

107. Notice that the reanalysis of *her* from NP specifier to head is predicted to be acceptable under the OLLC in contrast to the original version of the TRC as seen previously in note 74. Nothing crucial hinges on this, but some similar reanalyses are discussed in section 4.1.2.3.

108. This example might appear slightly more complicated than previous cases due to the N' rather than NP adjunction (e.g., $[_{NP}[_{NP}$ *the boat]* $[_{S'}$ *e floated down the river]]*) analysis of relative clauses adopted, since, as a result, *the boat* does not continue to exist as an exhaustive NP constituent within the final structure. This is certainly not a source of difficulty, however, since the same is true in the initial parse of any relativized or otherwise adjuncted NP. It may also be noted, as shown in (1), that the OLLC is equally violated with respect simply to the head N *boat:*

(1)

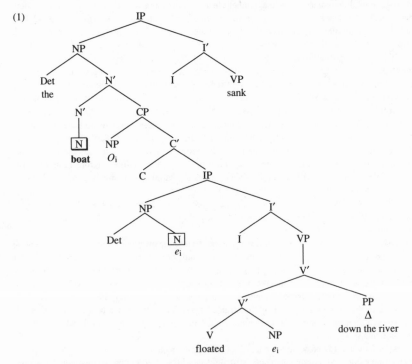

109. Such a reanalysis might be considered to hold from head to specifier, satisfying the government clause of the OLLC:

(1)

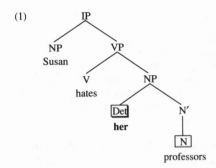

professors

However, this is inconsistent with the "highest projection" assumption of the text, is insufficiently general given examples like (294) or simply, *Susan hates the boys professors*, wherein no such head-to-SPEC analysis is obvious, and is unnecessary given that the dominance requirement is also satisfied. Some reanalyses of unambiguous heads are considered in §4.1.

110. It should be possible to empirically distinguish the two alternatives, given local ambiguities whose resolution immediately introduces additional nodes (other than IP) between the source and target position, thus satisfying dominance while violating government. If such examples do arise cross-linguistically, they could provide important evidence here, but the existence of relevant data is not obvious.

111. These results were confirmed in a survey conducted at Harvard University, alluded to in chapter 1, which also revealed that individuals are inconsistent across tokens of this sentence type. This may be readily reconfirmed by an appeal to hearers' intuitions, though I cannot offer experimental evidence to this effect.

112. The categorial status of the theta assigners also appears irrelevant as expected. Informal investigation reveals sentences like the following to be sporadic garden paths also:

(1)   ¿John warned the murderer of his enemy of the cops.

113. Notice that perceptual heuristics such as Minimal Attachment and Right Association, will have great difficulty accounting for such examples, as they should treat each identically, leading consistently to GP effects or their absence. Such sentences also provide strong evidence against a Steal-NP type strategy.

114. This is a reasonable structure on analogy with the rather clear status of *We voted the boys to be congressmen* as a Control rather than ECM construction. Notice however that when the secondary small clause argument is optional (unlike *vote*) the monotransitive interpretation is also readily available, as in the globally ambiguous:

(1)   We $\left\{ \begin{array}{l} \text{elected} \\ \text{prefer} \end{array} \right\}$ the boys congressmen.

Informally, it seems likely that this is attributable to the indisputably marked status of controlled (as opposed to ECM) small clause constructions, but a complete understanding of these facts must wait upon greater comprehension of the licensing and internal structure of this highly debated construction (cf. Bowers 1991 and references).

115. As alluded to in §2.3.2, a number of researchers have suggested that lexical recovery takes place in parallel (cf. Seidenberg et al. 1982; Gorrell 1987; Swinney 1979; and references). This is perfectly compatible with theta attachment, which could subsequently select among the alternatives.

116. Notice that it cannot be argued that *old train* is somehow a more plausible NP than *church pardons*, accounting for the differing initial interpretations (though not the differing reanalysis effects). Even very implausible Adj N ambiguities are still apparently resolved as NPs:

(1)   ¿The old baby the children.

An *old baby* is not a particularly sensible concept, yet the strong GP effect remains. This renders any "semantic" account of the initial preferences along the lines of Milne (1982) highly suspect.

Furthermore, it is important to recognize that the parallel behavior of (313) and (314) reveals that it is not the simple fact that the two senses of *train* in (314) are synchronically unrelated, while the two senses of *pardon* in (315) are, which is the source of the contrast. The two meanings of *number* are also related in (313) but the result is as problematic as the case in (314).

117. I am indebted to John Whitman for calling my attention to the potential relevance of these facts.

118. In fact, since a relationship of mutual government exists between a head noun and its modifying AP, adjective-noun ambiguity is predicted to be unproblematic regardless of the initial direction of resolution and subsequent restructuring.

(1)   I like green M&Ms.
(2)   I like green very much.
(2′)   AP to N *or* N to AP Reanalysis

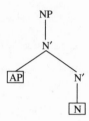

119. Notice that this also predicts the highly preferred but bizarre interpretation of the sentence

(1)   Japanese push bottles up Chinese.
       a.   The Japanese shoved bottles up the Chinese.
             [¿]The Japanese advance blocked the Chinese.

cited as an example of global ambiguity in chapter 1. In this instance the original verbal reading of *push* may continue unproblematically through the entire clause. Obtaining the alternative interpretation requires reanalysis of *push* from V (not VP given the additional lexical material) to subject NP, violating the OLLC and leaving the less plausible reading the only one available.

This reveals explicitly what has been tacitly quite clear throughout the previous discussion—that a perfectly processable globally ambiguous sentence may have an unobtainable garden path reading. However, as global ambiguity typically masks any GP effect, I have employed strictly local garden paths as the primary data, despite the fact that there is no important theoretical distinction between the two. Notice that there are of course globally ambiguous sentences in which the alternative reading may be easily obtained without violating the OLLC:

(2)   I mailed the boys sandwiches.
       a.   I mailed sandwiches to the boys. (*primary via theta attachment*)
       b.   I mailed the sandwiches of the boys. (*no OLLC violation*)

120. The structure posited in (324b′) is reasonable. Though I know of no explicit discussion of imperatives in the current generative literature, the proposed analysis should also hold of alternatives which conform to the X′ theory, including small clause constructions.

121. Similarly, were one committed to the notion that thematic roles such as GOAL, AGENT, THEME, etc. were relevant to syntactic phenomena, they too could be incorporated into the theory

as node features and their demonstrated irrelevance to processing effects attributed to free feature value relabeling. For example, given an ambiguous string such as, *I handed the duck* . . . , the post-verbal NP might be provisionally assigned the feature THEME, which could subsequently be changed to GOAL if the sentence were to continue, *a $20 bill*. A parallel account might also be applied to anaphoric indices.

122. Unfortunately, there is neither the time nor the space to even begin to adequately explore on-line chain formation here. As a brief example, however, consider how the case of unaccusatives would be handled by theta attachment. A string such as *the jockey raced* is ambiguous between a transitive (*the jockey raced the horse*) and an ergative reading. Theta attachment forces the pursuit of the former interpretation (given the maximal theta grid), and reanalysis as an unaccusative simply requires the insertion of a gap coindexed with the subject if no overt object is forthcoming (*the jockey$_i$ raced e$_i$*). See Pritchett (1991c) for an extension of some related ideas (though founded on the TRC rather than the OLLC) to A' chains.

123. The conclusions also hold of any theory of small clauses which conforms to the X' theory, including the various adjunction structures (cf. Stowell 1981, Fukui and Speas 1986).

In examples such as (326), theta attachment predicts the small clause interpretation to be primary since it allows an additional role to be discharged (from *duck* as a predicate rather than *duck* as an N). Some additional evidence for this comes from the bizarre first interpretation of sentences such as:

(1)   Man helps dog bite victim.

Notice that these Exceptional Case Marking (ECM) type small clause structures are perfectly acceptable and clearly distinct from the marked controlled small clauses previously discussed. Nevertheless, because proper grammatical analysis of small clauses remains a topic of ongoing research, I will investigate both initial small clause and initial NP resolutions of the ambiguity for completeness.

124. If one adopted a theory wherein a chain could receive more than one thematic role through a combination of predication and theta marking (cf. Williams 1980; Chomsky 1986b), it might also be argued that the adjectival reading of *fat* is pursued in order to allow *the boy* to receive some role as IP subject and another via predication, thus eliminating reference to *fat*'s derived status. As this requires a somewhat different set of structural and thematic assumptions, I simply note the possibility here.

125. This fact obviously correlates with their status as Object-Raising (ECM) or Equi (Control) verbs in infinitival constructions, but is of course more general.

126. A fundamental principle of Universal Grammar, the *Case Filter*, requires that, "Every phonetically realized NP must be assigned (abstract) Case," (Chomsky 1985a, p. 74). Case may be assigned structurally, under government, or inherently, correlating with theta role assignment (for example in dative and possibly genitive constructions). The [−N] categories V and P appear to be Case assigners, while N and A do not. Nominative case is assigned by tensed INFL. See Stowell (1981) for evidence that S' complements need not receive Case.

127. I will not entertain an alternative grammatical analysis of (332)–(335) which stipulates that the relevant verbs happen to subcategorize only for a secondary S' or PP argument since this merely describes the situation rather than explains it.

128. For example, recall the discussion in §4.0.4.2 of sentences like, *Katy gave the man who was eating the fudge*. There is no clear tendency for either the local matrix or embedded attachment of *the fudge*, despite the fact that the latter results in a fully grammatical construction. Like the original version, generalized theta attachment predicts no preference in such cases since in each representation every element is fully licensed and an equal number of licensing features (theta roles and now Cases) are locally discharged. The fact that the higher attachment results in a fully grammatical sentence is irrelevant.

129. It is not obvious that this is compatible with an account of the Case Filter in terms of a

visibility requirement on theta role assignment, but the status of that hypothesis is extremely uncertain (see Chomsky (1986b) and also see Epstein (1990) for arguments against reducing the Case Filter to visibility).

130. But recall from note 89 that certain problems arise in light of the acceptable status of double complement constructions containing subject rather than object relatives (I am grateful to Ted Gibson for pointing out this contrast):

(1)   (¿)The patient persuaded the doctor that disliked him to leave.

If attachment is made immediately at *that*, subsequent reanalysis should violate the OLLC, but such sentences seem improvements over examples like (340b). A possible solution might be sought in terms of the functional category–lexical category distinction, with lexical elements required as potential targets (and the ambiguity thus eliminated at the triggering verb). Interestingly, however, in other environments the GP effect appears to be realized as expected:

(2)   ¿The patient persuaded the doctor that disliked him of the danger.

Since it is not altogether clear whether the initial misanalysis is circumvented or, more likely, that reanalysis is simply facilitated for as yet unclear reasons, this question must temporarily remain open.

131. I am grateful to Ariel Cohen (personal communication) for this example.

132. See Pritchett (1991a) for a more explicit discussion of the role of head position in parsing as well as a detailed critique of Frazier's MA approach to Dutch head-final constructions (cf. Frazier 1987). As that article does not concern itself with processing failure per se, and the fundamental dependence of the theta attachment model on the position of licensing heads should be clear, I will not recapitulate the arguments here although many of the relevant issues are brought forward in the discussion which follows.

133. Generalized theta attachment deals with scrambling quite directly, though I will not discuss the issue in detail here. Whenever a head is capable of licensing an unattached scrambled argument, a trace coindexed with that argument will simply be inserted at the appropriate d-structure position, grammatical constraints otherwise permitting.

134. One issue which has not been considered in light of the primary emphasis on English is parsing in true *pro*-drop constructions. Both Japanese (and Korean discussed below) allow very free omission of arguments at the level of Phonological Form. One immediate influence of *pro*-drop on parsing performance is the bleeding of potential garden path environments since the "insertion" of a null argument rather than reanalysis of an attached constituent becomes a local grammatical option. The causative examples in (362) above and (365), below, were carefully chosen to disallow this possibility. However, for some speakers (of the Japanese Kansai dialect for example), null CAUSEES appear acceptable, and, as a result, such sentences are globally ambiguous. As predicted however, they continue to display an overwhelming preference for the interpretation where the NP-*ni* is construed with the embedded verb and a *pro* causee is inserted when required, obviating impossible reanalysis.

It should also be noted that theta attachment predicts, lexical requirements otherwise satisfied, that the preferred interpretation of a sequence, NP NP V COMP V will be as in (a) rather than (b):

(1)   a.   [*pro* [NP NP V COMP] V]
        b.   [NP NP [*pro* V COMP] V]

Null arguments should not be projected before a licensor which requires them appears since this would place unnecessary local strain on the theta criterion and Case theory. Furthermore, if overt arguments are available when a head occurs, they will of course be immediately licensed where possible as there is no obligation to project empty categories. This prediction is borne out in Korean as well as Japanese (example from Wonchul Park):

(2) Kelley-eykey Charles-ka tola o-ass-ta-ko   malhay-ss-ta.
     Kelley-DAT Charles-NOM return come-PST-IND-COMP say-PST-IND

where, according to native speakers, the interpretation, *pro said that Charles returned to Kelley*, is preferred to *Charles said to Kelley that pro returned*. Notice, however, that the syntactic topic prominence of such languages and its structural implications may interact with theta attachment in ways, which although entirely natural, have not become apparent in the investigation of English. There may also be a related subject-object asymmetry in reanalysis. This remains an open area of investigation.

REFERENCES

Abney, S. 1989. "A computational model of human parsing." *Journal of Psycholinguistic Research* 18.1.
————. 1987. "The English Noun Phrase in Its Sentential Aspect." Ph.D. diss., MIT.
————. 1986. "Licensing and parsing." In *Proceedings of NELS* XVII.
Aho, A., and J. Ullman. 1972. *The Theory of Parsing, Translation and Compiling.* New Jersey: Prentice-Hall.
Altmann, G., and M. Steedman. 1988. "Interaction with context during sentence processing." *Cognition* 30.
Baker, M. 1988. *Incorporation: A Theory of Grammatical Relation Changing.* Chicago: University of Chicago Press.
Barton, E., R. Berwick, and E. Ristad. 1987. *Computational Complexity and Natural Language.* Cambridge: MIT Press.
Berwick, R., S. Abney, and C. Tenny, eds. 1991. *Principle-Based Parsing: Computation and Psycholinguistics.* Dordrecht: Kluwer.
Berwick, R., and A. Weinberg. 1984. *The Grammatical Basis of Linguistic Performance: Language Use and Acquisition.* Cambridge: MIT Press.
Bever, T. 1970. "The cognitive basis for linguistic structures." In J. R. Hayes (ed.), *Cognition and the Development of Language.* New York: Wiley and Sons.
————. 1968. "A survey of some recent work in psycholinguistics." In W. Plath (ed.), "Specification and utilization of a transformational grammar." Scientific report, no. 3. T. J. Watson Research Center, New Jersey: IBM.
Bowers, J. 1991. "The syntax of predication." MS, Cornell University. Dept. of Modern Language and Linguistics.
Bresnan, J. 1978. "A realistic transformational grammar." In M. Halle, J. Bresnan, and G. Miller (eds.), *Linguistic Theory and Psychological Reality.* Cambridge: MIT Press.
Briscoe, E. 1983. "Determinism and its implementation in PARSIFAL." In K. Sparck Jones and Y. Wilks (eds.), *Automatic Natural Language Parsing.* West Sussex: Ellis Horwood.
Carlson, G., and M. Tanenhaus. 1988. "Thematic roles and language comprehension." In W. Wilkens (ed.), *Syntax and Semantics* 21: *Thematic Relations.* New York: Academic Press.

181

Chomsky, N. 1986a. *Barriers*. Cambridge: MIT Press.

———. 1986b. *Knowledge of Language: Its Nature, Origin, and Use*. New York: Praeger.

———. 1981. *Lectures on Government and Binding*. Dordrecht: Foris.

———. 1970. "Remarks on nominalization." In R. Jacobs and P. Rosenbaum (eds.), *Readings in English Transformational Grammar*. Waltham, MA: Ginn.

———. 1964. "The logical basis of linguistic theory." In H. Lunt (ed.), *Proceedings of the Ninth International Congress of Linguists*. The Hague: Mouton.

Chomsky, N., and H. Lasnik. (1977) "Filters and control." *Linguistic Inquiry* 8.

Clark, R. 1988. "Parallel processing and learnability." In S. Abney, (ed.), *The MIT Parsing Volume, 1987–88*. Cambridge: MIT Center for Cognitive Science.

Clark, R., and T. Gibson. 1988. "A parallel model of adult sentence processing." In *Proceedings of the Tenth Cognitive Science Conference*. Hillsdale, NJ: Lawrence Erlbaum Associates.

Clifton, C., and Ferreira F. (1989). "Ambiguity in context." *Language and Cognitive Processes* 4.

Correa, N. 1991. "Empty categories, chain binding, and parsing." In R. Berwick, S. Abney, and C. Tenny (eds.), *Principle-Based Parsing: Computation and Psycholinguistics*. Dordrecht: Kluwer.

Crain, S., and M. Steedman. 1985. "On not being led up the garden path: The use of context by the psychological syntax processor." In D. Dowty, L. Karttunen, and A. Zwicky (eds.), *Natural Language Parsing: Psychological, Computational, and Theoretical Perspectives*. Cambridge: Cambridge University Press.

Crocker, M. 1990. "Principle-based sentence processing: A cross-linguistic account." MS, University of Edinburgh, Human Communication Resource Centre.

Early, J. 1970. "An efficient context-free parsing algorithm." In *Communications of the ACM* 14.

Emonds, J. 1985. *A Unified Theory of Syntactic Categories*. Dordrecht: Foris.

Epstein, S. D. 1990. "Differentiation and reduction in syntactic theory: A case study." *Natural Language and Linguistic Theory* 8.

Ferreira, F. and Clifton, C. 1986. "The independence of syntactic processing." *Journal of Memory and Language* 25.

Fillmore, C. 1977. "The case for case reopened." In P. Cole and J. Sadock (eds.), *Syntax and Semantics* 8. New York: Academic Press.

Fodor, J. A. 1983. *The Modularity of Mind*. Cambridge: MIT Press.

Fodor, J. A., T. Bever, and M. Garrett. 1974. *The Psychology of Language*. New York: McGraw-Hill.

Fodor, J. D., and L. Frazier. 1980. "Is the human sentence parsing mechanism an ATN?" *Cognition* 8.

Fong, S. 1991. "The computational implementation of principle-based parsers." In R. Berwick, S. Abney, and C. Tenny (eds.), *Principle-Based Parsing: Computation and Psycholinguistics*. Dordrecht: Kluwer.

Ford, M., J. Bresnan, and R. Kaplan. 1982. "A competence-based theory of syntactic closure." In J. Bresnan (ed.), *The Mental Representation of Grammatical Relations*. Cambridge: MIT Press.

Frazier, L. 1989. "Against lexical generation of syntax." In W. Marslen-Wilson (ed.), *Lexical Representation and Process*. Cambridge: MIT Press/Bradford Books.

————. 1987. "Syntactic processing: Evidence from Dutch." *Natural Language and Linguistic Theory* 5.

————. 1985. "Syntactic complexity." In D. Dowty, L. Karttunen, and A. Zwicky (eds.), *Natural Language Parsing: Psychological, Computational, and Theoretical Perspectives*. Cambridge: Cambridge University Press.

————. 1978. "On comprehending sentences: Syntactic parsing strategies." Ph.D. diss., University of Connecticut.

Frazier, L., and J. D. Fodor. 1978. "The sausage machine: A new two-stage parsing model." *Cognition* 6.

Frazier, L., and K. Rayner. 1987. "Resolution of syntactic category ambiguities: Eye movements in parsing lexically ambiguous sentences." *Journal of Memory and Language* 26.

————. 1982. "Making and correcting errors during sentence comprehension: Eye movements in the analysis of structurally ambiguous sentences." *Cognitive Psychology* 14.

Fukui, N., and M. Speas. 1986. "Specifiers and projections." In *MIT Working Papers in Linguistics* 8, Cambridge.

Garfield, J. 1987. *Modularity in Knowledge Representation and Natural-Language Understanding*. Cambridge: MIT Press.

Gazdar, G., E. Klein, G. Pullum, and I. Sag. 1985. *Generalized Phrase Structure Grammar*. Cambridge: Harvard University Press.

Gibson, T. 1991. "A computational theory of human linguistic processing: Memory limitations and processing breakdown." Ph.D. diss., Carnegie Mellon University.

Goodall, G. 1987. *Parallel Structures in Syntax*. Cambridge: Cambridge University Press.

Gorrell, P. 1991. "Subcategorization and sentence processing." In R. Berwick, S. Abney, and C. Tenny (eds.), *Principle-Based Parsing: Computation and Psycholinguistics*. Dordrecht: Kluwer.

————. 1987. "Studies in human syntactic processing: Ranked-parallel versus serial models." Ph.D. diss., University of Maryland.

Gruber, J. 1976. *Studies in Lexical Relations*. Amsterdam: North Holland.

Hakes, D. 1972. "Effects of reducing complement constructions on sentence comprehension." *Journal of Verbal Learning and Verbal Behavior* 11.

Hawkins, J. 1990. "A parsing theory of word-order universals." *Linguistic Inquiry* 21.

Higginbotham, J. 1985. "On Semantics." *Linguistic Inquiry* 16.

Huang C.-T. J. 1982. "Logical relations in Chinese and the theory of grammar." Ph.D. diss., MIT.

Jackendoff, R. 1977. *X′ Syntax: A Study of Phrase Structure*. Cambridge: MIT Press.

Jenkins, J., J. A. Fodor, and S. Saporta. 1965. "An introduction to psycholinguistic theory." MS.

Johnson, M. 1991. "Deductive parsing: The use of knowledge of language." In R. Berwick, S. Abney, and C. Tenny (eds.), *Principle-Based Parsing: Computation and Psycholinguistics*. Dordrecht: Kluwer.

Kaplan, R., and J. Bresnan. 1982. "Lexical-functional grammar: A formal system for grammatical representation." In J. Bresnan (ed.), *The Mental Representation of Grammatical Relations*. Cambridge: MIT Press.

Katz, J., and P. Postal. 1964. *An Integrated Theory of Linguistic Descriptions*. Cambridge: MIT Press.

Keyser, J., and T. Roeper. 1984. "On the middle and ergative constructions in English." *Linguistic Inquiry* 15.

Kimball, J. 1975. "Predictive analysis and over-the-top parsing." In J. Kimball (ed.), *Syntax and Semantics*, vol. 4. New York: Academic Press.

———. 1973. "Seven principles of surface structure parsing in natural language." *Cognition* 2.

Koster, J. 1978. "Why subject sentences don't exist." In S. J. Keyser (ed.), *Recent Transformational Studies in European Languages*. Cambridge: MIT Press.

Kuno, S. 1973. *The Structure of the Japanese Language*. Cambridge: MIT Press.

Kuroda, S.-Y. 1987. "Whether we agree or not: A comparative syntax of English and Japanese." In W. Poser (ed.) *Papers from the Second International Workshop on Japanese Syntax*. Stanford: CSLI.

Kurtzman, H. 1985. "Studies in syntactic ambiguity resolution." Ph.D. diss., MIT.

Larson, R. 1988. "On the double object construction." *Linguistic Inquiry* 19.

MacDonald, M. 1989. "Priming effects from gaps to antecedents." *Language and Cognitive Processes* 4.1.

Marantz, A. 1984. *On the Nature of Grammatical Relations*. Cambridge: MIT Press.

Marcus, M. 1987. "Deterministic parsing and Description Theory. In P. Whitelock, M. Wood, H. Somers, R. Johnson, and P. Bennett (eds.), *Linguistic Theory and Computer Applications*. San Diego: Academic Press.

———. 1980. *A Theory of Syntactic Recognition for Natural Language*. Cambridge: MIT Press.

Marcus, M., D. Hindle, and M. Fleck. 1983. "D-Theory: Talking about talking about trees." In *Proceedings of the Association for Computational Linguistics* 21.

Mazuka, R., K. Itoh, S. Kiritani, S. Niwa, K. Ikejiru, and K. Naito. 1989. "Processing of Japanese garden path, center-embedded, and multiply-left-embedded sentences." *Annual Bulletin of the Research Institute of Logopedics and Phoniatrics* 23.

McCawley, J. 1988. *The Syntactic Phenomena of English*. Chicago: University of Chicago Press.

McClelland, J., and A. Kawamoto. 1986. "Mechanisms of sentence processing: Assigning roles to constituents of sentences." In J. McClelland and D. Rumelhart (eds.), *Parallel Distributed Processing*, vol. 2. Cambridge: MIT Press.

Miller, G., and N. Chomsky. 1963. "Finitary models of language users." In R. Duncan Luce, R. Bush, and Eugene Galanter (eds.), *Handbook of Mathematical Psychology*, vol. 2. New York: Wiley.

Milne, R. 1982. "Predicting garden path sentences." *Cognitive Science* 6.

Mitchell, D. 1987. "Lexical guidance in human parsing: Locus and processing characteristics." In M. Coltheart (ed.), *Attention and Performance* 12. Hillsdale, NJ: Lawrence Erlbaum Associates.

Nicol, J., and D. Swinney. 1989. "The role of structure in coreference assignment during sentence comprehension." *Journal of Psycholinguistic Research* 18.

Pereira, F. 1985. "A new characterization of attachment preferences." In D. Dowty, L. Karttunen, and A. Zwicky (eds.), *Natural Language Parsing: Psychological, Computational, and Theoretical Perspectives*. Cambridge: University of Cambridge Press.

Pollard, C., and I. Sag. 1988. *An Information-Based Approach to Syntax and Semantics*, Vol. 1, *Fundamentals*. CSLI Lecture Notes 13. Chicago: University of Chicago Press.

Pritchett, B. 1991a. "Head position and parsing ambiguity." *Journal of Psycholinguistic Research* 20. ←‐ *JPR*

———. 1991b. "Parsing with grammar: Islands, heads, and garden paths." In H. ←‐ Goodluck and M. Rochement (eds.), *The Psycholinguistics of Island Constraint Universals*. Dordrecht: Kluwer.

———. 1991c. "Subjacency in a principle-based parser." In R. Berwick, S. Abney, and C. Tenny (eds.), *Principle-Based Parsing: Computation and Psycholinguistics*. Dordrecht: Kluwer.

———. 1988. "Garden path phenomena and the grammatical basis of language processing." *Language* 64.

———. 1987. "Garden path phenomena and the grammatical basis of language processing." Ph.D. diss., Harvard University.

Pritchett, B., and J. Reitano. 1990. "Parsing with on-line principles, a psychologically plausible, object-oriented approach." In *Proceedings of COLING '90*.

Rizzi, L. 1990. *Relativized Minimality*. Cambridge: MIT Press.

Ross, J. R. R. 1967. "Constraints on variables in syntax." Ph.D. diss., MIT. Published as *Infinite Syntax*, Hillsdale, New Jersey: Lawrence Erlbaum Associates, 1986.

Schank, R., and L. Birnbaum. 1984. "Memory, meaning, and syntax." In T. Bever, J. Carroll, and L. Miller (eds.), *Talking Minds*. Cambridge: MIT Press.

Seidenberg, M., M. Tanenhaus, J. Leiman, and M. Bienkowski. 1982. "Automatic access of the meanings of ambiguous words in context: Some limitations of knowledge-based processes." *Cognitive Psychology* 14.

Shibatani, M. 1977. "Grammatical relations and surface cases." *Language* 53.

Simpson, G. 1984. "Lexical ambiguity and its role in models of word recognition." *Psychological Bulletin* 96.

Stabler, E. 1991. "Avoid the pedestrian's paradox." In R. Berwick, S. Abney, and C. Tenny (eds.), *Principle-Based Parsing: Computation and Psycholinguistics*. Dordrecht: Kluwer.

Steedman, M., and G. Altman. 1989. "Ambiguity in context: A reply." *Language and Cognitive Processes* 4.

Stowell, T. 1981. "Origins of phrase structure." Ph.D. diss., MIT.

Swinney, D. 1979. "Lexical access during sentence comprehension: (Re)consideration of context effects." *Journal of Verbal Learning and Verbal Behavior* 18.

Trueswell, J., M. Tanenhaus, and S. Garnsey. 1991. "Semantic influences on parsing: Use of thematic role information in syntactic disambiguation." MS, University of Rochester.

Wanner, E. 1980. "The ATN and the Sausage Machine: Which one is baloney?" *Cognition* 8.

Wanner, E., and M. Maratsos. 1976. "An ATN approach to comprehension." In M. Halle, J. Bresnan, and G. Miller (eds.), *Linguistic Theory and Psychological Reality*. Cambridge: MIT Press.

Wanner, E., R. Kaplan, and S. Shiner. 1975. "Garden paths in relative clauses." MS, Harvard University.

Wehrli, E. 1988. "Parsing with a GB-grammar." In U. Reyle and C. Rohrer, (eds.), *Natural Language Parsing and Linguistic Theories*. Boston: Reidel.

Weinberg, A. 1990. "A parsing theory for the nineties: Minimal Commitment." MS, University of Maryland.

———. 1988. "Locality principles in syntax and parsing." Ph.D. diss., MIT

Whitman, J. B. 1991. "String vacuous V to COMP," Paper presented at GLOW 1991, Leiden, Holland.

Williams, E. 1984. "Grammatical relations." *Linguistic Inquiry* 15.

———. 1983. "Against small clauses." *Linguistic Inquiry* 14.

———. 1980. "Predication." *Linguistic Inquiry* 11.

Woods, W. 1970. "Transition network grammars for natural language analysis." *Communication of the Association for Computing Machinery* 13.

Yngve, V. 1960. "A model and an hypothesis for language structure." In *Proceedings of the American Philosophical Society* 104.

INDEX OF NAMES

187

GENERAL INDEX